LINCOLN
AND HIS
GENERALS

LINCOLN AND HIS GENERALS

T. HARRY WILLIAMS

GRAMERCY BOOKS
NEW YORK

This 2000 edition is published by Gramercy Books™, an imprint of Random House Value Publishing, Inc. 280 Park Avenue, New York, N.Y. 10017, by arrangement with Alfred A. Knopf, Inc.

Gramercy Books™ and design are trademarks of Random House Value Publishing, Inc.

Random House
New York • Toronto • London • Sydney • Auckland
http://www.randomhouse.com/

Printed and bound in the United States of America.

Library of Congress Cataloging–in–Publication Data

Williams, T. Harry (Thomas Harry), 1909-
Lincoln and his generals / T. Harry Williams.
    p. cm.
Originally published: New York : Knopf, 1952.
Includes bibliographical references (p.) and index.
ISBN 0-517-16237-7
    1. Lincoln, Abraham, 1809-1865—Military leadership. 2. Generals—United
States—History—19th century. 3. United States--History—Civil War,
1861-1865—Campaigns. I. Title.

E457.2 .W7 2000
973.7'092--dc21

                                                    00-037571

9 8 7 6 5 4 3 2 1

for **S***tell*

Preface

I HAVE WRITTEN in this book the story of Abraham Lincoln the commander in chief. I have not written a military history of the Civil War or a group biography of the principal Union generals or a description of the military organization of the North, although there is something of all of these in the book. My theme is Lincoln as a director of war and his place in the high command and his influence in developing a modern command system for this nation. Always I have tried to describe and evaluate Lincoln's acts as a war director from the perspective of military developments since 1865 and to measure the correctness of his decisions by the standards of modern war.

Judged by modern standards, Lincoln stands out as a great war president, probably the greatest in our history, and a great natural strategist, a better one than any of his generals. He was in actuality as well as in title the commander in chief who, by his larger strategy, did more than Grant or any general to win the war for the Union.

Because Lincoln is at the center of the story and because the war is seen only as it unfolded before his eyes, the emphasis or proportion given to certain generals and events may trouble some readers. For instance, John C. Fremont occupies more pages than W. T. Sherman, although Sherman was worth ten Fremonts as a general. The incompetent N. P. Banks gets more space than the able George H. Thomas. Fremont and Banks loom larger than Sherman and Thomas because as commanders they were headaches to Lincoln and hence had intimate command relationships with him. Lincoln saw, militarily, much of Fremont and Banks, relatively little of Sherman and Thomas. Some readers may say that they could do with less of McClellan and more of Grant. So could have Lincoln, but it was his horrible predicament to be saddled with McClellan before he found Grant and to have to supervise nearly everything that McClellan did. Lincoln tried to use McClellan; but rightly distrusting the General's ability, he intervened frequently in the management of military matters. Rightly trusting in Grant's competence, Lincoln intervened less after Grant became general in chief, but even then he always exercised an over-all authority and never hesitated to check Grant when he thought the General was making a mistake. It might be said that before Grant, Lincoln acted as commander in chief and frequently as general in chief and that after Grant, he contented himself with the function of commander in chief. Consequently, as Grant assumed a larger role Lincoln took a smaller one—but he never left the stage entirely.

To the best of my knowledge, this book is the only work that treats of Lincoln as a war director—with him as the dominating figure—from the perspective of modern war. It is my hope that my discussion is a contribution both to the history of the American command system and to an understanding of it.

I am under obligation to the following people who gave me aid and comfort in preparing this book: Miss Mai Frances Lower, Dr. Philip D. Uzee, Mrs. George Herlitz, Mrs. Thomas Smylie, Mrs. Helen Bullock, Dr. Horace Merrill, Miss Catherine Heald, Dr. C. P. Powell, Miss Joan Doyle, and the staffs of the Louisiana State University Library and the Manuscript Division of the Library of Congress.

For searching criticism and helpful suggestions, I am deeply grateful to Dr. Charles E. Smith of Louisiana State University, a scholar of the Middle Ages who is also a profound and penetrating student of the Civil War.

Contents

LINCOLN

AND

HIS GENERALS

Chapter 1

The Pattern of Command

THE Civil War was the first of the modern total wars, and the American democracy was almost totally unready to fight it. The United States had in 1861 almost no army, few good weapons, no officers trained in the higher art of war, and an inadequate and archaic system of command. Armies could be raised and weapons manufactured quickly, but it took time and battles to train generals. And it took time and blunders and bitter experiences to develop a modern command system. Not until 1864 did the generals and the system emerge.

In 1861 the general in chief of the army, which at the beginning of the war numbered about 16,000 men, was Winfield Scott. He was a veteran of two wars and the finest soldier in America. But he had been born in 1786, and he was physically incapable of commanding an army in the field. He could not ride, he could not walk more than a few steps without pain, and he had dropsy and vertigo.[1] The old General dreamed wistfully of taking the field. "If I could only mount a horse, I—" he would say sadly and pause, "but I am past that." [2] He was one of two officers in the army as the war started who had

[1] Winfield Scott to Simon Cameron, October 31, 1861, *War of the Rebellion . . . the Official Records of the Union and Confederate Armies*, Ser. 3, I, 611. Hereafter cited as *Official Records;* unless otherwise noted, all citations are to Ser. 1.

[2] Frederick W. Seward, *Reminiscences of a War-Time Statesman and Diplomat, 1830–1915*, 167–168.

ever commanded troops in numbers large enough to be called an army. The other was John E. Wool, who was two years older than Scott. Wool had been a good soldier in his time, but he too showed the effects of age. He repeated things he had said a few minutes before, his hands shook, and he had to ask his aides if he had put his hat on straight.[3] Besides Scott and Wool, not an officer in the North had directed the evolutions of as large a unit as a brigade.[4] The largest single army that most of the younger officers had ever seen was Scott's force of 14,000 in the Mexican War.

There was not an officer in the first year of the war who was capable of efficiently administering and fighting a large army. Even Scott, had he been younger and stronger, would have had difficulty commanding any one of the big armies called into being by the government. All his experience had been with small forces, and he might not have been able to have adjusted his thinking to the organization of mass armies. The young officers who would be called to lead the new hosts lacked even his experience. Not only had they never handled troops in numbers, but they knew almost nothing about the history and theory of war or of strategy. They did not know the higher art of war, because there was no school in the country that taught it. West Point, which had educated the great majority of the officers, crammed its students full of knowledge of engineering, fortifications, and mathematics. Only a minor part of its curriculum was devoted to strategy, and its graduates learned little about how to lead and fight troops in the field. They were equally innocent of any knowledge of staff work: the administrative problems of operating an army or the formulation of war plans. Most of them never learned anything of it in the army, except for those few who

[3] Henry M. Flint to Frederic Hudson, September 10, 1862, James Gordon Bennett MSS.

[4] Charles W. Elliott, *Winfield Scott: The Soldier and the Man*, 718.

could read French or who went abroad.[5] They spent most of their army careers fighting Indians or building forts, and there was not much of a staff organization in America for them to get any experience with.

The staff of the army, such as it was, consisted of Scott and the heads of the important departments and bureaus in the military organization—the adjutant general, the quarter-master general, the chief of engineers, the chief of ordnance, and others. Some of these officers were men of ability and would do good work in the war. Their agencies were going concerns with years of experience behind them when hostilities started and needed only to be expanded to meet the larger needs of a larger army. None of the staff chiefs had made any plans for war, and none of them was accustomed to thinking in terms of supplying the needs of mass armies. Some of the departments, notably the quartermaster general's, made the shift from peace to war with efficiency; others never got completely adjusted. All of them were unready for war in 1861, and in that year and even later were not able to furnish field commanders with the technical information or advice or supplies which they were suddenly called on to provide. One of the most ironic examples of American military unreadiness was the spectacle of Northern—and Southern—generals fighting in their own country and not knowing where they were going or how to get there. Before the war the government had collected no topographical information about neighboring countries or even the United States, except for the West. No accurate military maps existed. General Henry W. Halleck was running a campaign in the western theater in 1862 with maps he got from a book store. With frenetic haste, the general set topographical officers and civilian experts to work

[5] Arthur Latham Conger, "President Lincoln as War Statesman," *Wisconsin Historical Publications, Proceedings,* 1916, 12; Jacob Dolson Cox, *Military Reminiscences of the Civil War,* I, 177–180.

making maps, but the resulting charts were generally incorrect. Benjamin H. Latrobe, the civil engineer, drew a map for a general going into western Virginia, but the best he could promise was that it would not *mislead* the expedition. General George B. McClellan had elaborate maps prepared for his Virginia campaign of 1862 and found to his dismay when he arrived on the scene that they were unreliable; "the roads are wrong . . . ," he wailed. Not until 1863 did the Army of the Potomac have an accurate map of northern Virginia, its theater of operations.[6] Poor staff work continued in some departments until the end of the war. As late as 1864 there was not an office in Washington that could tell a general organizing a campaign what railroads were under military control, what the condition of their equipment was, or how many men and supplies they could transport.[7]

In no section of the staff organization was there any person or division charged with the function of studying strategy or formulating war plans for even a theoretical war. The work of the staff was completely technical and routine. Scott, the general in chief, had done no thinking before the war about what strategy should be adopted if war came. He had busied himself chiefly with devising political schemes to avert civil conflict. When the shooting started, he had no strategic design in mind to subdue the South. No other officer had one. Nobody in the army had thought it was important to think of war in strategic terms.

At the head of the American military organization was the

6 Henry W. Halleck to D. C. Buell, February 13, 1862, *Official Records*, VII, 609; B. H. Latrobe to Frederick W. Lander, January 4, 1862, Lander MSS.; George B. McClellan, *McClellan's Own Story*, 253, 264; Emerson Gifford Taylor, *Gouverneur Kemble Warren* . . . , 106–107.

7 Herman Haupt to Lincoln, January 16, 1864, the Robert Todd Lincoln Collection of the Papers of Abraham Lincoln, vol. 138. Hereafter cited as Lincoln MSS.

president, the commander in chief of all the armed forces of the nation. The man who was president when the war began had been a civilian all his life, had had no military experience except as a militia soldier in a pygmy Indian war, and in 1861 probably did not even know how to frame a military order. The president of the rival nation, the Confederate States, was a graduate of West Point, he had been in the regular army and had seen battle service in the Mexican War. Abraham Lincoln was a great war president; Jefferson Davis was a mediocre one. Nowhere in the history of war is there a better illustration of Clausewitz's dictum that an acquaintance with military affairs is not the principal qualification for a director of war but that "a remarkable, superior mind and strength of character" are better qualifications.[8]

With no knowledge of the theory of war, no experience in war, and no technical training, Lincoln, by the power of his mind, became a fine strategist. He was a better natural strategist than were most of the trained soldiers. He saw the big picture of the war from the start. The policy of the government was to restore the Union by force; the strategy perforce had to be offensive. Lincoln knew that numbers, material resources, and sea power were on his side, so he called for 400,-000 troops and proclaimed a naval blockade of the Confederacy. These were bold and imaginative moves for a man dealing with military questions for the first time. He grasped immediately the advantage that numbers gave the North and urged his generals to keep up a constant pressure on the whole strategic line of the Confederacy until a weak spot was found —and a break-through could be made. And he soon realized, if he did not know it at the beginning, that the proper objective of his armies was the destruction of the Confederate armies and not the occupation of Southern territory. His

[8] Karl von Clausewitz, *On War*, 599, Modern Library Edition.

strategic thinking was sound and for a rank amateur astonishingly good.[9]

During the first three years of the war, Lincoln performed many of the functions that in a modern command system would be done by the chief of the general staff or by the joint chiefs of staff. He formulated policy, drew up strategic plans, and even devised and directed tactical movements. Judged by modern standards, he did some things that a civilian director of war should not do. Modern critics say that he "interfered" too much with military operations. He and his contemporaries did not think that he interfered improperly. In the American command system it was traditional for the civilian authority to direct strategy and tactics. The Continental Congress in the Revolution and the president and cabinet in the War of 1812 and the Mexican War had planned extensive and detailed campaigns. Lincoln was acting only as the civil authority had acted in every previous war. He was doing what he and most people thought the commander in chief ought to do in war.

Sometimes Lincoln made excellent plans and decisions; sometimes he made bad mistakes. Some of his mistakes resulted from his initial ignorance in 1861–62 of how to translate his strategical concepts into workable instructions for his generals. His first generals, especially McClellan, were equally ignorant of how to establish relations with the head of the government so that they could find out his ideas about strategy and counsel him. When Lincoln asked them for advice, he usually got *ipse dixit* opinions. McClellan, who succeeded Scott as general in chief, did not seem to know that he ought to offer guidance to his political chief.[1] If McClellan

[9] Colin R. Ballard, *The Military Genius of Abraham Lincoln: An Essay*, 2–3, 6, 28–29, 239; John C. Ropes, *The Story of the Civil War*, I, 111.

[1] Sir Frederick Maurice, "Lincoln as a Strategist," *Forum*, LXXV, 1926, 164.

and other generals had known how to talk to Lincoln or had wanted to talk with him about the military situation, the President would have interfered in military affairs less than he sometimes did. On several occasions, he intervened because the generals had not frankly told him what they were going to do or had not explained their purposes to him in terms that he could understand. Sometimes Lincoln "interfered" without meaning to. He had the type of mind that delighted to frame a plan of military operations. He loved to work up a plan and spring it on a general. The mental exercise gave him pleasure, and he liked to get the reactions of soldiers to his schemes. He did not mean for the generals to adopt his designs, but they did not always understand this. What he intended as a presentation of his ideas or a suggestion to be considered sometimes came through to the military mind as an order from the commander in chief.[2]

Much of Lincoln's so-called interfering with the conduct of the war occurred in the first years of the conflict, when he believed, with some reason, that he was more capable of managing operations than were most of the generals. When the war started, he was inclined to defer to the judgments of trained soldiers. He soon came to doubt and even scorn the capabilities of the military mind. He asked of the generals decision, action, fighting, victory. They replied with indecision, inaction, delay, excuses. He became oppressed by the spectacle, so familiar in war, of generals who were superb in preparing for battle but who shrank from seeking its awful decision. "Tell him," he wrote in preparing instructions for one general, "to put it through—not to be writing or telegraphing back here, but put it through." [3] He wanted victories, but he

[2] Sir Frederick Maurice, *Statesmen and Soldiers of the Civil War*, 95–96.

[3] Lincoln to Simon Cameron, June 20, 1861, John G. Nicolay and John Hay (eds.), *The Complete Works of Abraham Lincoln*, VI, 294. Hereafter cited as *Works of Lincoln*.

got more letters than victories, letters from generals who wrote back that they could not put it through unless Lincoln provided them with more men and more guns . . . and still more.

One of the most important functions Commander in Chief Lincoln had to perform was choosing generals to manage the armies. He never had to worry that too few would apply for commissions. At the beginning of the war especially, he was showered with requests and demands for appointments from would-be generals and their political and military supporters: from officers who had spent weary years in the regular army in junior rank and now saw a chance to get their stars; from former officers who had resigned from the army to take lucrative civilian jobs and now wanted to return as generals; from politicians who thought military heroes would be popular after the war; from men who were ambitious, patriotic, able, mediocre, and incompetent. The rush for rank impressed, amused, and irritated the President. A popular jest of the war, one with a bitter undertone, was his reported remark about a brigadier general who got himself captured along with some horses and mules: "I don't care so much for brigadiers; I can make them. But horses and mules cost money." [4]

Lincoln handed out many commissions at the start of the war for reasons that were completely political but completely sound in a military sense. He used the military patronage to unite discordant groups in support of the war and to keep down divisions in the North. Creating and maintaining national unity was a necessary and vital phase of war-making in 1861, and Lincoln performed brilliantly with his appointments. He had to satisfy his own Republicans, who thought he gave too many commissions to Democrats, and he had to soothe the Democrats, who thought he was letting Republicans

[4] James Harrison Wilson, *Under the Old Flag*, I, 349.

run the war.[5] He dispensed commissions to ambitious political chieftains with large personal followings, especially if they were Democrats, like Nathaniel P. Banks, John A. McClernand, and Ben Butler. These selections saddled the army with some prize incompetents in high places, but they were good investments in national cohesion.[6] Some of Lincoln's appointments went to men who were leaders of important nationality groups like the German-Americans. Lincoln realized the importance of enlisting the Germans in support of the war, but he was amused by their eagerness to get their prominent men on the list of generals. Once a staff officer heard a conversation between the President and Secretary of War Edwin M. Stanton about some appointments of brigadier generals. Lincoln said he agreed with most of Stanton's recommendations, but, continued the President, "there has got to be something done unquestionably in the interest of the Dutch, and to that end I want Schimmelfennig appointed." Lincoln uttered the name with great enjoyment. Stanton said there were German officers who were better recommended. "No matter about that," said Lincoln; "his name will make up for any difference there may be." It had to be Schimmelfennig, and he went off repeating the name.[7]

With Schimmelfennig, Lincoln was getting a saving laugh out of a serious situation. He was escaping momentarily from the grimness of war in the same way he did when he told one of his stories to a pompous senator or read Artemus Ward in a Cabinet meeting. Selecting generals was a galling, dull busi-

[5] George W. Julian, *Speeches on Political Questions, 1850–1868,* 202–204; Senator Henry Wilson in *Congressional Globe,* 2 Sess., 38 Cong., pt. 1, 164; P. A. Ladue to Lincoln, January 6, 1862, Lincoln MSS.; Joseph Medill to Lincoln, February 17, 1864, *ibid.*

[6] Fred Harvey Harrington, *Fighting Politician, Major General N. P. Banks,* 54–56.

[7] Allen Thorndike Rice (ed.), *Reminiscences of Abraham Lincoln by Distinguished Men of His Time,* 391–392.

ness, and he seized every chance he had to get some fun out of it. He liked to have attractive wives of officers besiege him for promotions for their husbands. In the Lincoln Papers is a list he made in 1861 of officers he wanted to remember when he made appointments. After the name of Lieutenant Slemmer is the notation: "His pretty wife says a Major, or first Captain." [8] Of another wife who wanted him to make her husband a brigadier general, he wrote: "She is a saucy woman and I am afraid she will keep tormenting me until I may have to do it." [9]

In dealing with the applicants for appointments and promotions, Lincoln demonstrated his most skilled techniques in managing men and situations. Once the Pennsylvania Congressional delegation came buzzing angrily at Lincoln to get a promotion for the state's son, General Samuel P. Heintzelman. They extolled him, said he was a fine general, a good man. Seizing on the last claim, the President agreed that Heintzelman certainly was a good man; in fact he was "a good egg," and therefore he would keep. "You must trust me," he said, "to see that the General has justice done him." There was a pause, and then one of the delegation said: "We have trusted you a long time on this." "Gentlemen, you must do so longer," said Lincoln, and bowed them out.[1]

Lincoln probably enjoyed his exchange with the Pennsylvanians. But sometimes he got terribly angry when people criticized his military appointments. Once General Carl Schurz, the ebullient and incompetent German-American officer, wrote Lincoln that the administration was failing politically because the war was failing and that Lincoln was to blame for it all because he had entrusted the important com-

[8] Memorandum, April, 1861, Lincoln MSS., vol. 44.
[9] Memorandum, August 23, 1862, *ibid.*, vol. 85.
[1] MS. Journal of Samuel P. Heintzelman, entry of June 22, 1862. There are no quotation marks around the spoken statements in Heintzelman's account.

mands to men whose hearts were not in the war. By men without hearts, Schurz meant Democrats. With a dramatic reference to his brave boys dying in an aimless war, he concluded: "I do not know whether you have ever seen a battlefield. I assure you, Mr. President, it is a terrible sight." [2] Lincoln liked Schurz, but he was angered by the General's letter. And he had no intention of letting Schurz patronize him. In a cutting reply, one of the best of his war letters, he read Schurz a lecture on how to pick generals. Who is to decide who shall be generals? he asked. "If I must discard my own judgment and take yours, I must also take that of others; and by the time I should reject all I should be advised to reject, I should have none left, Republicans or others—not even yourself. For be assured, my dear sir, there are men who . . . think you are performing your part as poorly as you think I am performing mine." Republican and Democratic generals had been about equally successful, continued Lincoln, naming some officers from each party who had performed well. Then came the crusher: "I will not perform the ungrateful task of comparing failures." [3] Anybody else but Schurz would have been demolished. He kept on writing letters.

Lincoln never discarded his judgment to others in choosing generals. But he was willing to discard his judgment of what was good strategy and take the opinion of any general whom he considered to be able. He was willing to yield the power to direct strategic operations to any general who could demonstrate that he was competent to frame and execute strategy. Lincoln sensed that there was something wrong in the command system. Somewhere, he thought, there ought to be a division of function between him and the military. But where should the line be drawn? And who was the general to whom

[2] Carl Schurz to Lincoln, November 8, 1862, Lincoln MSS., vol. 92.
[3] Lincoln to Schurz, November 24, 1862, *Works of Lincoln*, VIII, 84–87.

he could confide the power to control? Lincoln was to go through some bitter and agonizing experiences before he got the answers to these questions. In the process, he and the army and the nation were to learn a lot about command. By 1864 the United States would have a modern command system. Lincoln did not know it in 1861, but he was going to make a large and permanent contribution to the organization of the American military system.

Chapter 2

Two Men of Destiny

IT was a humble little note that Lincoln wrote to General Scott on April 1, 1861. He asked whether it would impose too much labor on the General to send him short daily reports of the military situation. "If not, I will thank him to do so." [1] In the first frantic days of the war Lincoln approached the ancient warrior with grateful humility. Ignorant of war himself, he wanted to use the knowledge of one who was supposed to be a master of the art. He found no established machinery for communication between him and the commanding general; his note to Scott was an attempt to place their relationship on an institutional basis.

Scott started sending the reports immediately and continued to do so for weeks, until more formal contacts between the President and the military were established. The documents repose today in the Lincoln Papers, each report about two or three small pages in length and on the outside of each envelope in Lincoln's writing, "Gen. Scotts daily report No.—." [2] Lincoln was too human and curious to be satisfied with written accounts when he could talk to the author. He would frequently call at Scott's office during the day or, accompanied by a few cabinet members, drop in at night at the General's quarters, where Scott, enthroned in a huge arm-

[1] *Works of Lincoln*, VI, 238.
[2] Lincoln MSS., vols. 39–45.

chair, would be dispensing maxims of war to his staff. Always then Scott would insist that the President take the big chair, and after the exchange had been made he would recount the military happenings of the day.[3]

The daily reports dealt with routine matters of troop movements and the like, but the important thing Lincoln wanted to know was what general plan Scott had in mind for subduing the Confederacy. The President talked about a tentative scheme of his own—he would hold Fortress Monroe on the eastern flank of Virginia, blockade the Southern ports, make Washington safe, and then go down and attack Charleston.[4] This is the earliest recorded example of Lincoln's strategic thinking. Although he probably devised his plan hastily, it contained elements of soundness, notably the proposals to wage economic warfare through a naval blockade and to maintain Fortress Monroe as a base for future moves. As a strategic design, it lacked completeness because it contemplated movements in only one theater of war. At this stage Lincoln apparently did not envision operations in the Mississippi Valley.

The occupation of the line of the Mississippi was an important part of the plan which Scott prepared for the government. He proposed to establish a tight blockade of the Confederacy's ports and then to move an army of 60,000, accompanied by gunboats, down the river to seize and hold it from Cairo to the Gulf. For the commander of the expedition, he had decided on young George B. McClellan, with some "rough-vigor fellows" to assist him. The Confederacy would be enveloped, sealed off from the world politically and economically. This done, Scott would halt and wait. He would wait for the Unionist sentiment he thought existed in the

[3] E. D. Townsend, *Anecdotes of the Civil War in the United States,* 42.

[4] Tyler Dennett (ed.), *Lincoln and the Civil War in the Diaries and Letters of John Hay,* 11, diary entry of April 25, 1861.

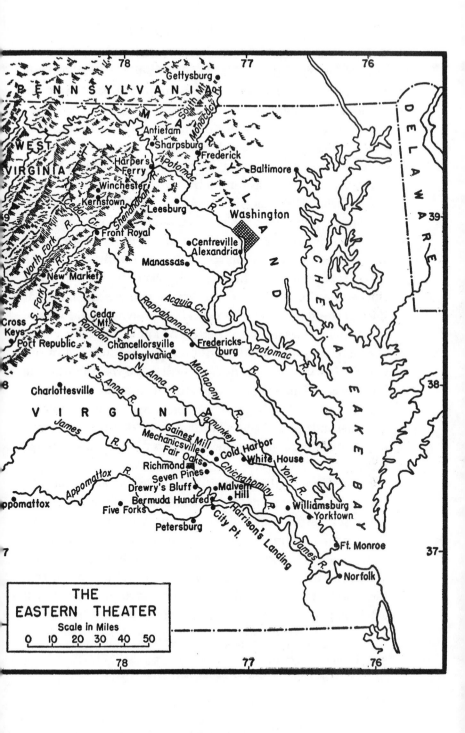

THE
EASTERN THEATER
Scale in Miles
0 10 20 30 40 50

South to assert itself and force the Confederate authorities to treat for peace and reunion. Don't invade the South, he advised Lincoln, that will exasperate the Unionists, we can win without attacking.[5]

This was the famous and often ridiculed Anaconda plan that was to squeeze the South to military death. In its calculations on the existence of a strong Unionist element in the Confederacy and its assumption that this group would seize control when the Anaconda began to constrict, it was more a diplomatic policy than a plan of strategic action. Lincoln did not adopt it because he could not afford to rely on a policy alone. Even if the Anaconda worked, it would take years to make its effect felt, and he wanted quicker results. The defect in the thinking of Scott, the military man, was the idea that the war could be won by a single effort of some kind. Lincoln, the civilian strategist, knew better; he knew that many efforts of different kinds would be required. But, as surely as Lincoln saw the fallacy in Scott's design, he saw also the one strategic jewel in it. If Lincoln had not realized before the military importance of the Mississippi River, he grasped it after studying the Anaconda plan. From that time on, the occupation of the line of the great river became an integral part of his strategic thinking.[6]

At the moment there was little Lincoln and Scott could do except to consider plans. Action would have to wait until men and resources were mobilized. Around Washington the government was assembling an army, made up mostly of volunteers, that by early summer would number slightly over 30,000. As its commanding general Lincoln appointed Irvin McDowell from the regular army. Although powerful political influences led by Secretary of the Treasury Salmon P.

[5] Scott to McClellan, May 3, 1861, *Official Records,* LI, pt. 1, 369–370; Townsend, *Anecdotes of the Civil War,* 55–56.

[6] Conger, "Lincoln as War Statesman," 112–121.

Chase had suggested McDowell as commander, the reasons for his appointment were military. It was thought that he had the right military background to enable him to organize and lead an army of recruits. Much of his experience had been in staff work, a field of which most American officers knew little. He had gone to military school in France, had spent a year there observing French practices, and had served on Scott's staff.[7]

The new general was to have a tragic career in the war. He had ability, he was modest and honest, but everything he tried went amiss. He was one of those generals of whom Grant said later that they got started wrong and never recovered. He was about six feet in height, square and strongly built; his hair was thick and dark, his eyes were small and blue, and he wore his beard in the French style. He put on weight easily because he was a gargantuan eater; awed observers gaped as he ate a whole watermelon for dessert. In his conversation he was impulsive and often censorious and dogmatic; hence he offended many people. There was a large amount of the prig in him. He was a prohibitionist. Once his horse reared and fell on him, knocking him unconscious. A surgeon tried to get some brandy in him, but his teeth were too rigidly set. Later, when told what happened, he said he was glad that even when he was unconscious liquor could not be forced down him.[8]

McDowell had no idea of fighting that summer. He was oppressed with his difficulties, and they were real. He was the first general in American history to command an army of 30,000 men. He had a small and inexperienced staff, he lacked a decent map of Virginia and knew only the direction of the main roads, and he had a green force to train. Scott too was opposed to battle because he believed the army was unready,

[7] J. H. Stine, *History of the Army of the Potomac*, 2–3, 7; Kenneth P. Williams, *Lincoln Finds a General*, I, 67.

[8] Wilson, *Under the Old Flag*, I, 66; William H. Russell, *My Diary, North and South*, 389; Carl Schurz, *Reminiscences of Carl Schurz*, II, 383; Herman Haupt, *Reminiscences of General Herman Haupt*, 63.

and he feared bloodshed would stop the rise of Union sentiment in the South.[9] Yet McDowell had to fight because Lincoln ordered an immediate offensive. The first big Northern
strategic movement was initiated and planned by the President and forced by him upon his generals. It was the first important exercise of his power as commander in chief. Late in
June, Scott, at the insistence of the President, gave McDowell
verbal instructions to prepare a plan of operations against the
Confederate army at Manassas, about thirty miles southwest
of Washington. McDowell responded with a proposal to move
30,000 men toward Manassas and turn the enemy position.[1]

Strategist Lincoln made the decision to undertake an offensive for reasons he considered militarily sound and not because the politicians, the press, and the public were screaming,
"Onward to Richmond." In the Virginia theater were about
50,000 untrained Union troops and 30,000 untrained Confederates. Slightly over 20,000 of the Confederates were at
Manassas, the rest in the Shenandoah Valley facing a larger
Northern force. If the Union troops in the Valley could neutralize the enemy there, McDowell could move on Manassas
with a superior force. If he smashed the Confederates, he
could disperse the remaining Southern forces in the state, take
Richmond, and end the war. It seemed to Lincoln a chance
worth taking.[2] The fallacy in his thinking was the notion that
the South would quit after an initial defeat. The South was
as unlikely to do this as the North was after it was whipped at
Manassas.

McDowell brought his plan to Scott, and the two worked

[9] Russell, *My Diary*, 395–396; Heintzelman, MS Journal, June 8,
1861; Stine, *Army of the Potomac*, 8–9; Townsend, *Anecdotes of the
Civil War*, 57.

[1] McDowell to E. D. Townsend, June 24, 1861, *Official Records*,
II, 719–721; McDowell in testimony to the Committee on the Conduct
of the War, *Reports of the Committee on the Conduct of the War*, 1863,
II, 35, hereafter cited as *C. C. W., Reports*.

[2] Ballard, *Military Genius of Lincoln*, 49–50.

it over carefully, studying what maps they had. Scott approved McDowell's arrangements. On June 29 they were asked to come to the White House to discuss the plan with Lincoln, the Cabinet, and the senior generals in Washington. At the meeting Scott made a final plea for the Anaconda but yielded when he saw how firm the President was for an immediate advance. McDowell then presented his design to move on Manassas and flank the Confederates out of their defensive works. One of the generals said the success of the plan depended on the Federal forces in the Valley being able to prevent the Confederates there from joining the army at Manassas, and Scott assured him he would see that this was done. McDowell made bitter objections to his own plan. He thought it was wrong to force him to organize, discipline, march, and fight at the same time; he wanted more time to prepare his army. Lincoln replied, "You are green, it is true; but they are green, also; you are all green alike," and he directed McDowell to put his plan into execution.[3]

McDowell was not ready to move until the middle of July. Then the general who did not believe in his plan and his army marched toward Manassas. The newspapers published accounts of his numbers and line of march; crowds of civilian spectators accompanied the army; the whole North thrilled with anticipation. On a hot Sunday, the twenty-first, McDowell crossed Bull Run and started to turn the Confederate left. At first he drove the Confederates from one position after another, but finally they formed a line that held. The Union general in the Valley had not carried out his part of the plan; the Confederates there slipped away and came to Manassas, some of them arriving during the battle. With these reinforcements, the Confederates had as many men as McDowell had. They halted his last thrust and then counterattacked. As

[3] *C. C. W., Reports*, 1863, II, 35–38, 55, 62; Townsend, *Anecdotes of the Civil War*, 57.

the Unionists fell back, the spark of panic spread through their green ranks, and they milled back over Bull Run, losing morale and organization with every backward leap. Some officers, including McDowell, vainly tried to stop the stampede. On the north side of the Run a measure of order was restored, but McDowell knew he had to get his demoralized army back to the Washington defences. He ordered a retreat, a movement many of his men were already starting to execute. The battle that Lincoln had wanted had ended in defeat. But the decision might well have been the other way. McDowell had come close to victory.

That Sunday morning in Washington Lincoln asked Scott how he thought the battle would go. Old Fuss and Feathers said McDowell was certain to win and the President was not to worry. At eleven o'clock Lincoln went to church. In the afternoon he was at the White House receiving telegrams about the battle from an operator at Fairfax Station. At about three the operator sent in some despatches in which he said that, judging by the sound of the firing, he thought the Federals were falling back. Disturbed, Lincoln walked to Scott's office. He found the General asleep, woke him up, and told him things looked bad. Scott said that nobody at a distance from a battle could tell how it was going by its noises; the operator was wrong and McDowell would triumph. Then Scott prepared to go to sleep again! Lincoln went back to the White House and read the telegrams that continued to come in. Between four and six the despatches indicated a victory, and a relieved President went for an evening drive. While he was gone, Secretary of State Seward, pale and haggard, appeared at the executive mansion with the news that the battle was lost and McDowell in retreat. Find the President, he begged Lincoln's secretaries, and tell him to come to Scott's office. Lincoln returned soon, and the secretaries gave him Seward's message. Without a word or a change of expression, he walked to army headquarters, where the Cabinet was gathered. A telegram from McDowell came confirming the report of the defeat. Later Lincoln returned to the White House and lay down on a lounge. Civilian spectators of the battle were reaching the city, and some of them came to describe the fighting to Lincoln. He stayed on the lounge all night.[4]

Two days after the battle Lincoln rode out to Arlington to visit McDowell and the troops. Supposedly he said to the General, "I have not lost a particle of confidence in you," and McDowell replied, "I don't see why you should, Mr. President."[5] The story may be true or partially true. It would have been characteristic of Lincoln to say something kind to the General, but he had decided that McDowell's job was too large for him. He was probably beginning to have some doubts about Scott too. A Pennsylvania visitor in the capital described a conversation he heard between Lincoln and Scott. The old man kept repeating that Confederate General Beauregard at Manassas had more troops than he had, yet Beauregard could not capture the capital. Lincoln sat twirling his spectacles in his fingers. Finally he said: "It does seem to me, general, that if I were Beauregard I could take Washington."[6]

He had no real fears that Washington would fall, nor was he discouraged by the failure of the offensive he had planned. Neither was he disposed to doubt his ability to formulate general strategy or to abrogate his authority as commander in chief. On the day that he visited McDowell he prepared a "Memoranda of Military Policy Suggested By the Bull Run

---

[4] John G. Nicolay to Therena Bates, July 21, 1861, Nicolay MSS.; John G. Nicolay and John Hay, *Abraham Lincoln: A History*, IV, 352–356.

[5] E. D. Townsend to McDowell, July 23, 1861, *Official Records*, II, 758; Russell, *My Diary*, 507.

[6] Alexander K. McClure, *Lincoln and Men of War-Times*, 60–61.

Defeat." He proposed to push forward plans for the block-ade, strengthen the various Union forces and the points they held, and increase the size of the army by bringing in more volunteers. A few days later he added that when the fore-going had been accomplished, two offensives should be launched: one, to seize Manassas or a point on the railroads near it; and the other, a joint movement from Cairo against Memphis and from Cincinnati into East Tennessee.[7] He was thinking in big strategic terms, and he wanted a bigger man than McDowell in command in the East, a man who could bring order out of the confusion that followed Bull Run and organize an invasion of Virginia, and maybe a man who could succeed Scott in command of all the armies when the old general had to retire. On July 22 Lincoln summoned George B. McClellan to Washington.

Out in western Virginia, where he was clearing Confeder-ates out of the mountains, McClellan received a telegram di-recting him to report in Washington. He knew it was the call of destiny. He rode on horseback sixty miles to the near-est railroad station, caught the train to Wheeling, where he saw his adoring wife for a few moments, and continued on to Washington. He arrived on the twenty-sixth. With becoming respect for age and military etiquette, he first called on Scott and then reported to the adjutant general, who told him to see Lincoln. The President invited him to attend a Cabinet meeting but did not ask Scott. The old man was enraged, and McClellan felt amused and superior.[8] Everything that hap-pened made him feel more superior. The President, the Cabinet, Scott—everybody seemed to defer to him. "By some strange operation of magic I seem to have become the power of the land," he confided to his wife. He believed that he had been called to save his country. He was thirty-five years old,

---

[7] *Works of Lincoln*, VI, 331–333.
[8] McClellan, *Own Story*, 55, 66–67.

and his official title was commander of the Division of the Potomac.[9]

McClellan is the problem child of the Civil War. People reacted to him in violent extremes but rarely in terms of realistic evaluation. His contemporaries revered or reviled him, and historians have defended or attacked him. There was a duality in his character that made him at once honest and deceitful, simple and cunning, modest and arrogant, attractive and distasteful. Some people saw one McClellan; some, the other. Lincoln saw both, and labored patiently to bring the good McClellan uppermost. The job was too difficult even for his talents of human management.

McClellan always saw Lincoln as a person of inferior antecedents and abilities, who unfortunately was his superior officer. He regarded Lincoln as an oaf, sometimes a hostile or boring one, but always lubberly. McClellan felt superior to most people; he was a natural patronizer. His career before 1860 had been a sustained success. Born in Philadelphia of a well-to-do family, he had attended the best schools there before entering West Point. He graduated from the academy in 1846 and went immediately into the Mexican War as an engineer officer on Scott's staff. His work in the war was good, and his superiors marked him as an officer with a future. In 1855 the War Department sent him and two other officers to Europe to study the organization and methods of continental armies. He resigned from the army two years later to take the post of chief engineer of the Illinois Central Railroad. Later he became president of the Eastern Division of the Ohio and Mississippi Railroad. While he was with the Illinois Central, he met Lincoln, then running against Stephen A. Douglas for a Senate seat. McClellan voted for Douglas; Lincoln impressed him merely as a good storyteller. When the war started, McClellan, then living in Cincinnati, offered his services and re-

---

[9] *Ibid.*, 82–83; *Official Records*, II, 766.

ceived a commission as major general. He commanded the Department of the Ohio. His department was huge, his army small; but he was the only Union general who won any battles in 1861. He crossed the Ohio River and drove the Confederates out of western Virginia. His campaign was a minor one in every sense—the size of the forces engaged, the results—but it was victorious. When Lincoln looked for a general for the Eastern command, he thought of the young officer who had managed an independent command and given the Union its only success.

McClellan would have been a better man had he encountered some humbling reverses in his early years. He would have been a better general when he took over the Eastern command had he been tested in his first battles by possible or actual defeat. In his campaign in western Virginia, he triumphed too easily; he was readily convinced that he was a great soldier. The public, eager for a hero, went wild over him. He looked and acted as a soldier and a hero ought to act. Handsome and magnetic, he was of average height, but so stockily built he seemed short. His features were regular, his hair dark auburn, his eyes blue. In manner he was courteous, modest, sometimes boyish; and, like a proper American hero, he smoked and chewed tobacco. Admirers pointed out that he looked like Napoleon, and photographers got him to pose standing with folded arms. Soon the press began to call him the Young Napoleon.[1] The vast adulation clouded his sense of reality. Wherever he went in Ohio and Virginia, crowds gathered to stare at him. He felt then as he would always feel when people in numbers, civilians or soldiers, looked at him —that they saw him as a savior, the man, the one man, who could protect them from danger. He developed a Messianic

[1] Russell, *My Diary*, 479–480, 520–521; O. O. Howard, *Autobiography of Oliver Otis Howard*, I, 167; Albert D. Richardson, *The Secret Service . . .* , 143; Cox, *Military Reminiscences*, I, 57.

complex.[2] Later, when he was about to become general in chief, he wrote his wife in what he thought were words of sincere modesty: "I was called to it; my previous life seems to have been unwittingly directed to this great end. . . ." [3]

In the western Virginia campaign, McClellan revealed most of the military and personal characteristics he would later manifest in his operations in larger commands. He was a fine organizer and trainer of troops; and his men, sensing that he identified himself with them, idolized him. In preparing for battle he was confident and energetic, but as he approached the field of operations he became slow and timid. He magnified every obstacle; in particular, the size of the enemy army increased in his mind the closer he got to it. In battle he tended to interpret sights and sounds in his front as unfavorable to him; he hesitated to throw in his whole force at the supreme moment; and he withdrew when bolder men would have attacked.[4] In his strategic thinking, he demonstrated an ability to formulate big and daring plans that he did not relate to the realities of the strategic situation. He laid a scheme before Scott in April, 1861, when the Union forces were hardly larger than a corporal's guard, in which he proposed that two large armies move on Richmond and Nashville and after capturing them crush their way to Montgomery, Mobile, and New Orleans, ending the war in one magnificent stroke.[5] He could conjure up a grandiose design based on conditions that existed mainly in his imagination, and at the same time devote serious attention to a thimble-sized matter. From Camp Dennison, where he was organizing

[2] McClellan, *Own Story*, 57, 82–83.

[3] *Ibid.*, 172.

[4] McClellan to E. D. Townsend, June 22, 1861, *Official Records*, II, 194; Peter S. Michie, *General McClellan*, 90–91; Cox, *Military Reminiscences*, I, 57–58.

[5] McClellan to Scott, April 27, 1861, *Official Records*, LI, pt. 1, 338–339.

his army, he once telegraphed to the War Department asking for authorization to use boards to erect chapels if local parties provided the nails and labor. Amazed and amused by the request, the Secretary replied: "The Lord's will be done." [6]

Early in the western Virginia campaign McClellan demonstrated a trait that would get him into trouble later. He assumed that, beyond his function of framing strategy, he had the right to pronounce political policy for the government without first ascertaining the views of government or getting permission from his superiors to speak. When he invaded Virginia, he issued proclamations saying that his army would not interfere with slavery and would repress any attempted servile insurrection. Then he sent copies to Lincoln and said he had expressed what he thought were Lincoln's views and he hoped the President would approve.[7] As a matter of fact, he had reflected Lincoln's policy; he and the President were in accord on the slavery issue, both being gradual emancipationists and opponents of the wartime destruction of slavery. In making a policy announcement on slavery, McClellan merely did what many generals would do in the war. The line between policy and strategy was dimly drawn; just as Lincoln believed he was capable of making strategy, so generals thought they were qualified to form policy. McClellan differed from other officers only in his sublime conviction that the government would fall if it refused to adopt his ideas. In policy as in strategy, he assumed that he could deal with the government on an equal basis as a sort of contracting party.[8]

When the Young Napoleon assumed command, he found Washington and the military organization affected by the

[6] Simon Cameron to McClellan, May 22, 1861, *ibid.*, 388.

[7] McClellan, *Own Story*, 50–52; McClellan to Lincoln, June 1, 1861, McClellan MSS., Ser. 1.

[8] McClellan, *Own Story*, 33–35; John C. Ropes, *The Army under Pope*, 12.

aftermath of the defeat at Bull Run. Soldiers absent from their units straggled along the streets; people talked hysterically about a Confederate advance over the Potomac; demoralization seemed to be in the air. The situation was not nearly as perilous as he would later in all sincerity describe it, but it was bad enough. He gave it what he liked to call the hand of the master; and at such a juncture he was truly masterful. A brilliant administrator and a fine trainer of troops, he was at his best in getting an army ready to fight. Lincoln could not have picked a better man to reorganize McDowell's defeated troops and to organize the masses of recruits the government began to move into the Washington area. McClellan took hold of affairs with a calm confidence that imparted itself to all who saw him; he worked with a feverish energy that would have killed a weaker man. He sat at his desk drawing up plans of organization; he rode all over the camps making inspections, sometimes spending twelve hours in the saddle; he conferred with Lincoln and Scott and the Cabinet; he slept hardly at all. System and efficiency appeared in everything he controlled. In those months of summer and early fall, he forged out of the volunteer hosts placed under his command the Army of the Potomac, one of the finest fighting armies in the history of war. Whatever else he failed to do in the war, he created that army, and gave it a belief in itself that nothing could destroy. Its record will always stand as a tribute to McClellan's organizing abilities. No other army fought so well or so long under so many mediocre commanders—the first of whom was its creator.

About a week after McClellan took the command of the Eastern department, he presented to Lincoln a plan of strategic action for all theaters of the war. He prepared it, he said later, at the President's request, and his recollection was probably correct. When Lincoln called McClellan to Washington, he undoubtedly had considered that the young general might be the man to succeed Scott as general in chief. He would want to know whether McClellan could think in terms of grand strategy, and it would be characteristic of him to ask the general to draw up a plan immediately. The document he received was a perfect revelation of the workings of McClellan's mind. McClellan could always devise big projects, but he rarely related them to the resources at his disposal. His imagination ran away with him and from the facts; he created situations in his mind and believed they were real.

In the memorandum he gave Lincoln, he started out with a realistic statement and became more and more unrealistic with every sentence he wrote. At the end he was rambling from one recommended operation to another, apparently writing each one down as it came to mind. He began soundly enough by saying the object of the war differed from ordinary wars in that the Union had to crush a whole population and not just to conquer a peace. The principal effort of the North, he advised, should be made in the Virginia theater, with subsidiary operations being conducted on the Mississippi and in Missouri and Tennessee. The force in Virginia should number 273,000. He would move it by water to the seacoast and advance inland and capture Richmond; then he would apply the same treatment to other parts of the Confederacy by seizing Charleston, Savannah, Mobile, Montgomery, and New Orleans. His thoughts soared as he mentally occupied the South. He told Lincoln it would be a smart move to send a force from Kansas and Nebraska down through the Indian Territory to take over west Texas; that suggested Mexico to him, and he instructed the President that it would be good policy to make an alliance with that nation! In a rosy glow of confidence as he finished composing his hodgepodge scheme, McClellan asserted that if the government gave him the 273,000 men he asked for he would crush the rebellion at one blow. "I shall carry this thing *en grand* . . . ," he exulted to his wife.[9]

The plan he was so proud of was a defective one in almost every respect. It was fundamentally wrong because it proposed to concentrate the military effort in one theater to the neglect of others and because it would have made places instead of enemy armies the objectives. It was wrong in other ways. McClellan seemed to think the huge host he wanted for his own army could be recruited immediately. Even if the government could have raised such a force, it could not have housed and fed it, especially if collected in one area. And even if by some miracle this condition had been met, there was not enough water transport available to have carried the army to the Southern coast. Lincoln's reactions to McClellan's fantasia are not known. He may have been impressed by it, or he may have been appalled. Or he may have thought the Young Napoleon was merely a little flighty and would settle down with experience.

McClellan continued to slave away at his work, going without sleep or relaxation and wearing his nerves to the snapping point. He also continued to create imaginary situations, and now he began to fill them with enemies and dangers. He became convinced that the Confederates in Virginia numbered at least 100,000 and were preparing to attack him. Actually their army was about half as big as he thought, and they had not the slightest intention of advancing; but he insisted that he needed large reinforcements.[1] Always he was conscious that he was the only man who could preserve the nation. "The

---

[9] McClellan, *Own Story*, 101–105; *Official Records*, V, 6–8. McClellan wrote his "Memorandum" on August 2, 1861, but erroneously dated it August 4 in his report. McClellan to Mrs. McClellan, August 2, 1861, *Own Story*, 83–84.

[1] McClellan to Scott, August 8, 1861, *Official Records*, X, pt. 3, 3–4; McClellan to Mrs. McClellan, August 8, 16, McClellan, *Own Story*, 84, 87.

people call on me to save the country," he wrote to his wife. "I must save it, and cannot respect anything that is in the way." People were writing him that he ought to be dictator, he told her. ". . . I have no such aspiration. I would cheerfully take the dictatorship and agree to lay down my life when the country is saved." [2]

His fears and frustrations demanded a scapegoat, and he found one in Scott. Before he came to Washington, he could not praise the old General enough, even going so far as to tell Scott that all he knew of war he had learned from him.[3] Almost immediately after he arrived, he began to quarrel with Scott and to accuse the general in chief of throwing obstacles in his way. The old man always comes in my way, he understands nothing, I can do nothing as long as he controls—so McClellan complained to his wife.[4] He started to ignore and bypass Scott, communicating directly with Lincoln and members of the Cabinet. Scott was infuriated and, denouncing McClellan as "an ambitious junior," asked to be retired. Lincoln tried to patch up the squabble. Scott agreed to stay on, mainly because he liked the President and wanted to please him. McClellan backed out of a fight when he saw Lincoln supporting Scott, but he was yielding only temporarily. He was determined to be free from Scott's control.[5]

As the beginning days of autumn came to Washington, McClellan felt that his military position was safer. He now thought he could hold Washington against an attack, even though he estimated his forces to be inferior to those of the enemy. He had an army of 70,000 ready for the field, but the

[2] McClellan to Mrs. McClellan, August 9, 1861, *ibid.*, 85.

[3] McClellan to E. D. Townsend, July 5, 1861, *Official Records*, II, 199; McClellan to Scott, July 18, McClellan MSS., Ser. 1.

[4] McClellan to Mrs. McClellan, August 8, 9, 15, 16, 1861, *Own Story*, 84–87.

[5] Scott to Simon Cameron, August 9, 12, 1861, McClellan to Lincoln, August 10, *Official Records*, XI, pt. 3, 3–4, 5–6.

Confederate army had grown in his mind to 130,000. Still, he was thinking about taking the offensive.[6] Lincoln too was thinking it was time to undertake offensive movements. The President had a plan in mind for two minor thrusts into the Confederacy, intended as diversionary attacks to prepare the way for bigger moves. About October 1, he wrote in what he called a "Memorandum for a Plan of Campaign" that he wanted the Union forces in Kentucky to move and seize a point on the railroad connecting Virginia and Tennessee near the Cumberland Gap. At the same time the navy would send an expedition to occupy Port Royal, off the coast of South Carolina. After these movements had been completed, Generals McClellan in the East and Fremont in the West were to "avail themselves of any advantages the diversions may present." [7]

In 1861 Lincoln selected as commanders of his two most important departments two generals who believed they were men of destiny. John C. Fremont was the western counterpart of McClellan. Like the Young Napoleon, he was a handsome and magnetic man. He gave at the same time an impression of wise maturity and of buoyant youth. Although he was forty-eight and his dark hair and beard were tinged with gray, he seemed much younger. Of medium height, he was slender, muscular, graceful. His features were regular, his eyes piercing, his voice musical; and his every action was dramatic.[8] He was a person of note before the war. As an explorer of the West for the army's corps of topographical engineers, he had won national fame for his crossings of the Rockies and the title of Pathfinder. In the Mexican War he had helped conquer California; in 1856 he was the first presidential candidate of the Republican party. When the war began he was eager

[6] McClellan, *Own Story*, 90, 105–107.
[7] *Works of Lincoln*, VII, 3–6.
[8] Richardson, *Secret Service*, 194–195; Schurz, *Reminiscences*, II, 344.

to get into the army, and powerful political interests backed him for a commission. He commanded the support of the anti-slavery wing of the Republican party, and he was a popular hero with the German-Americans. The influential Blair family—the father an adviser of several presidents, a son in the Cabinet and another the boss of Missouri—pushed his cause with Lincoln.

Fremont was in France when the shooting started. He rushed home and came to Washington to see Lincoln about getting a command. The President was willing to give him something. Whatever feeling Lincoln had about Fremont's military ability, he knew the Pathfinder could bring influential groups to the support of the war effort. And at that stage he had no reason to doubt Fremont's capacity as a soldier; rather, he had reason to think that this man of experience and exploits would make him a good general. Fremont wanted to go to the West, which he knew and where he was known; and that was where the Blairs, worried about a Confederate threat to their bailiwick of Missouri, wanted him sent. To Lincoln, the West seemed like an ideal theater for Fremont, and on July 3 the President made the appointment. Orders were drawn creating the Western Department, composed of Illinois and the states and territories west of the Mississippi to the Rockies, under the command of Major General Fremont, with headquarters at St. Louis.[9]

Lincoln did not at the moment assign Fremont a specific objective to accomplish in the West. In discussions between the President, Scott, and Fremont, it was decided that the General should go out to Missouri and use his name and energy to raise an army. When he felt that the state was safe from Confederate invasion and his army large enough for

[9] *Works of Lincoln*, VI, 296; *Official Records*, III, 390; Allan Nevins, *Fremont, Pathmarker of the West*, 473–474; William E. Smith, *The Francis Preston Blair Family in Politics*, II, 55; C. C. W., *Reports*, 1863, III, 154, 161.

offensive operations, he was to start a movement down the Mississippi, with Memphis as his objective. Although Lincoln was anxious for Fremont to get to St. Louis and take hold of affairs, the Pathfinder stayed in the East three weeks before leaving. On the day he departed, he called on Lincoln and discussed his plan to occupy the Mississippi line. At the end of the conference Lincoln walked with Fremont to the portico of the White House. The General asked whether Lincoln had any instructions. "No," replied the President, "I have given you *carte blanche;* you must use your own judgment and do the best you can." Lincoln meant only that he was giving Fremont extensive and undefined authority to organize his department, but it was a dangerous remark to make to a weak and unstable man. Fremont understood that he could exercise any power he thought necessary, even beyond the limits of his commission. Somebody had told him that Lincoln had said he had given Fremont more power than he had himself, and the Pathfinder believed the absurdity.[1]

Fremont arrived in St. Louis on July 25. Almost immediately he began to act as nearly every general in the war did after taking over a command. At first he brimmed with confidence and optimism, but soon he imagined himself surrounded on all sides by dangers and difficulties. His shrill complaints poured into Washington. He was faced by an enemy superior in numbers and steadily increasing; he lacked supplies for his troops; he had to have reinforcements or he would be overwhelmed. Lincoln had sent a boy to do a man's work. Fremont was a sincere and attractive person, but a giddy and fumbling general. With no previous military training or knowledge, he stepped into a complex military situation. He did not have the capacity to handle it or to learn by experience from his mistakes. If he had been smart enough

---

[1] Nevins, *Fremont,* 476–477; *C. C. W., Reports,* 1863, III, 33, 43–44, 154–155.

to appoint a good staff, he might have got along better; but his staff was like himself—showy and futile. It was made up mostly of Hungarian and German officers; bedecked in fancy uniforms, they encircled the General's headquarters and made it almost impossible for people, even those with important business, to see him. Inefficiency and failure marked every phase of Fremont's conduct of affairs in Missouri. Confederate troops in the state whipped a part of Fremont's forces at Wilson's Creek. Fremont spent a lot of time and money building fortifications around St. Louis and making contracts for the purchase of horses and guns. The General was honest but innocent; much of the money went into the pockets of crooked contractors. In Washington the government was appalled by the costs he ran up. He got into a bitter quarrel with Frank Blair, Jr., the Missouri representative of his sponsors, and brought the powerful family down on his back. Finally, he attempted to frame policy and so ran afoul of Lincoln.

Politically Fremont was associated with the faction of the Republican party known as the radicals, who wanted to make the abolition of slavery one of the official objectives of the war. Fremont was sincerely antislavery, and his desire to strike a blow at that institution, coupled with his opinion that Lincoln had given him a blank check, caused him to set up as a policy maker. On August 30 he issued a proclamation establishing martial law in the state, one section of which freed the slaves of all persons resisting the government.[2]

Like McClellan, the Pathfinder had assumed that he could define policy without consulting the government. Unlike McClellan, he had announced a policy which ran counter to the one proclaimed by the government. Lincoln and Congress, in order to keep the border slave states in the Union and to unite Northern opinion on one issue, had said the war was being conducted to restore the Union. The President knew

[2] *Official Records,* III, 466–467.

that Fremont's proclamation would alienate conservative support of the war; besides, he had no intention of letting generals make policy. Unofficially he asked Fremont to modify the section of the proclamation dealing with slavery. The General refused, but graciously said he would obey an order from Lincoln to change it. His attack on slavery was as much a military movement as a battle, he explained; and his judgment as to when and how to attack the enemy should be trusted. Lincoln then publicly revoked the slavery part of the ukase.[3]

By now Lincoln was beginning to distrust Fremont's judgment generally, but he hoped the Pathfinder might still be saved and made useful. After talking to Scott, he decided to ask General David Hunter, an old regular army officer, to go out to Missouri to assist Fremont. It was Lincoln's hope that Hunter's professional knowledge would keep Fremont from making any bad military blunders.[4] At about the same time Lincoln sent Postmaster General Montgomery Blair and Quartermaster General M. C. Meigs to St. Louis to advise with Fremont and to investigate affairs in the Western Department.[5]

While the President's agents were traveling west, an emissary from Fremont was on the way east. It was Jessie Benton Fremont, the General's intelligent, intrepid wife. The Fremonts knew there was dissatisfaction in Washington with the General, and when Montgomery Blair had headed west they decided their enemies were getting ready to strike. Jessie caught the first train to Washington and Lincoln. After a trip

[3] Lincoln to Fremont, September 2, 11, 1861, *Works of Lincoln,* VI, 350–351, 353; Lincoln to O. H. Browning, September 22, *ibid.,* 357–361; Fremont to Lincoln, September 8, *C. C. W., Reports,* 1863, III, 151–152.

[4] Scott to Lincoln, September 5, 1861, Lincoln MSS., vol. 54; Lincoln to Hunter, September 9, *Works of Lincoln,* VI, 352.

[5] *C. C. W., Reports,* 1863, III, 155–156; M. Blair to Lincoln, September 14, 1861, Lincoln MSS., vol. 55.

of three days, she arrived at night on September 11 and went to Willard's Hotel. Although it was late, she sent her card to the White House. A reply came at once that Lincoln wanted to see her.

After sitting up two nights on the train, Jessie walked to the executive mansion. She was tired and fearful and ready to fight, and Lincoln sensed her mood. In a later account of the interview, she said he was harsh in manner and did not ask her to sit down. Apparently she broke into a defense of all Fremont's acts and demanded to know why Montgomery Blair had gone to St. Louis. Lincoln said Blair had been sent as a friend and adviser. The President said Fremont should not have issued his proclamation, and Jessie flared back with an antislavery argument. Nettled, Lincoln replied: "You are quite a female politician." Jessie said something—the accounts do not quite agree—to the effect that if her husband wanted to try conclusions with Lincoln he could set up for himself, or that if Fremont were removed it would be difficult to persuade his army and friends to accept it as an act of authority. On that note the conference ended. She had done Fremont much harm and no good.[6]

No advisers, not Hunter nor anybody else, could help Fremont. He did not ask Hunter for counsel and would not have understood it if Hunter had given him any. Confederate forces continued to operate in Missouri, and late in September, to Lincoln's dismay, captured a Federal garrison at Lexington.[7] Lincoln's patience was now about run out. He sent Secretary of War Cameron to St. Louis, ostensibly to inspect fortifications, but Cameron bore an order from Lincoln direct-

[6] Nevins, *Fremont,* 516–519; Nicolay and Hay, *Lincoln,* IV, 415; Jessie Fremont to Lincoln, September 12, 1861, Lincoln MSS., vol. 54; Jessie Fremont to W. H. Lamon, October 25, *ibid.,* vol. 59.

[7] Scott to Fremont, September 23, 1861, *C. C. W., Reports,* 1863, III, 151.

ing Fremont to turn over his command to Hunter. When Cameron got to Missouri, he found Fremont in the field and moving after the Confederates, who were retreating south. He showed Lincoln's order to the General. Fremont was pained and humiliated, and begged the Secretary not to deliver it officially. He said he was on the point of catching up to the enemy and would then destroy him. Cameron consented to withhold the order until his return to Washington, but told Fremont that failure would mean removal.[8]

There was little likelihood that Fremont could run down the Confederates. They were merely eluding battle with him while slipping away to safety. Lincoln knew that the General's big words to Cameron meant nothing. In a Cabinet meeting he said it was plain Fremont was unfit for command and must be removed. On October 24 he sent an order to General Samuel Curtis, in command at St. Louis, removing Fremont and appointing Hunter in his place. Curtis was to transmit the order to Fremont and Hunter. Even then Lincoln was willing to give the Pathfinder one last slender chance. The order was not to be delivered if Fremont had won a battle, or was in one, or was in the presence of the enemy ready to fight one.[9]

The removal order was carried from Washington to Curtis by Leonard Swett, a political friend of the President's. Since it had been published in the newspapers that the order was on its way, and since Swett was known to be close to Lincoln, Curtis decided that if Swett tried to deliver the order he would be refused entrance into Fremont's lines. To make sure the order would get to Fremont without his knowing that it was coming, Curtis gave it to an Iowa captain, J. C. McKenney,

[8] Simon Cameron to Lincoln, October 12, 14, 1861, Lincoln MSS., vol. 58.

[9] Howard Beale (ed.), *Diary of Edward Bates, 1859–1866*, 198–199; *Works of Lincoln*, VII, 10–11.

who dressed himself as a farmer and started for Fremont's camp, trusting that his disguise and a pass from Curtis would get him through the lines. Curtis feared that Fremont would refuse to obey the order even if the courier delivered it, and had duplicate copies prepared so that he could promulgate it in the event that Fremont made any opposition.

McKenney reached Fremont's headquarters at five in the morning on November 2. He waited five hours to see whether there was any prospect of a battle and then asked to see Fremont. An aide told him he would have to state his business first. He said his business was with the General alone. Finally he was taken to Fremont. He handed the order to the General. Fremont tore open the envelope and read the document. Trembling with rage, he snapped at McKenney: "Sir, how did you get through my lines?" [1]

Undoubtedly Fremont, deluded by the idea that he was on the heels of the enemy, had known that a removal order was coming through and had wanted to prevent its delivery until he had won a victory, which would have saved him his command. But there was no possibility that he would do what his enemies feared he would do and what some of his friends hoped he would do—defy the order. Fundamentally he was too good and too weak a man to refuse to obey an official injunction. While some of his officers talked wildly of mutiny, he issued a dignified address to the troops asking them to support the government and his successor. Then he left for St. Louis. [2]

Lincoln had no idea of keeping Hunter in command of the Western Department. He appointed him because at the time of Fremont's removal Hunter was the officer in the Department best qualified to take over. But Lincoln doubted that

[1] Samuel Curtis to Lincoln, November 1, 6, 16, 1861, Lincoln MSS., vols. 59, 60, 61; Leonard Swett to Lincoln, November 9, *ibid.*, vol. 60.
[2] *Official Records*, III, 560; Thomas J. McCormack (ed.), *Memoirs of Gustave Koerner, 1809–1896*, II, 189.

Hunter had the ability to command permanently the large and complex Western area. While he studied the list of generals to find a man for the West, he was faced with a command crisis in the East. McClellan was finally demanding the removal of Scott as general in chief.

Chapter 3

"I Can Do It All"

PEOPLE were sniping at General McClellan in October, 1861. The weather was wonderful; the roads to Virginia were hard and dry. From the politicians and the press came nasty remarks about his inaction and demands that he move his army on Richmond. Flustered by the barrage of criticism, the Young Napoleon begged Lincoln for more time to train the troops. The President assured him that he could have his own way. Late in the month three of the leading Republicans in the Senate went to Lincoln and demanded that he order McClellan to fight. Lincoln defended the General, but after his visitors left, even though it was night, he went to McClellan's headquarters. There he talked with McClellan about the mounting popular impatience for action. Although Lincoln deprecated the pressure for a battle, he tried to make the General see that it was a real force and something that in a democracy the military had to take into account. McClellan replied dramatically that he had everything at stake in the offensive he was mounting, and that if he failed nobody would see him again. Impulsively Lincoln said: "I have a notion to go out with you and stand or fall with the battle." [1]

McClellan definitely indicated to the President that he meant to fight soon. He said the same thing to the Senators

[1] Dennett, *Diary of John Hay*, 26–27, 31, entries of October 10, 26, 1861.

when he met them in a three hour session later that same night at the home of Montgomery Blair. He wanted to fight, he said; but he was held back by Scott. The old General was for a defensive policy; he would not let McClellan attack; but if Scott were retired—. For months McClellan had brooded over the injustice of his young genius being controlled by Scott. Now he saw the way to free himself: to make the politicians believe Scott was to blame for the inaction of the Eastern army. The Senators were convinced; they agreed to make a desperate effort to get Scott retired.[2]

Old Fuss and Feathers was perfectly willing to step out. Sick and tired, he knew he was not able to perform his duties properly, and he was enraged beyond endurance at the way McClellan ignored him and his orders. But if he could, he was going to see that McClellan did not become general in chief. Scott wanted Major General Henry W. Halleck for that post. Halleck was on his way to Washington from California, and Scott intended to hang on until he arrived.[3] But the pressure against him—from McClellan, the Cabinet, Congress—was too great. Even Lincoln thought it was time for him to ask for retirement. On the last day of October, Scott wrote a formal application to be placed on the retired list, saying in his letter that he regretted to leave the service of a president as kind and considerate as Lincoln. The next day Lincoln named McClellan "to command the whole army."[4] Now that he had won the victory, the Young Napoleon professed to feel no great elation. In one of the curious reversions of mood of which he was capable, he was moved by pity for the man whose career he had helped to end.[5]

[2] McClellan, *Own Story*, 170–172.

[3] Scott to Simon Cameron, October 4, 1861, *Official Records*, LI, pt. 1, 491–493; Townsend, *Anecdotes of the Civil War*, 62.

[4] Scott to Cameron, October 31, 1861, *Official Records*, Ser. 3, I, 611–612; McClellan, *Own Story*, 200; *Works of Lincoln*, VII, 13–14.

[5] McClellan, *Own Story*, 173.

Lincoln went to McClellan's headquarters on the night of November 1 to talk with the General about the duties of his new position. The President said he was relieved that a change had been made, but that he feared the increase in responsibility would embarrass McClellan. Lincoln was trying to make McClellan realize the vast importance of being general in chief. All that McClellan could think about was that he was free from Scott. "I am now in contact with you . . . ," he said; "I am not embarrassed by intervention." Patiently Lincoln returned to the point: "In addition to your present command, the supreme command of the Army will entail a vast labor upon you." At last McClellan caught it. "I can do it all," he said quietly.[6]

All through November, Lincoln conferred every day with McClellan. Sometimes he summoned the General to meetings at the White House, but mostly he went to McClellan's quarters. To Lincoln, it did not seem strange that he, the superior, should go to McClellan, the inferior. Lincoln spent far more time in other people's offices than he did in his own. That was how he found out what was going on, how he sized up people. In his visits with McClellan, he often did nothing but tell stories; but he was studying the General, trying to determine whether McClellan could handle the job of supreme command. He was likely to drop in at headquarters at any hour of the day or night. He would inquire about the latest military news, discuss some projected movement, or just talk.[7] McClellan was amused or bored by the visitations. He thought the President was honest and well-meaning; he considered Lincoln's anecdotes pertinent though unrefined—but the fellow was such a simpleton and such a nuisance.[8] Once

[6] Dennett, *Diary of John Hay*, 32–33.

[7] McClellan, *Own Story*, 161–162; Heintzelman MS. Journal, November 4, 1861.

[8] McClellan, *Own Story*, 170, 176; Malcolm Ives to James Gordon Bennett, January 15, 1862, Bennett MSS.

General Samuel Heintzelman came to see McClellan and found Lincoln present. In his journal, Heintzelman described the scene. Lincoln was examining a map of Virginia and making suggestions about operations. McClellan obviously thought the President's ideas were absurd but listened as if much edified. When Lincoln left, McClellan saw him to the door. The Young Napoleon came back into the room, closed the door and, looking back over his shoulder, said, "Isn't he a rare bird?" [9]

He was a rare bird as long as he did not try to exercise any real control over McClellan. When that happened, McClellan's amusement turned to anger and scorn. About the middle of November, Secretary of the Navy Gideon Welles and David D. Porter, a naval lieutenant, presented to Lincoln a scheme to capture New Orleans. Lincoln liked the idea and, taking Welles and Porter with him, proceeded to McClellan's house. The President directed McClellan to confer with Porter and draw up a formal plan. Going to a map, Lincoln expounded on the importance of getting control of the Mississippi line. After New Orleans, he said, Vicksburg, the key center of the Confederacy: "The war can never be brought to a close until that key is in our pocket." [1] McClellan resented Lincoln's taking a hand in strategic planning. Right after Lincoln lectured McClellan about the Mississippi, the General administered to the President the famous snub described by the presidential secretary, John Hay. Lincoln, Seward, and Hay went to McClellan's quarters at night. Finding the General absent, they decided to wait. McClellan came in and was told that Lincoln was there. Without even deigning to greet the commander in chief, the General went upstairs to bed. Also about this time, McClellan introduced a new and sneering note in his correspondence in his references to Lincoln.

[9] Heintzelman MS. Journal, November 11, 1861.
[1] David D. Porter, *Incidents and Anecdotes of the Civil War*, 95–96.

Before, the President had been a good-natured bumpkin; now, he was "the original Gorilla" and a teller of low stories.[2] Lincoln had made the mistake of being humble with a super-egoist. The egoist mistook humility for weakness.

As he went in and out of McClellan's headquarters, Lincoln might well have met certain prominent leaders of the opposition party. Some of the Democratic bosses had decided that McClellan would be the hero of the war and a likely presidential candidate. They were flitting around him all autumn, sounding him out on the presidency and urging him to oppose an antislavery policy. The General was silent about his political ambitions, but he was vocal in his political views. He was a Democrat, he was opposed to wartime emancipation, and he did not care who knew it. "Help me to dodge the nigger—we want nothing to do with him . . . ," he wrote to the Democratic politico who was directing the move to make McClellan president. McClellan seemed to think that the government had no right to announce a policy he did not like and that the adoption of such a policy would in some way hamper him in his conduct of operations.[3]

Although McClellan spent some time talking politics with Democratic callers, he devoted most of his attention to the job of being supreme commander. He could do it all, he had told Lincoln, and he was out to prove his word. He found there was a lot to do. The government had no master plan for action on all fronts and had made no arrangements to co-ordinate movements in the West with those in the East. He discovered that the Federal forces in the West were small, poorly organized, and unable to cooperate with each other,

[2] Dennett, *Diary of John Hay*, 34–35; William Starr Myers, *A Study in Personality: General George Brinton McClellan*, 339; McClellan, *Own Story*, 175–176.

[3] Frank A. Flower, *Edwin McMasters Stanton . . .* , 122–123; McClellan to S. L. M. Barlow, November 1, 1861, McClellan MSS., Ser. 1.

let alone with the Eastern army. With a characteristic burst of energy, McClellan tackled the problem of organizing the West. There should be two departments in the vast area, he decided: one, Fremont's old Department of the West, to which would be added the western part of Kentucky; the other, the Department of the Ohio, consisting of the rest of Kentucky and Tennessee. As commander of the first, McClellan recommended to Lincoln Henry W. Halleck; to command the second, Don Carlos Buell. McClellan probably picked Halleck for one department because he felt he had to give something big to the man who had been his rival for the chief command; he selected Buell because he believed that that officer would be one of the great men of the war.

As the two commanders prepared to go to their posts, McClellan gave them formal written instructions. To Halleck he said: restore order from the chaos left by Fremont; impress on the people that we are fighting only to restore the Union; concentrate your army near the Mississippi for "ulterior" operations. To Buell he wrote: hold Kentucky; impress on the people that we are fighting for the Union and the Constitution; prepare your army for a move into East Tennessee to rescue the Union-loving people there from rebel oppression.[4] There was more policy than strategy in these instructions, and Lincoln and McClellan were both responsible for the emphasis. The statements about the objective of the war being the restoration of the Union and not the destruction of slavery embodied the political ideas of both men. The direction to Buell to move into East Tennessee and occupy Knoxville emanated from Lincoln, who wanted it done for political reasons, and was agreed to by McClellan for military reasons. In the early part of the war there was nothing Lincoln desired more desperately than the liberation of East Tennessee. It

[4] McClellan to Buell, November 7, 1861, and to Halleck, November 11, McClellan, *Own Story,* 207-210.

was intolerable to him that the strongest Union area in the South should be controlled by the Confederacy. Although his motives for wanting it freed were political, he always tried to argue that there were great military benefits to be derived from seizing Knoxville and cutting the East Tennessee and Georgia Railroad, thus getting, as he said, between the rebels and their "hog and hominy." [5] McClellan fell in with Lincoln's ideas about East Tennessee because they promised to aid the future operations of the Army of the Potomac. A Federal army at Knoxville would be in a position to threaten the flank of the Confederates in Virginia and might cause them to detach from the forces opposed to McClellan when he moved on Richmond. In all his strategical planning the Young Napoleon never lost sight of himself and his own army.

Don Carlos Buell was a McClellan without charm or glamor. Maybe that was why McClellan liked him so much. He was cold, reserved, harsh, and thoroughly unpopular with most people. As a soldier, he duplicated many of McClellan's qualities. He was industrious, methodical, a good organizer and disciplinarian, and a loud opponent of wartime emancipation. At the start of the war, he was regarded as one of the best officers in the service, but he turned out to belong in Grant's category of generals who never got started right. [6]

Lincoln and McClellan expected Buell to strike for Knoxville that fall. After he arrived on the scene, Buell saw rightly that he could not take East Tennessee by moving directly into it from the north. There were no railroads from his base at Louisville to the gaps opening into the mountains of East Tennessee; he would have to haul his supplies in wagons a long distance over poor roads. The logistics problem made it

[5] R. W. Johnson, *A Soldier's Reminiscences in Peace and War*, 322; Ballard, *Military Genius of Lincoln*, 177.

[6] Johnson, *A Soldier's Reminiscences*, 184, 196–197; Harvey S. Ford (ed.), *Memoirs of a Volunteer, 1861–1863*, 131; Lew Wallace, *Lew Wallace, An Autobiography*, II, 644–645.

unlikely that Buell could get into the area or that if he got there, he could hold it. Buell presented McClellan a plan of his own to secure East Tennessee, a plan, in fact, to secure all Tennessee. He proposed simultaneous movements by his and Halleck's armies: Halleck to move from western Kentucky up the Tennessee and Cumberland rivers and Buell to move on Nashville. This would force the Confederates to fight or retreat. If they were defeated or forced out of their lines in Kentucky and Tennessee, the Confederates in East Tennessee would have to give up the region or be taken in flank. The Federals could walk in almost unopposed.[7]

There was a lot of sound military thinking in Buell's scheme, but McClellan saw none of it. In his letters to Buell, he exhibited the trait that was one of his greatest weaknesses —that of insisting that a situation he had created in his own mind was the real one. He wanted Buell to go into East Tennessee to aid his own operations in Virginia. Therefore it was possible for Buell to go in, and McClellan refused to believe that it was not. He could not adjust his mind to the actual situation as presented by Buell. Ignoring all the hard facts of the problem, he insisted that Buell must liberate East Tennessee, even though military advantages were sacrificed in the process. At the time he sent Buell to the West, McClellan had been planning a move of his own into Virginia. As a part of his scheme, Buell was to appear on the Confederate flank and so Buell had to be there. Military realities were not going to hinder the plans of McClellan as long as somebody else had to overcome them.[8]

Before he took over the supreme command, McClellan had contemplated an advance by the Army of the Potomac against the Confederates at Manassas, the movement to take place in

[7] Buell to McClellan, November 16, 30, 1861, McClellan MSS., Ser. 2; Buell to McClellan, November 27, *Official Records*, VII, 450–451.

[8] McClellan to Buell, November 20, December 3, 1861, *ibid.*, VII, 457–458, 468.

the latter part of November.[9] For a while after he became generalissimo, he continued to talk about an offensive. But soon his customary timidity and aversion to decision took hold of him. He began to see all kinds of obstacles in front of him and all sorts of reasons why he should not fight. The biggest obstacle was the size of the Confederate army—the size that existed only in his mind. He now demonstrated the quality that was his greatest deficiency as a soldier: perpetual exaggeration of the numbers opposed to him. His estimate of the size of the Confederate forces was based on the reports of the poorest intelligence service any general ever had. He had engaged Allen Pinkerton, head of a private detective agency, to provide him with analyses of the composition of the enemy army. Pinkerton, who mysteriously signed his reports "E. J. Allen," informed McClellan that the Confederates had about 126,000 troops in Virginia and that their army at Manassas numbered from 80,000–90,000 men. Either Pinkerton was completely incompetent, or he sensed that McClellan wanted the enemy army magnified as an excuse for inaction, for the reports almost doubled the actual numbers of the Confederates. McClellan believed, or made himself believe, Pinkerton's calculations. As he reckoned that the largest force he could put in the field was 76,000, McClellan could argue plausibly to Lincoln that he was not ready to advance.[1]

He found other reasons for delay. The roads were getting bad, the army needed more training, Buell was not ready to cooperate by striking East Tennessee. McClellan got morbid as he contemplated the obstructions before him. Forgetting that he had created most of them himself, he began to im-

[9] *Ibid.*, V, 9–11; McClellan to S. L. M. Barlow, November 8, 1861, McClellan MSS., Ser. 1; William Swinton, *Campaigns of the Army of the Potomac*, 69–70.

[1] E. J. Allen to McClellan, October 4, 28, November 15, 1861, McClellan MSS., Ser. 1; McClellan, *Own Story*, 75–79.

agine that the government had withheld resources from him and that it would try to place the blame for failure upon him. To protect himself in the record, he prepared a paper for the War Department evidencing that the necessity for delay was not his fault. To his wife he wrote: "I have a set of men to deal with unscrupulous and false; if possible they will throw whatever blame there is on my shoulders, and I do not intend to be sacrificed by such people." [2]

It is probable that McClellan had never really intended to attack the Confederates at Manassas. He may have thought he wanted to, he may have talked about it, but actually he shrank from the decision of a showdown battle. What he most wanted to do was to capture Richmond without fighting a battle, although his military sense should have told him that the occupation of the Confederate capital without defeating the Confederate army would be a barren achievement. Late in November, General John G. Barnard, Chief of Engineers of the Army of the Potomac, was alone at headquarters with McClellan. Almost casually, McClellan said he had a plan to take Richmond. He unfolded it to Barnard. He would transport his army by water down the Potomac River and Chesapeake Bay to the mouth of the Rappahannock River, go up the Rappahannock a short distance, and land his troops at Urbana on the southern bank, about fifty miles northeast of Richmond. From there he would march rapidly to Richmond and have the place before the Confederate army at Manassas could arrive to defend it. [3] The more he thought about his new plan, the better McClellan liked it, but while he was working over the details he kept it largely to himself.

He told Lincoln nothing of the scheme but revealed the whole thing to Secretary of the Treasury Chase. He said later

[2] McClellan to Mrs. McClellan, latter part of November, *Own Story*, 176–177.

[3] John G. Barnard, *The Peninsula Campaign and Antecedents* . . . , 51; McClellan, *Own Story*, 202–203.

that Chase was hindered in his financial operations by the un-
certainties of the military situation and he wanted to relieve
the Secretary's mind.[4] Apparently it did not occur to Mc-
Clellan that there was any impropriety in his informing a
Cabinet member about an important strategic design before
he told the commander in chief. Nor did he seem to think
that Lincoln too might be worried, and worried about bigger
things than bond issues.

If not worried about McClellan's inaction, the President was
at least curious about it. He had given McClellan almost complete freedom to direct strategic movements in all theaters.
He had upheld the General against the popular pressure for
an autumn advance into Virginia. There had been no strategic movements any place and no advance or even an intima-
tion of one in Virginia. Lincoln thought it was time for Mc-
Clellan to be doing something in Virginia while the weather
was still good and before winter set in. In characteristic fashion, the President tried to stir McClellan to action by produc-
ing a plan of his own. About the first of December he sent
the General a scheme he had worked out for a combined
frontal and flank attack on the enemy at Manassas and asked
McClellan to provide information as to when the move could
be made and with how many men. McClellan responded with
the information but indicated that he did not approve of the
project. He added: ". . . I have now my mind turned ac-
tively toward another plan of campaign that I do not think at
all anticipated by the enemy nor by many of our own people." [5] This mysterious hint was apparently all that McClellan chose to tell Lincoln about the Urbana scheme. In verbal
conferences later he may have given the President a general
idea of the proposed movement, but it is doubtful that he did

<hr>

[4] *Ibid.*, 203; Jacob W. Schuckers, *Life and Public Services of Salmon
Portland Chase*, 445.

[5] *Works of Lincoln*, VII, 24–26. McClellan replied to Lincoln December 10.

even that. Certainly he did not take his superior officer as fully into his confidence as he should have.

When McClellan first thought of the Urbana movement, he had planned to start it immediately. But in December the weather turned bad. The rains came, the roads were deep in mud, the army could not move. For once McClellan had a real reason for not advancing. Then late in the month he became ill with typhoid fever. He took to his bed and remained there for three weeks. Although he later claimed that his mind was not affected by the fever and that he was able to transact army business every day, he did not tell the entire story. He had to sleep and rest a great deal, and he could not exercise all the functions of command. His subordinates could administer the Army of the Potomac, but they could not make strategic decisions for armies in other theaters. Lincoln was deeply disturbed by the situation. In particular, he was worried about the two departmental commanders in the West. Were Buell and Halleck acting together under the terms of previous instructions from McClellan, or were they awaiting orders from a general in chief temporarily unable to issue any? Lincoln decided to find out.

During December affairs in the West had been at a standstill. Buell kept saying that he wanted to free East Tennessee, but that he preferred a move on Nashville, with Halleck aiding him by moving up the Tennessee and Cumberland rivers. Halleck said little except that he did not have enough men to assist Buell. Now with McClellan sick, Lincoln intervened in the situation. He took over the function of general in chief. On the last day of the month he telegraphed Buell and Halleck, informing them of McClellan's illness and asking whether they were acting in concert. Buell replied that there was no arrangement for concert, that McClellan had said he would attend to that matter at the proper time. From Halleck came the response that he knew nothing of Buell's plans and that he was not ready to cooperate with Buell. Lincoln told both generals to get into communication with each other at once and to act in concert.[6] The two exchanged some letters, but they were unable to get together on anything. Buell proposed to strike the Confederates at Bowling Green and wanted Halleck to attack them at the same time in western Kentucky; Halleck insisted that he lacked the resources to undertake an offensive.[7]

Lincoln knew about Buell's desire to go after Nashville, but he understood that the General also intended a move into East Tennessee. Buell now told the President frankly that an advance on Knoxville would have to be entirely subordinate to an attack on the Confederate forces in his front. This announcement hit Lincoln hard. In a letter to Buell, he conceded that he was not competent to criticize the General's views, but said that he would rather have Knoxville than Nashville. Union seizure of Knoxville would cut an important artery of the enemy's communications, he contended, and free the loyalists of the mountains. Apparently Lincoln did not realize the comparative smallness of Buell's army, for he urged the General to attempt the impossible—advances against both Nashville and Knoxville. Lincoln ended his letter to Buell with an expression that in varied form would appear in many of his despatches to generals: "I do not intend this to be an order in any sense, but merely . . . to show you the grounds of my anxiety." [8] His anxiety was so great that he showed Buell's letter to McClellan. From his

[6] Lincoln to Buell and Halleck, December 31, 1861, *Official Records,* VII, 524; Lincoln to Buell, January 1, 1862, Buell to Lincoln, January 1, Lincoln to Halleck, January 1, Halleck to Lincoln, January 1, *ibid.,* 526; Lincoln to Halleck, January 1, *Works of Lincoln,* VII, 71.

[7] Halleck to Buell, January 2, 1862, *Official Records,* VII, 527; Buell to Halleck, January 3, *ibid.,* 528–529; Halleck to Buell, January 6, *ibid.,* 533.

[8] Buell to Lincoln, January 5, 1862, *ibid.,* VII, 530–531; Lincoln to Buell, January 6, *Works of Lincoln,* VII, 73–74.

sickbed, the Young Napoleon wrote plaintively to Buell that his own advance depended on Buell's being established in East Tennessee and that his plans must not be deranged. While Lincoln was cast down by the news from Buell, he got another jolt from Halleck, who said his force was too small to enable him to help Buell and that Buell's plan of a cooperative movement was no good anyhow. Sadly Lincoln indorsed on Halleck's letter: "It is exceedingly discouraging. As everywhere else, nothing can be done." [9]

On January 10, the day that he received Halleck's despatch, Lincoln, discouraged and despondent, went to the office of Quartermaster General Meigs. Seating himself in a chair in front of the open fire, the President said: "General, what shall I do? The people are impatient; Chase has no money . . . ; the General of the Army has typhoid fever. The bottom is out of the tub. What shall I do?" Meigs said typhoid fever meant an illness of six weeks and that if in that period the Confederates should attack the Army of the Potomac, the situation would be critical. He advised Lincoln to consult the ranking officers in the army so as to be ready to select a commander if a crisis came, or, insinuated Meigs, perhaps Lincoln could choose a man to lead an offensive.[1] Lincoln acted on Meigs' counsel immediately. He sent word to Generals McDowell and William B. Franklin to come to the White House that night for a conference; he also invited Seward, Chase, and T. A. Scott, Assistant Secretary of War. Lincoln told them his troubles: McClellan was sick, Buell and Halleck were not in concert—he had to talk to somebody. Turning to the Generals, he said he wanted to get their opinion about the possibility of starting active operations with the Army of the Potomac. According to McDowell, the President said that if

[9] Halleck to Lincoln, January 6, 1862, *ibid.*, VII, 75–78.
[1] "General M. C. Meigs on the Conduct of the Civil War," *American Historical Review*, XXVI, 1921, pp. 292–293, 302.

McClellan did not want to use the Army, he would like to borrow it. McDowell suggested a move on Manassas, while Franklin, who was to some extent in McClellan's confidence, recommended operating on one of the water routes east of Richmond. As Lincoln adjourned the meeting, he asked them to return the next night.[2] The second conference was short. The Generals said that for the present McDowell's plan was the best, and Lincoln told them to work on it. On the twelfth Lincoln called them together again, and this time he announced that McClellan was better and would meet with them the next day.[3]

McClellan had heard about the conferences going on at the White House, and had decided that there was a plot afoot to get him removed. In a rage that gave him strength, he got up from his bed to face the conspirators. The meeting on the thirteenth was tense, angry, and awkward. Accounts of it were left by Meigs, McDowell, and McClellan. Although they differ in details, they agree in the main outline of what happened. Lincoln explained why he had called the two generals and the others together in the first place, and McDowell said something apologetic to McClellan about his role in the affair. McClellan, who thought McDowell was at the bottom of the move against him, cut him off coldly. Then a long silence followed. Everybody thought McClellan would say something about his future plans, but he sat mute. Lincoln and Chase started to whisper together. Meigs moved his chair closer to McClellan and in a low voice urged him to speak. McClellan replied that Lincoln could not keep a secret and that if he told his schemes they would be in the newspapers tomorrow. Finally Chase bluntly asked McClellan what he intended to

[2] McDowell's memorandum of the meeting in Henry J. Raymond, *Life and Public Services of Abraham Lincoln*, 772–774.

[3] *Ibid.*, 774–776; "General Meigs on the Conduct of the War," 292–293. As the conferences continued, Meigs and Montgomery Blair had been invited to attend them.

do and when. McClellan answered that he did not want to reveal his plans to the group and would not do so unless ordered by the President. He would say, however, that he meant to move Buell's army forward very soon. This faint hint of action was enough to appease Lincoln. Rising, he said: "Well, on the assurance of the General that he will press the advance in Kentucky, I will be satisfied, and will adjourn this council."[4] Lincoln was beginning to have some doubts about McClellan, but he still wanted to believe in the General.

The Secretary of War had not attended the councils, because during the time they were held Lincoln was in process of easing the Secretary out of office. Simon Cameron had been an inefficient and corrupt administrator, and Lincoln had had enough of him. With some difficulty, the President persuaded Cameron that he ought to resign and accept an appointment as ambassador to Russia, and on January 13 Lincoln named Edwin M. Stanton as head of the War Department. The advent of Stanton would have far-reaching effects on the organization of the system of command and on the fortunes of McClellan and other generals. The new Secretary was honest in a financial sense, energetic almost to the point of frenzy, and as industrious as a hive of bees. He was also arbitrary, passionate, excitable, and chronically dishonest in his human relationships. He was scornful of professional military training and delighted to bully professional soldiers. Although he was supposed to be a friend of McClellan, he disliked and distrusted the General and would be his most relentless enemy.[5]

There would be occasions during the war when Stanton would try to bully and browbeat Lincoln as he did his subordinates and those generals who would take it. Lincoln never

[4] "General Meigs on the Conduct of the War," 292–293; Raymond, *Lincoln,* 776–777; McClellan, *Own Story,* 155–159.

[5] Donn Piatt, *Memories of the Men who Saved the Union,* 57–58; Stanton to C. A. Dana, January 24, 1862, Dana MSS.; T. Harry Williams, *Lincoln and the Radicals,* 91–92.

took it. He put up with a lot from the Secretary in order to utilize his talents, but he never let Stanton dominate him. In any clash of wills on an important issue, Stanton always came off second best. During the remainder of the war the two men lived in close daily association. The White House was not connected by telegraph with the War Department, where all military and Western Union telegrams relating to the war, including those to Lincoln, were received. Every day Lincoln would walk from the executive mansion to Stanton's offices, located on Pennsylvania Avenue at Seventeenth Street. He went in the morning, in the afternoon, and at night. The first thing he did after entering was to read the war bulletins. Often he came over late at night to get the most recent news before retiring. If a particular situation seemed critical, he would stay there all night, and during a battle he almost lived in the telegraph office.[6]

After the Young Napoleon had got up to face down his enemies, he stayed up, although he was still weak. He brought increased pressure on Buell and Halleck to do something.[7] Lincoln too kept urging action in the West and urging it directly on Buell and Halleck. His grasp of strategy was getting better all the time. He proposed that Halleck menace the Confederate forces in western Kentucky and on the Mississippi while Buell menaced those in eastern Kentucky and East Tennessee. The Confederates would have to weaken one point or another of their line and the Federals could break through the weakened point. We have the greater numbers, he told Buell, and we should threaten the enemy "with superior forces at different points at the same time. . . ." [8] His

[6] David H. Bates, *Lincoln in the Telegraph Office*, 42; McClure, *Lincoln and Men of War-Times*, 160–161.

[7] McClellan to Buell, January 13, 1862, *Official Records*, VII, 547; Buell to McClellan, January 13, *ibid.*, 548–549.

[8] Lincoln to Buell, January 13, 1862, *Works of Lincoln*, VII, 83–84.

reasoning was so sound that not even Halleck and Buell could object to his plan.

Buell finally did attempt an advance of a part of his army in eastern Kentucky. He defeated the Confederates at Mill Springs but could not move any farther toward East Tennessee because of the miry roads.[9] At the same time, Halleck began to demonstrate sudden and unsuspected offensive inclinations. During the weary months when Lincoln and McClellan had sought to get things moving in the West, Halleck had insisted that he could do nothing but hold Missouri. He had derided Buell's plan of moving up the Tennessee and Cumberland and had hintingly said that all forces in the West ought to be under a single command. Now, in the latter part of January, he announced that he favored operations on the Tennessee-Cumberland line, and when he heard that the Confederates in western Kentucky were about to be reinforced, he ordered his own forces there under Ulysses S. Grant to advance against Fort Henry on the Tennessee.[1]

Halleck's decision to attack was made precipitately; he did not tell Buell about the movement until it had got started. Buell asked whether Halleck wanted him to cooperate in any way. At first Halleck said no, but when the going got tougher, he besought Buell to make a diversion in his favor. When the going got easier and he saw a chance to win a bigger victory if he had a bigger army, Halleck asked Buell to come and serve under him. There was certainly room for the inferences drawn then and later that Halleck had started his movement to advance his military fortunes. In an interesting display of martial contrariness, Buell, who had first suggested the Tennessee movement and who earlier had wanted Halleck to

[9] Buell to Lorenzo Thomas, January 27, 1862, *Official Records*, VII, 568.
[1] *Ibid.*, VII, 508–511, 572, 574, 586–587.

assist him with a diversion, now began to find reasons and excuses why he could not aid Halleck. When he finally moved, he marched toward Nashville and not to join Halleck.[2]

Grant captured Fort Henry and then moved against Fort Donelson on the Cumberland and took it. The double victory cracked the center of the Confederate line in Kentucky. With their flanks endangered, the Confederates had to pull completely out of Kentucky, and they fell back through Tennessee to northeastern Mississippi. The man who was really responsible for the first smashing Union success of the war was Grant. Halleck had sat at his desk in St. Louis, ostensibly directing the offensive, but actually, as his despatches reveal, understanding very little of what was going on. Now he claimed all the credit. He demanded of McClellan that as a reward for Henry and Donelson, he be made commander of all the armies in the West and that McClellan lay his request for promotion before Lincoln. Tartly McClellan replied that Buell could direct his own army better than Halleck could from St. Louis and that he would not place Halleck's request before the President.[3] Halleck then got the issue before Stanton through the intervention of Assistant Secretary of War Scott. The Secretary liked the idea and promised to submit it to Lincoln. But McClellan still had influence with the President. On February 22 Stanton telegraphed Halleck that that morning Lincoln had decided no change was necessary in the system of command in the West and that Halleck and Buell were to continue acting in cooperation.[4]

After the completion of the Henry and Donelson campaign, Halleck recommended Grant for promotion to major general

---

[2] *Ibid.*, VII, 574, 576, 583–584, 587–588, 593, 605, 617, 632–633.

[3] Halleck to McClellan, February 17, 20, 1862, *ibid.*, VII, 628, 641; McClellan to Halleck, February 21, 1862, *ibid.*, 645.

[4] T. A. Scott to Stanton, February 17, 1862, Stanton MSS.; Halleck to Stanton, February 21; Stanton to Halleck, February 21, 22, *Official Records*, VII, 648, 652, 655.

of volunteers, but he lavished most of his praise for the victories on himself and other officers. He also asked promotion
for Buell and John Pope, who had done nothing in compari-
son with Grant's achievements. In the correspondence of
Halleck, McClellan, and Buell, there was barely an intima-
tion that Grant had been responsible for the recent successes
but a strong suggestion that they had resulted from the super-
planning of great brains in Washington and St. Louis. But on
the receipt of the news of the fall of the forts, Lincoln, on his
own initiative, nominated Grant to be major general. The
President was interested in Grant. Here was a general who
moved and won victories with the resources he had and without crying that he needed more men.[5]

[5] Arthur L. Conger, *The Rise of U. S. Grant,* 191–192.

Chapter 4

"You Must Act"

LINCOLN wrote the order on January 27 without consulting anybody. General War Order Number 1, he called it. It was the first order of a general nature issued in his name. It directed that February 22 be the day for a general movement of the land and naval forces against the enemy.[1] In many ways it was a curious and quaint document, and it brought much ridicule upon Lincoln then and later. One section commanded particular armies to be ready to move on the twenty-second and solemnly instructed the soldiers of others to obey existing orders for the present and additional ones when given! Certainly there was a measure of absurdity in ordering an advance on a national holiday four weeks hence without considering what the weather might be then or what the Confederates might do in the interim. But undoubtedly Lincoln did not intend the order to be taken too seriously as a program of action. His probable purpose was to stir McClellan to some kind of action. The pressure on Lincoln from Congress and the public for an offensive was tremendous, but McClellan had not moved nor had he indicated that he meant to move. All winter the Army of the Potomac had lain idle in its camps. McClellan had not even tried any minor movements: no probing reconnaissances across the Potomac, no strikes at exposed Confederate points like Norfolk, no attempts to break the

[1] *Works of Lincoln*, VII, 89–90; Dennett, *Diary of John Hay*, 36.

blockade of the lower Potomac which the Confederates had established. And it was not until about this time that he took the President into his confidence about his future plans.

McClellan knew the pressure on Lincoln, but he made little attempt to advise or help the President. Either he did not know how to establish confidential relations with his political superior or he did not want to. During the winter months, he had been maturing in his mind the plan for the move to Urbana, but he had said nothing about it to Lincoln—at least nothing definite. Soon after Stanton became head of the War Department, McClellan verbally described the Urbana scheme to him, and the Secretary told him to lay it before Lincoln. McClellan did, and Lincoln promptly disapproved it.[2] Not only did Lincoln veto McClellan's plan; he ordered one of his own put into execution. He directed McClellan to move the Army of the Potomac toward Manassas and seize a point on the railroad southwest of that place and to begin the operation not later than February 22. The President was sticking to his conviction, expressed to McClellan on December 1, that the best point of attack was the Confederate army in northern Virginia.[3]

But McClellan was not ready to give up. He asked Lincoln if he could present in writing his objections to the President's plan and the reasons why he thought his was better. Lincoln said he could.[4] While McClellan was composing his document, in the shape of a letter to Stanton, he received a communication from Lincoln in which the President asked the General to answer five questions. If, said Lincoln, you can answer these questions to my satisfaction, I will yield my plan to yours. The questions were:

[2] McClellan's report, *Official Records*, V, 41.

[3] President's Special War Order No. 1, January 31, 1862, *Works of Lincoln*, VII, 91.

[4] McClellan, *Own Story*, 228–229.

Does not your plan involve a larger expenditure of time and
      money than mine?

Wherein is a victory more certain by your plan than mine?

Wherein is a victory more valuable by your plan than mine?

Would it not be less valuable in that yours would not break
      a great line of the enemy's communications, while
      mine would?

In case of disaster, would it not be more difficult to retreat
      by your plan than mine? [5]

These were posers for McClellan, but he set himself to answer them. His big purpose, he said, was to strike at the vitals
of the enemy, not to win a barren victory near Washington.
If the Army of the Potomac moved against the Confederates
at Manassas, it might defeat them, but it could not win a decisive victory. The enemy would retreat, to fight again and
again. On the other hand, a movement by the lower Chesapeake Bay promised quick and smashing success. Here the
army could operate on the shortest possible land route to
Richmond over roads that were passable all year and in an
area less defensible than northern Virginia. A movement on
this line would force the Confederates to evacuate Manassas
in order to cover Richmond. The Army of the Potomac, however, would be between them and the city, in position to operate on their line of communications and make them fight a
battle on ground favorable to the Federals; or McClellan
could seize Richmond and force the Confederates to attack
him. If he was beaten, said McClellan, he had a safe line of
retreat down the peninsula between the York and James
rivers to Fortress Monroe on the coast. If he was successful, he
would have all Virginia in his grasp. At the same time Halleck
and Buell would move on into Tennessee and Alabama and

[5] Lincoln to McClellan, February 3, 1862, *Works of Lincoln*, VII,
93–94.

down the Mississippi. The rebellion would be ended. If the lower Chesapeake line was chosen as the one on which to operate, McClellan advised that the point of landing be Urbana; if for any reason Urbana could not be used, he recommended Mob Jack Bay or Fortress Monroe.[6]

In the letter to Stanton, McClellan took the administration fully into his confidence about his strategic designs. It was the first time he had done so, and his frankness won Lincoln's approval of his plan. Without being fully convinced of the merits of the Urbana movement, Lincoln yielded his plan to the General's. The President never formally revoked the order of January 31, but he dispensed with it by not requiring its execution. Lincoln and McClellan got together in a number of verbal conferences in which they discussed the problems of procuring water transport for the move to Urbana. That Lincoln had serious doubts about the scheme was evident when he delayed until February 27 issuing an order to accumulate ships to take the army to the lower Chesapeake.[7]

The Young Napoleon was in a wonderful mood now that he was going to have his way. He even liked Lincoln again. "You have been a kind true friend to me . . . during the last few months," he wrote the President. "Your confidence has upheld me when I should otherwise have felt weak." [8] Actually he had much less of Lincoln's confidence than he thought. The President did not really like the idea of attacking Richmond by going down Chesapeake Bay. With a Confederate army estimated by McClellan to number over 100,000 poised at Manassas only thirty miles from Washington, Lincoln thought it dangerous business to shift the Army of the Potomac to the vicinity of Richmond. While McClellan was moving to Urbana, the Confederates might pounce on Wash-

[6] McClellan to Stanton, February 3, 1862, *Official Records*, V, 42–45.

[7] McClellan, *Own Story*, 236–237; *Official Records*, V, 45–46.

[8] McClellan to Lincoln, February 22, 1862, Lincoln MSS., vol. 69.

ington. For the moment Lincoln, probably out of deference to McClellan's supposed better judgment, kept his misgivings to himself, but later he would give them full expression.

Lincoln undoubtedly made a mistake in grudgingly approving a plan which he distrusted. If he did not like the Urbana scheme, he should have said so and either asked McClellan for another one or relieved the General. On his part, in his dealing with the administration, McClellan committed several bad errors which showed that he lacked the qualities of a supreme commander. After six months of inactivity which had brought a storm of criticism upon the government and for which he was largely responsible, McClellan should have attacked the Confederates at Manassas when Lincoln ordered him to. He probably would have won a victory, but even if he had not he would have strengthened the administration with the public and gained Lincoln's easy assent for the Urbana movement later. Instead, McClellan blindly insisted upon using a plan to which the political authorities objected. He depended upon them for material assistance, and he should have realized that their opposition meant that he would not have their full support and cooperation in executing his plan.[9]

During the rest of February and in early March, McClellan went ahead with his preparations for the movement of the army to Urbana. He was also making plans, at Lincoln's request, to open communications on the Baltimore and Ohio Railroad near Harper's Ferry and to capture the Confederate batteries blockading the lower Potomac. Early on the morning of March 8 Lincoln sent for McClellan. After telling the General that he was dissatisfied with the conduct of affairs around Harper's Ferry, Lincoln renewed all his former objections to the Urbana plan. McClellan repeated his defense

[9] Michie, *McClellan*, 197; Swinton, *Army of the Potomac*, 93–94; Maurice, *Statesmen and Soldiers*, 75–77.

of it and then told the President that he would lay it before
the generals of divisions that day for their decision.[1] The idea
of subjecting the plan to the scrutiny of a military council
pleased Lincoln. If the division commanders in their collec-
tive wisdom indorsed it, the scheme must be all right. At least
the responsibility for its success would be on the military and
not on him.

McClellan called his generals into conference that morning,
and they spent most of the day going over his plan, which
many of them now learned about for the first time. Finally
they voted eight to four in favor of the Urbana move; the
minority favored an advance toward Manassas. They had been
told that when they reached a conclusion Lincoln wanted to
see them, and they repaired to the White House. Their secretary read an account of the meeting to the President. After
some discussion of various aspects of the plan, Lincoln said
that he was not a military man and that he would, therefore,
accept the opinion of the majority.[2] Later he said to Stanton:
"We can do nothing else than accept their plan and discard
all others. . . . We can't reject it and adopt another without
assuming all the responsibility in the case of the failure of the
one we adopt."[3]

Once again Lincoln, against his judgment, had yielded to
McClellan and accepted a plan he considered dangerous. The
events of March 8 demonstrated the strained and unhealthy
relations existing between Lincoln and McClellan; there was
something bizarre in the spectacle of the President refusing
to adopt the plan of his chief general until it had been ap-

[1] *Official Records,* V, 49–50; McClellan, *Own Story,* 195–196.

[2] *C. C. W., Reports,* 1863, I, 270, 360, 387, 597, 681; Heintzelman
MS. Journal, March 7, 8, 1862. General Heintzelman put the date of
the council as March 7 and said the generals met with Lincoln the next
day, but as he wrote this section of his journal later than the event, it is
probable he was mistaken.

[3] Flower, *Stanton,* 139.

proved by a majority vote of subordinates. Right after he acceded to the decision of the council in favor of McClellan and on the same day, Lincoln issued two orders that showed he distrusted the General and disliked the Urbana move. One directed that the twelve divisions of the Army of the Potomac be organized into four corps, to be commanded by the senior major generals, McDowell, E. V. Sumner, S. P. Heintzelman, and E. D. Keyes.⁴ Lincoln made the order without consulting McClellan and knowing that the General would be opposed to it. The question of corps organization had been discussed for weeks between Lincoln, Stanton, McClellan, and the radical Republican leaders in Congress. It should have been approached as a technical military problem, but it was all tangled up with politics—political and military. The officers of the Army of the Potomac were divided into two factions. In one group were the senior generals and their followers. They were Republicans in politics and believed in wartime emancipation. Several of the senior officers were older than McClellan and resented his being their superior. In the council of March 8, McDowell, Sumner, and Heintzelman had voted against the Urbana plan. The other faction consisted of younger officers devoted to McClellan. He had brought them into the army and raised them to their present high positions. In them he trusted, and to them and not to the older generals he confided his plans. They were gentlemen and Democrats, his kind of people. In the factionalism of the officers, the radical bosses saw an opportunity to hamstring McClellan's authority. They urged a corps organization upon Lincoln because the important new commands would go to the senior and Republican generals. To Lincoln the corps idea seemed militarily sound, but McClellan raised objections to it. He did not want to appoint corps commanders until actual operations disclosed which generals were fit to head corps. Like

⁴ *Works of Lincoln,* VII, 116–117.

the radicals, McClellan was thinking in political terms. He did not want to be checked by a council of Republican officers.[5] Lincoln had listened to the arguments of the General and the radicals without announcing a decision. Then suddenly at the same time that he agreed to let McClellan try the Urbana move, he issued the corps order. It was as if he said to the General: I will let you do what you want but I don't like it, and I am going to set some older heads to watch you.

Lincoln's second order of March 8 dealt directly with the movement of the army to Urbana and revealed even more directly than the first his doubts about McClellan. In it he officially accepted the General's plan, but he added conditions to be observed in its execution that McClellan and the council of division generals had not contemplated. The President directed that no change be made in the base of operations of the Army of the Potomac without leaving in and about Washington such a force as in the opinion of McClellan and *all* the corps commanders should leave the capital "entirely secure" and that not more than half the army be moved to a new base until the enemy blockade of the lower Potomac was removed. And to make sure that McClellan would not delay any more, Lincoln ordered that the move to Urbana must start on March 18.[6]

The Young Napoleon had gone to such trouble to get his scheme approved, and then on March 9 he received such discouraging news. On that day the Confederates evacuated their lines around Manassas and Centreville and fell back behind the Rappahannock. They did so to be in a better defensive position to meet any advance McClellan might make and not because, as he claimed later, they had heard about the projected movement to Urbana. But by shifting their army farther south, they made it impossible for McClellan to carry

[5] Williams, *Lincoln and the Radicals*, 118–122.
[6] *Works of Lincoln*, VII, 117–118.

out the Urbana plan. McClellan had based his whole strategic design on the assumption that the Confederates would
remain in northern Virginia while he got between them and
Richmond. Now they were on the south side of the Rappahannock in the very area where he had expected to start his
operations. Because McClellan was badly upset when he
heard the enemy had left the Manassas area, he did something
foolish. He marched his army out and occupied the abandoned Confederate positions. His purpose, he said, was to
give the troops some experience on the march. From the
strictly military view, there was nothing wrong with his
move; indeed, it was a good move for the Federals to seize
Manassas and the important railroad communications around
it. Yet, after refusing to attack the Confederates when they
were at Manassas, McClellan looked silly when he paraded
the whole army there after they had gone. Furthermore, reporters and other observers following the army could tell
from the camp remains that the Confederate forces had
not been as large as McClellan had estimated. The country
learned that the army that had held McClellan at bay for
months numbered only about 50,000 men and not over 100,-
000 as McClellan had claimed.

McClellan's advance to the deserted Confederate redoubts
was bloodless, but at least he had taken the field. Lincoln
chose this moment to relieve the Young Napoleon as general
in chief, leaving him in command of only the Department of
the Potomac. The President made the change in an order of
March 11, which also placed all forces in the West under
Halleck's command and created a new department, the
Mountain Department, made up of western Virginia and
East Tennessee, for Fremont.[7] Lincoln had excellent military
reasons for stripping McClellan of supreme command. With
the General about to lead the Army of the Potomac into an

[7] *Ibid.,* VII, 129–130.

important campaign, it was obvious that he could not exercise an over-all supervision of operations in other theaters. The field command of his own army would be all he could handle. The language of the removal order—that McClellan was relieved of the chief command "until otherwise ordered" —implied that Lincoln intended the demotion to be temporary. One of the President's close friends said later that Lincoln meant to restore McClellan to his former position if he captured Richmond.[8] According to the presidential secretary, John Hay, Lincoln said he was doing McClellan a kindness by permitting him to retain command of the Army of the Potomac and by a successful campaign retrieve his past errors.[9] As out of patience with the General as Lincoln was, he was undoubtedly ready to give McClellan any reward for a victory.

Although Lincoln had acted from the best of motives in relieving McClellan, he, or Stanton, bumbled the announcement of the removal order. In some way it got into the newspapers before it was delivered to McClellan. After the war, McClellan said he first learned of his demotion in a Washington paper, and implied that he had been treated very badly. This was not quite an accurate statement. His friends in the capital telegraphed him that the order had appeared in the press.[1] So far was Lincoln from any desire to hurt McClellan's feelings that he sent William Dennison, an intimate friend of McClellan's, out to the Army to explain the order to the General. Dennison arrived on the twelfth, the day McClellan received the bad news by telegraph from Washington. After Dennison talked to him, McClellan felt all right about being relieved. He wrote Lincoln a manly letter, say-

[8] McClure, *Lincoln and Men of War-Times,* 204–205.

[9] Dennett, *Diary of John Hay,* 37.

[1] McClellan, *Own Story,* 224–225; R. B. Marcy to McClellan, March 12, 1862, McClellan MSS., Ser. 1; Anson Stager to McClellan, March 12, *ibid.*

ing he was ready to serve in any capacity and would let no considerations of self interfere with his work. This was the better side of McClellan coming to the fore. Lincoln was much pleased with the letter.[2]

As he marched his men around northern Virginia, McClellan was considering what plan of operations he should follow now that the Confederates had retired behind the Rappahannock. Although the Urbana scheme seemed to be out, he was still obsessed with the idea of moving against Richmond along one of the water routes from the east. In his letter of February 3 to Lincoln, he had said that, if Urbana could not be used as a landing point, Mob Jack Bay or Fortress Monroe offered the next best bases. Now he was turning over in his mind a plan to land the army at Fortress Monroe and move up the region between the York and James rivers known as the Peninsula, using one of the rivers as his line of communications. He decided to submit this plan to his corps commanders and called them to meet with him on March 13 at Fairfax Court House. After listening to McClellan's explanations of the Fortress Monroe plan, the council voted unanimously to adopt it, provided that certain conditions could be met. The conditions were that the Confederate ironclad ship, the *Merrimac*, which on March 8 had come out of Norfolk and slaughtered a Federal squadron, could be neutralized; that sufficient water transport to take the army to its new base could be quickly procured; and that the Navy could cooperate in a move to destroy the enemy batteries on the York River. Acting on Lincoln's injunction of March 8 about the safety of Washington, the council resolved that a force be left to cover the capital large enough to make it entirely secure. The generals differed among themselves as to how large the

[2] McClellan to Lincoln, March 12, 1862, Lincoln MSS., vol. 70; Marcy to McClellan, March 14, McClellan MSS., Ser. 2; Dennison to McClellan, March 14, McClellan, *Own Story*, 250.

covering force should be, the minimum figure being 40,000 and the maximum over 50,000. If the conditions prescribed could not be met, the council advised an advance against the Confederates on the Rappahannock line.[3]

McClellan, perhaps remembering that McDowell was close to Stanton, sent that General to Washington with a copy of the proceedings of the council.[4] McDowell got to Washington that afternoon and delivered the document to Stanton. Testily the Secretary telegraphed McClellan that McDowell was there with a paper purporting to be the opinion of the corps generals but that it contained nothing to indicate that it was McClellan's plan. Specifically, what is your plan? asked Stanton. McClellan replied that the paper McDowell bore was his plan, and if the government approved it, he would start operations immediately.[5] Stanton then took the document to Lincoln for approval or rejection. Later that night the Secretary telegraphed the President's decision to McClellan. Lincoln's reaction was far from enthusiastic. He did not formally approve the plan, but as Stanton phrased his opinion, he "makes no objection" to it. Lincoln gave these directions to be observed in the execution of the movement: McClellan was to leave Washington secure from attack; to leave a force at Manassas large enough to make it certain the Confederates could not recapture it; and to move the remainder of the army to Fortress Monroe or some other base, "or, at all events, move . . . at once in pursuit of the enemy by some route." [6] Lincoln did not like the Fortress Monroe plan any more than he had the Urbana movement, and yet he accepted it. Again he was making a mistake. If he objected to McClellan's plan, he should have required the General to make another or

[3] *Official Records*, V, 55–56.

[4] *Ibid.*, LI, pt. 1, 551.

[5] Stanton to McClellan, March 13, 1862, *ibid.*, V, 750; McClellan to Stanton, March 13, *C. C. W.*, *Reports*, 1863, I, 312–313.

[6] Stanton to McClellan, March 13, 1862, *Official Records*, V, 56.

should have removed him. Instead, he did as he had done on March 8. He assented to the plan but added another condition to be met by McClellan, this time the detachment of a force sufficient to hold Manassas. If Lincoln was going to let McClellan carry out the plan, he should have given the General a free hand in working out the details. Feeling as he did about McClellan and the Peninsula scheme, Lincoln would have done better to remove the General.

McClellan was about to embark on a campaign to which the government was opposed but one which would largely depend for success upon the support and cooperation it got from several agencies of government. The procuring of water transport to take the army to the Peninsula would have to be done by the War Department; the neutralizing of the *Merrimac* and the destruction of the enemy batteries on the York required action by the Navy and would necessitate the framing of plans for coordinated action by the Navy and War Departments. If ever a general taking the field needed the complete trust of his superiors, McClellan did, and if ever a general lacked it, he did. McClellan was leaving behind him in Washington a President who believed the plan of operations of his commanding general was dangerous and a Secretary of War who thought the commander ought to be removed.

After McClellan had been relieved as general in chief, all the functions of command reverted to Lincoln; but as the order relieving McClellan had directed all department commanders to report to Stanton, the Secretary exercised tremendous power over the military machine. Stanton thought he ought to have a military man as adviser, and he called to Washington Ethan Allen Hitchcock, an ancient officer who was unfit for active service. Hitchcock was an interesting figure. He had never wanted to be a soldier, but his family had forced him to become one because they thought the grandson of Ethan Allen ought to be a warrior. The study of war was of little interest to Hitchcock, but he was fascinated by such subjects as mysticism, philosophy, and spiritualism and had written books about Christ, Swedenborg, and alchemy. When he arrived in Washington, Stanton amazed him by asking him if he would like to be commander of the Army of the Potomac. Hitchcock refused the offer. Stanton then took him to Lincoln, who said he wanted to have the benefit of Hitchcock's advice. The President said he knew nothing of military affairs, and yet he had to exercise control. Lincoln's appeal did not convince the old officer that he ought to accept a job in Washington, but Stanton kept working on him. The Secretary recounted such awful tales of McClellan's incompetence that Hitchcock felt "positively sick." Finally he agreed to become a staff officer under Stanton. The Secretary appointed him chairman of a new agency, the Army Board, composed of the heads of bureaus in the War Department. Lincoln and Stanton would frequently turn to this body for counsel.[7]

McClellan started to embark his army on the seventeenth from Alexandria. As he was superintending the departure of the troops, he received from Stanton a request to submit to the government in official form a statement of his plan. McClellan responded by saying his purpose was to operate from Fortress Monroe as a base, using the York River as a line of communications and making Richmond his objective. He intended to establish his main depot at West Point on the York and expected to fight a decisive battle with the enemy between that place and Richmond. There were two ways of reaching West Point. One was to move from Fortress Monroe and take Yorktown and Gloucester by a siege; the other was to make a combined land and naval attack on Yorktown, reducing it in a few hours, and then under cover of the Navy

[7] W. A. Croffut (ed.), *Fifty Years in Camp and Field: the Diary of Major-General Ethan Allen Hitchcock*, 437–440.

to push a corps up the river to West Point. McClellan wanted to employ the second method, and he strongly urged that the Navy be ready to throw its most powerful vessels against York-town.[8]

He was counting heavily on the aid of the Navy, but one of the serious breakdowns in his plan occurred because the Navy was not able to cooperate with him. The fault was partly McClellan's, partly the government's, and partly the inadequacies of the command system, which was not equipped in 1862 to manage a complicated operation calling for common action by two branches of the service. After McClellan made his request for naval support, a lot of talking took place about enlisting it, but everybody seems to have misunderstood everybody else. Lincoln came to Alexandria to talk with McClellan, and Stanton sent agents to talk to the Navy. The Navy promised cooperation but understood that McClellan wanted it only to keep the *Merrimac* from entering the York River. This was about all the Navy could do anyway. It had enough force to neutralize the *Merrimac* but not enough to attack Yorktown also. McClellan blissfully assumed that the Navy would do what he wanted. Despite his insistence that a naval attack on Yorktown was essential, he went to the Peninsula without any definite assurances from the Navy that it could help him.[9]

When Lincoln talked with McClellan at Alexandria about naval cooperation, he told the General that a great deal of pressure was being exerted on him to detach Blenker's division from the Army of the Potomac and give it to Fremont. According to McClellan, Lincoln said then that he was opposed to taking Blenker away. A few days later the President wrote McClellan that he was ordering the division to join Fremont. With characteristic consideration, Lincoln ex-

[8] McClellan to Stanton, March 19, 1862, *Official Records*, V, 57–58.
[9] *C. C. W., Reports*, 1863, I, 628–634.

plained why he had issued the order: ". . . I write this to assure you I did so with great pain, understanding you would wish it otherwise. If you could know the full pressure of the case, I am confident that you would justify it, even beyond a mere acknowledgment that the commander-in-chief may order what he pleases." [1]

The pressure of the case was indeed great. After Fremont had been removed from command of the Western Department, the radicals had insisted that their favorite be given another chance. Lincoln did not want to risk a disrupting fight in the Republican ranks by disregarding their demands, and he had conceived the idea of creating the Mountain Department for Fremont.[2] The radical chieftains, eager for Fremont to make a good showing, kept pressing Lincoln to provide the Pathfinder with more troops. The President had a motive of his own in wanting to strengthen Fremont. The General, naturally, trying to get all the men he could, had dangled the bait of East Tennessee before Lincoln. If he were reinforced, said Fremont, he could take Knoxville. This was more than Lincoln could resist, but he should have resisted. Fremont had more than enough troops to hold western Virginia; he did not have enough, even with Blenker, to take East Tennessee. Blenker's ten thousand should have remained with the Army of the Potomac; McClellan could have used them. They were so wearied by their long march to the Valley that they were no good to Fremont. McClellan took the departure of the division in good spirit. He wrote Lincoln that he appreciated the circumstances of the case and the frankness of Lincoln's note and that he would work all the harder to make up for the loss of Blenker.[3]

[1] Lincoln to McClellan, March 21, 1862, *Works of Lincoln*, VII, 138; McClellan, *Own Story*, 164–165.

[2] Journal of Ethan Allen Hitchcock, Hitchcock MSS., entry of March 23, 1862.

[3] McClellan to Lincoln, March 31, 1862, Lincoln MSS., vol. 72.

By April 1, part of the army had landed at Fortress Monroe, and the remainder was awaiting embarkation at Alexandria. On that day McClellan decided to go to the Peninsula. As he was about to get on a steamer, he was informed that Lincoln was coming to see him. In a note to a staff officer, the General said he would await his superior's arrival if the President was not going to stay very long! [4] The interview must have been short, for McClellan was eager to be away—away from Washington, away from men who tried to control him. "I did not feel safe until I could see Alexandria behind us," he wrote his wife. [5] McDowell, whose corps was still at Alexandria, rode back to Washington with Lincoln. He noted that the President seemed disturbed about the safety of Washington now that the army was leaving for the Peninsula. [6] Although McDowell did not know it, Lincoln also was disturbed about McClellan's ability to conduct a big offensive. The next day, the President, in a penetrating criticism, told one of his close friends that he had taken McClellan's measure: the General had talent and was great at preparation, but he lacked aggressiveness and became nervous and oppressed as the hour for action approached. But he had given McClellan peremptory orders to move fast, said Lincoln, and he hoped for the best. [7]

Lincoln might well have felt alarm for the security of Washington, because he knew nothing of McClellan's arrangements for its protection. In a remarkable display of secretiveness, the General waited till he got aboard ship on April 1 to furnish the government with a statement of the forces he had left for the defence of the city in accordance

[4] McClellan to Seth Richardson, April 1, 1862, McClellan MSS., Ser. 1.

[5] McClellan, *Own Story*, 306.

[6] *C. C. W., Reports*, 1863, I, 260–261.

[7] Theodore C. Pease and James G. Randall (eds.), *The Diary of Orville Hickman Browning*, I, 537–539.

with the President's order of March 8 and the recommendations of the council at Fairfax Court House. Then, steaming
away from Washington and anybody who might check his
figures, McClellan sent to the Adjutant General a letter summarizing the number and the disposition of the troops he was
leaving behind. According to McClellan's computations, they
numbered over 73,000 men; he advised bringing up 4,000
more from New York to make a grand total of 77,000. They
were to be stationed thus: at Manassas, 10,859; at Warrenton,
just south of Manassas, 7,780; in the Shenandoah Valley, 35,-
467; on the lower Potomac, 1,350; and in and around Washington itself, 22,000.[8] The force at Warrenton and Manassas
was to meet Lincoln's condition that Manassas be made secure against recapture. Originally McClellan had intended
this force, under the command of General Banks, to be larger.
But in late March a small Confederate army under Stonewall
Jackson had appeared in the Valley, and McClellan had sent
Banks and a part of the Manassas-Warrenton troops to face
Jackson. When McClellan wrote his letter, Manassas was practically empty of Union soldiers. To bring the Manassas group
up to the strength required by Lincoln's order, McClellan directed that 4,000 men from the Washington garrison be sent to Manassas, leaving 18,000 in the capital defences, and he advised that 6,000 more be brought in from
Maryland and Pennsylvania. That was how he got his 10,859
for Manassas! The 4,000 lost to the Washington garrison was
to be made up from troops that could be brought from New
York. McClellan played fast and loose and careless with all
his figures. In determining the number at Manassas he
counted men who were not there. The 7,780 at Warrenton he
counted twice, once as a part of the Manassas force and again
as a part of Banks' army. He included Blenker's division, on

8 McClellan to Lorenzo Thomas, April 1, 1862, *Official Records,*
V, 60–61; McClellan, *Own Story,* 240–241.

its way to Fremont, in the total figures for Banks. It was true
that Blenker was in the Valley and could be detained by Banks
if necessary, but Blenker was not supposed to be a part of the
Washington defence forces.[9] Actually, not counting Blenker
or the Warrenton group twice and the troops supposed to be
on the way, McClellan had left about 50,000 men at the most
to guard Washington and the approaches to it. About 29,000
of these were in the city or on its front at Manassas and Warrenton.

Out of the April 1 letter arose one of the great controversies of the war. Had McClellan obeyed Lincoln's order to
leave enough men "in and about" Washington to make the
capital secure? Had he followed the recommendations of the
council of corps commanders on March 13? Had he left Washington safe or in danger? There is no doubt that McClellan,
intent on taking the largest possible army to the Peninsula,
gave little thought to the defence of Washington or little consideration to the natural fears of Lincoln for the safety of the
capital. The General assumed what was true, that the safety
of the city would be assured by his offensive against the enemy capital, but he never made this truth clear to Lincoln.
The President had stipulated that as many troops be left in
and about Washington as, in the opinion of the corps generals, would make the place secure. The generals had differed
about the size of the defending force and had been a little
vague about it, but 40,000 seems to have been their minimum
figure. Undoubtedly this was the figure Lincoln thought they
had set, and undoubtedly he also thought they meant 40,000
men in the Washington forts and just south of the Potomac
—not at Warrenton or in the Valley. Therefore McClellan,
knowingly or unknowingly, did not obey the President's

[9] Ballard, *Military Genius of Lincoln*, 74–76; Ropes, *Story of the
Civil War*, I, 262–265.

order of March 8 or follow the recommendations of the council of March 13.

On the other hand, the General had left the capital secure. The forces he had left were adequate to meet any thrust the enemy could prepare. The only possible threat to Washington could come from Jackson in the Valley, and Banks should have been able to deal with it. Banks in the Valley was an integral part of the Washington defensive forces, but it never occurred to McClellan to go frankly to Lincoln and explain this. The troops at Warrenton and Manassas formed a protective screen in front of Washington, but McClellan never thought of explaining this to Lincoln. He knew Lincoln's fears about the Peninsula plan and the safety of Washington. Before he ever left for the field, he should have gone over with the President face to face every detail of his arrangements for the defence of the city. He should have given Lincoln a sense of security. In the last analysis, most of McClellan's difficulties stemmed from his failure to take Lincoln into his confidence. McClellan said in his official report that before he left he sent his chief of staff to Hitchcock with a list of the troops he was detailing to guard Washington and that Hitchcock said the arrangements looked all right. McClellan seemed to think that by this proffer of information he had done his duty by the government. But he had no business dealing through a subordinate with a subordinate. He should have opened his heart to Lincoln. Lincoln wanted him to. In view of the President's fears about Washington, it is surprising that he did not require from McClellan before the General went to the field a statement about the defensive arrangements for Washington. Undoubtedly he assumed that McClellan would do exactly what he had been ordered to do.

On the day after McClellan left for the Peninsula, General James Wadsworth, commander of the capital defences, appeared at the War Department. He gave Stanton a report, charging that his forces were poor in quality and too few in numbers to hold the city against an attack and complaining because he had to send 4,000 of them to Manassas. Stanton sent the report to Hitchcock and Adjutant General Lorenzo Thomas, and asked whether McClellan had complied with the President's order to leave Washington secure. Hitchcock and Thomas replied that McClellan had not obeyed the order and that the capital was in danger.[1] Now Stanton saw a chance to strike McClellan. He, Wadsworth, and some of the radical Congressional leaders descended on Lincoln. They charged that McClellan, out of incompetence or disloyalty, had left the capital defenceless. The Congressional bosses believed the disloyalty accusation, but Lincoln did not. He was convinced, however, by the evidence of Stanton and Wadsworth that McClellan had disobeyed the order of March 8 and that Washington was in danger. As the political chief of the nation, he was aware of the importance of the capital; and he had no intention of exposing it to any menace while a general who had never fought a big battle took the main army far away to seek a doubtful decision. On April 3 Lincoln came to the War Department and conferred with Stanton and the Army Board. Then he directed Stanton to detain one of the two corps of the Army of the Potomac awaiting embarkation at Alexandria and to hold it in front of Washington. Stanton ordered McDowell's fine corps of over 30,000 to stay.[2]

McClellan was in the Peninsula making his first contact with the enemy when he received the news about the detachment of McDowell. Already convinced that he faced an army greatly superior to his, he protested bitterly to Lincoln and

[1] *Official Records*, XI, pt. 3, 60-62; James Greenleaf Pearson, *James S. Wadsworth of Geneseo*, 118-120; C. C. W., *Reports*, 1863, I, 304-305.

[2] *Works of Lincoln*, VII, 138-139; C. C. W., *Reports*, 1863, I, 304-305.

Stanton that he needed all the men he could get.[3] The President curtly replied that McClellan had over 100,000 troops and that he ought to break the Confederate lines at once. The General was enraged and was tempted to tell Lincoln to come do it himself.[4]

Lincoln's own anger against McClellan passed away in a few days, and he wrote the General a long, considerate, and wise letter. He was not offended but pained, he said, by McClellan's despatches complaining that he was not being properly sustained. Then Lincoln explained why he had detained McDowell's corps. Demonstrating that he did not understand that Banks' force was a part of the Washington defences, the President chided McClellan for leaving only 20,000 men to guard the city: "My explicit order that Washington should, by the judgment of all the commanders of corps, be left entirely secure, had been neglected." The safety of the capital, he said, was a question the country would not allow him to evade. McClellan had not made adequate arrangements for its safety, and he, the President, had been constrained to make them himself. Having kindly yet firmly explained the detachment of McDowell, Lincoln proceeded to give McClellan some military advice. The General was then stalled before Yorktown, insisting he could not assault the enemy lines without reinforcements. Lincoln urged him to attack at once. He tried to make McClellan see that the enemy would gain more by delay than he would and that in a democracy generals could not wait for perfect military conditions:

And once more let me tell you that it is indispensable to you that you strike a blow. I am powerless to help this. You will do me the justice to remember I always insisted that going down

[3] McClellan to Stanton, April 5, 7, 1862, McClellan, *Own Story*, 262, 266–267; McClellan to Lincoln, April 7, *ibid.*, 266.

[4] Lincon to McClellan, April 6, 1862, *Works of Lincoln*, VII, 140; McClellan to Mrs. McClellan, April 8, McClellan, *Own Story*, 308.

the bay in search of a field, instead of fighting at or near Manassas, was only shifting and not surmounting a difficulty; that we
would find the same enemy and the same or equal entrenchments
at either place. The country will not fail to note—is noting now—
that the present hesitation to move upon an intrenched enemy is
but the story of Manassas repeated.

I beg to assure you that I have never written you or spoken
to you in greater kindness of feeling than now, nor with a fuller
purpose to sustain you, so far as in my most anxious judgment,
I consistently can. But you must act.[5]

During the weeks when the strategy for the Eastern campaign was being worked out in Washington, things were happening in the West. Halleck prepared to send Grant's army
up the Tennessee to cut Confederate communications. As
the expedition was about to move, Halleck decided he would
have to relieve Grant from command. For two weeks he had
received no despatches or reports from Grant. Then Halleck
heard that Grant, without asking permission, had gone to
Nashville in Buell's department. Rules and ritual were important to Halleck, and he immediately concluded that Grant
and his army were demoralized by victory, a cause of de-
pravity which Halleck had not yet experienced. From his
hazardous desk in St. Louis, he peevishly informed McClellan, then still general in chief, that he was worn out by
Grant's neglect of duty. McClellan authorized Halleck to
arrest Grant. Halleck replied that he had learned the awful
truth: Grant had gone back to his "old habits"—he was
drinking again. Hesitating to arrest Grant, Halleck removed
Grant from command and put another officer in his place.
Grant, however, was able to explain everything to Halleck.
He had sent frequent reports to his superior, but the telegraph operator apparently had deserted, taking all the despatches with him. Instead of going to Nashville to get drunk,

[5] Lincoln to McClellan, April 9, 1862, *Works of Lincoln*, VII,
141–143.

Grant had gone to confer with Buell about cooperative action. Halleck, well aware of Grant's standing with the public, then restored him to command of the army going up the Tennessee.[6]

Grant went up the river and disembarked at Pittsburg Landing. In the meantime, Lincoln had given Halleck command of all the armies in the West, and Halleck had ordered Buell to join Grant on the Tennessee. Early in April, the Confederates moved in on Grant and struck him in a surprise attack at Shiloh near the Landing. Grant was guilty of a familiar military sin, that of expecting that the enemy would do what he wanted, which meant in this case that the enemy would wait for Grant to attack. Undeniably, he had not taken proper precautionary measures, and he was caught completely unawares by the Confederate assault. At first the battle went all in favor of the Confederates, but Grant rallied his troops and with the aid of part of Buell's army, which had arrived, he drove the foe from the field. Shiloh was the first great bloody battle of the war. The list of Union killed and wounded was long, and there were charges that Grant, by his incompetence or neglect or drunkenness, was responsible for the heavy losses.

Lincoln took official notice of the accusations. He instructed Stanton to ask Halleck whether misconduct on the part of Grant or any other officer had contributed to the number of casualties. Halleck refused to pin any blame on Grant and pointed out that most of the casualties were due to the Confederates.[7] Privately, Halleck was very critical of Grant. In a letter to Hitchcock, he said he had never seen a general more deficient in organizational skill: "Brave & able on the field, he has no idea of how to regulate & organize his forces

[6] McClellan, *Own Story*, 215–217; James Harrison Wilson, *Life of John A. Rawlins*, 74–79; Grant to Halleck, March 7, 1862, Stanton MSS.; Halleck to Lorenzo Thomas, March 15, Hitchcock MSS.

[7] *Official Records*, X, pt. 1, 98–100.

before a battle or how to conduct the operations of a campaign." [8]

Lincoln, though, was satisfied with Grant, even after Shiloh. He was not worried about Grant's neglect of army red tape. A friend called on the President to advise that Grant ought to be removed because of Shiloh and because he was hurting the administration with the public. Lincoln sat and listened. The friend finished. There was a long silence. Then Lincoln gathered himself up in his chair and perhaps with thoughts of the Peninsula in his mind, said: "I can't spare this man; he fights." [9]

[8] Halleck to E. A. Hitchcock, April 18, 1862, Hitchcock MSS.
[9] McClure, *Lincoln and Men of War-Times*, 178–180.

Chapter 5

"I Give You All I Can"

LINCOLN went to the War Department on April 11 and talked with Stanton and the Army Board. The President was worried about McClellan's complaints that he did not have enough men to break the Confederate lines; he wanted to reinforce McClellan if he could do so without endangering Washington. The General had asked for Franklin's division of McDowell's corps, and Lincoln asked Hitchcock whether sending Franklin to the Peninsula would weaken the capital defences. Hitchcock said no, and Lincoln immediately wrote an order for Franklin, with about 11,000 men, to join McClellan.[1] At first the Young Napoleon professed to be completely satisfied with the addition of Franklin, but a few days later he demanded that McCall's division of McDowell's corps be sent to him.[2] In a letter to Stanton, McClellan said that he was weaker by five divisions than he had expected to be and that if the government had not weakened his army he would be in front of Richmond instead of before Yorktown. Give me McCall, he pleaded, and I will shake the rebels out of Yorktown.[3]

[1] *Official Records*, XII, pt. 1, 220; *C. C. W., Reports*, 1863, I, 304–305.

[2] McClellan to Lincoln, April 14, 1862, McClellan MSS., Ser. 1; McClellan to Lincoln, April 18, *Official Records*, LI, pt. 1, 578.

[3] McClellan to Stanton, April 20, 1862, McClellan, *Own Story*, 281–283.

The number of troops that McClellan had in the Peninsula campaign is one of the great mysteries of the war. "A curious mystery," Lincoln called it, and it has continued so ever since. Students of the Civil War have tried to estimate the size of the Union army by studying the sometimes incomplete and often contradictory documents, but without coming to any common agreement. McClellan had intended to operate with about 156,000 troops. He claimed that after the government had detached McDowell and other units from him he had only 93,000 left. Deducting from this total, unfits and extra duty men, he asserted that he began the campaign with only 70,000 effectives.[4] One of the best authorities on numbers in the Civil War calculated that McClellan fought the biggest battle of the campaign with only about 91,000 effective troops.[5] On the other side of the statistics, McClellan, on April 1, had under his command in round numbers 158,000 troops, his "aggregate present and absent"; on June 20 he had 156,000; on July 10, by his own figures, 157,000; and on July 20, 158,000.[6] The two government officials who had charge of transporting troops to the Peninsula testified that the total number sent was 159,000 or 160,000.[7] The aggregate totals included sick and wounded, legal or illegal absentees, and men on extra duty, such as teamsters and cooks. On June 20, right before the decisive engagement of the campaign, McClellan had "present for duty," 105,000, according to one estimate; and 115,000, according to another.[8] Right

[4] *Ibid.*, 163–164.

[5] Thomas L. Livermore, *Numbers and Losses in the Civil War in America, 1861–1865*, 84–86.

[6] Williams, *Lincoln Finds a General*, I, 216–217; *Official Records*, XI, pt. 3, 312, 329.

[7] *C. C. W., Reports*, 1863, I, 296. Testimony of John Tucker, Assistant Secretary of War, and Quartermaster General Meigs.

[8] Williams, *Lincoln Finds a General*, I, 415; *C. C. W., Reports*, 1863, I, 345.

after the close of the campaign, McClellan stated that his aggregate present was 117,000 and his present for duty equipped was 98,000. The adjutant general's office estimated that his present for duty was 101,000.[9]

It seems certain that during the course of the campaign McClellan received over 150,000 men, about the number he had intended to start with. He did not, however, have this many when he began his operations or in the first engagements he fought or at any one time in later stages of the campaign. The reinforcements he received while he was in the Peninsula came at different times. For example, most of the troops he lost when the government took part of his army away were later restored to him, but not all at once. He recovered over 20,000 of McDowell's corps. He got Franklin's division right away, in April, but he did not receive McCall's until June. Any estimate of the average size of McClellan's army must take into account that he received his reinforcements in parcels and that from his total at any given time there must be deducted casualties, absentees, extra duty men, and a large number of soldiers rendered unfit by sickness. Probably the largest fighting army that McClellan could ever have committed to battle would have numbered slightly under 100,000. As the largest army that the Confederates put in the field numbered about 85,000, McClellan's army was only a little larger than the enemy's at the supreme moment of the campaign. For the kind of offensive operation he had planned, his numerical superiority was none too great. In the initial stages of the campaign, however, McClellan had overwhelming superiority in numbers. When he landed in the Peninsula, the main enemy army was moving to Richmond from the Rappahannock. The Confederates on the Peninsula held a line from Yorktown to the James with about 11,000

---

[9] *Official Records,* XI, pt. 3, 312, 329.

troops. Undoubtedly McClellan could have broken through these defenders and driven up the Peninsula. But instead of attacking, he settled down for a siege of the Confederate works that lasted a month and gave the Confederates time to concentrate their forces.

McClellan's original intention had been to take Yorktown immediately with the aid of the Navy and then send a force up the York River, flanking the Confederates out of their defensive positions on the Peninsula. After he arrived at Fortress Monroe, he found that the Navy could not cooperate in an attack on Yorktown. His next idea was to send McDowell's corps to operate on the north side of the river and accomplish the same objective of flanking the enemy out of their works. Then he learned that McDowell had been detained at Washington. All that McClellan could do now was to move directly against the Confederate lines. Although the works of the defenders were strong, they were not complete and were lightly held. Almost certainly McClellan, who then had about 70,000 troops, could have smashed through them had he attacked. But here he acted just like McClellan. Without probing the enemy positions with reconnaissances in force, he decided they were too strong to assault and that he would take them by siege methods. He called for siege machinery and started operations all along the line, directing his main efforts at the strong works around Yorktown.

McClellan was confident and happy during the siege of Yorktown. He liked siege warfare, with its slowness, its engineering problems, and its small loss of life. He seemed to think that when he took the Confederate defences he would take the defenders also and win a decisive victory. "I am confident of success . . . of brilliant success," he assured Lincoln.[1] He told the President not to worry about the apparent inaction of the army. "Gigantic" works had been built, roads

[1] McClellan to Lincoln, April 20, 1862, Lincoln MSS., vol. 74.

constructed, and batteries moved up. Victory was certain—
but he did need some more heavy guns.[2]

Lincoln had thought from the first that McClellan should
have attacked the Confederate works, and when he heard
about the General's request for guns he lost some of his ordinary patience. In a sharp telegram, Lincoln said: "Your call
for Parrott guns from Washington alarms me, chiefly because
it argues indefinite procrastination. Is anything to be done?"
McClellan replied that the guns were intended to hasten, not
delay, operations.[3] Lincoln's telegram threw McClellan into
one of his morbid moods. To his wife, the General wrote that
his enemies in Washington were pursuing him remorselessly
and that he had not a single friend in the government.[4] He
did not win any friends by the outcome of the siege. After a
month of preparation, he was ready to breach the enemy
works with artillery and follow up with an infantry assault.
The operation was certain to succeed, but the Confederates
had no intention of waiting in the trap. They were content
to have held McClellan off for weeks while they organized
their defences. On May 5 they evacuated their lines and fell
back up the Peninsula. As had been the case at Manassas, the
Young Napoleon marched into abandoned works.

Right after the fall of Yorktown, Lincoln came to Fortress
Monroe. Accompanied by Stanton and Chase, he arrived on
May 6 and did not return to Washington until the twelfth.
The President's reasons for making the trip seem to have
been partly personal, a sort of vacation jaunt, and partly military, to see how things in the Peninsula were going. Stanton
invited McClellan to come down from the front to confer

[2] McClellan to Lincoln, April 23, 1862, McClellan MSS., Ser. 1;
McClellan to General J. W. Ripley, Chief of Ordnance, April 26, *Official
Records*, LI, pt. 1, 584.

[3] Lincoln to McClellan, May 1, 1862, *Works of Lincoln*, VII, 152;
McClellan to Lincoln, May 1, McClellan, *Own Story*, 295.

[4] McClellan to Mrs. McClellan, May 1, 3, 1862, *ibid.*, 316–317.

with Lincoln, but the General was too busy.[5] The commander in chief watched Union gunboats shell Confederate batteries at Sewall's Point, and ordered Admiral L. M. Golds-
borough, over that officer's objections, to send some of his
vessels up the James. Then Lincoln discussed plans to take
Norfolk with General Wool, the commander at Fortress
Monroe. Lincoln, Wool, and the Cabinet members steamed
around the coast in a boat looking for a landing place for the
troops to be sent against Norfolk. The President stayed at
the Fortress when Wool made his attack, which turned out to
be no attack, for the Confederates had evacuated the city on
news of the abandonment of Yorktown. Lincoln could return
to Washington well pleased. He had seen his forces fire at
the enemy, and he had influenced the planning of an operation. Perhaps he felt as Chase did, that Norfolk would not
have been taken if the President had not been there.[6]

After he occupied the Yorktown defences, McClellan
moved slowly toward Richmond, using the York River as his
line of communications. He intended to make West Point on
the York or the White House on the Pamunkey, a tributary
of the York, his field base of supplies. He met little resistance
from the enemy. The Confederate commander, Joseph E.
Johnston, wanted to fight the decisive battle for Richmond
near the capital, so he fell back as McClellan came on. About
halfway up the Peninsula, McClellan came to the Chickahominy River. This stream started above Richmond, flowed
east for a distance, and then turned south and emptied into
the James. As McClellan advanced, he put his army north
of the Chickahominy, which meant he would have to cross it
again near Richmond. He would claim later, in his official

[5] Stanton to McClellan, May 6, 1862, and McClellan to Stanton,
May 7, Stanton MSS.

[6] Stanton to P. H. Watson, May 7, 10, 1862, Stanton MSS.; Beale,
Diary of Edward Bates, 255–258; Pease and Randall, *Diary of O. H.
Browning*, 545; Schuckers, *Chase*, 368–374.

report and in his writings after the war, that he had never wanted to use this route, that he had planned to cross the lower Chickahominy and reach the James and advance along the line of that river to Richmond. He would charge that the administration had prevented him from doing so by offering to send him reinforcements from Washington by land but refusing to send any by water. In order to reach out to make contact with the expected help coming overland, said McClellan, he had to place his army in an unfavorable position north of the Chickahominy. The accusation was completely an afterthought. Everything in McClellan's correspondence and despatches indicates that he had always intended to use the York as his line of operations and that he had put himself north of the Chickahominy by his own decision.

As he got closer to Richmond, he became characteristically nervous and oppressed. The Confederates were concentrating an immense army against him, he complained to his wife, and his government was giving him no aid. "Those hounds in Washington are after me again," he said in one letter.[7] Frantically he implored the War Department to send him more men. Getting no response, he wrote directly to Lincoln. He told the President he could not put more than 80,000 troops into battle, while the enemy had about double that number. He asked Lincoln to reinforce him with all the disposable troops in the Washington area, no matter who their commander was. Even if it was McDowell, he meant. McClellan blamed McDowell for the detachment of the latter's corps, but now he wanted the corps and was willing to take its commander along with it. The reinforcements should be sent by water, he said. Again he was showing his inability to understand realities. McDowell was then at Fredericksburg in command of the new Department of the Rappahannock. He was

[7] McClellan to Mrs. McClellan, May 12, 15, 18, 1862, McClellan, *Own Story*, 356–357, 359.

about sixty-five miles and three days of marching from Richmond. The easiest way for him to join McClellan was by land, but in McClellan's original plan all troops were to move to the Peninsula by water. Therefore, McDowell had to come that way now, even though the original conditions no longer existed. All through the campaign, when McClellan asked for reinforcements, for McDowell or anybody else, he would insist that they come by water. He could not change the plan to meet changed situations. McClellan closed his letter with a curious sentence: "They [the soldiers] have confidence in me as their general, and in you as their President. Strong reinforcements will at least save the lives of many of them." Presumably this meant that more men would be left alive to admire Lincoln and McClellan. The President must have pondered over that one.[8]

Lincoln answered McClellan's plea by saying that he would do all he could to sustain the Army of the Potomac, but that he was still unwilling to uncover Washington by sending McDowell to the Peninsula.[9] The President was anxious, however, to aid McClellan if he could do so without endangering the capital, and he hit upon a plan. This was to send McDowell to join McClellan by land. McDowell was to move south from Fredericksburg toward McClellan's army, and McClellan was to extend his right wing north of Richmond to meet McDowell. Moving directly between Washington and Richmond, McDowell would always be in position to turn back to defend the capital against any Confederate attack. The distance between him and McClellan's right wing would be only fifty miles. Lincoln's instructions to McDowell were interesting. The General was to retain command of his forces, about 40,000, and his Department. While cooperating with McClellan, he was to obey the latter's orders, except that

8 McClellan to Lincoln, May 14, 1862, *ibid.*, 343–345.
9 Lincoln to McClellan, May 15, 1862, *Works of Lincoln*, VII, 163.

he was not to allow his force "to be disposed otherwise than so as to give the greatest protection" to Washington.[1] Stanton wrote to McClellan to tell him McDowell was coming and to explain Lincoln's plan. The President wanted to accomplish two things, said the Secretary: to give McClellan an increased force for the final push on Richmond and to maintain the security of Washington. Sending McDowell to the Richmond area by land would aid McClellan and keep Washington covered; furthermore, said Stanton, remembering McClellan's request that reinforcements be sent by water, McDowell could reach McClellan faster by land than by water. In emphatic words, Stanton charged McClellan not to give McDowell any order, either before or after they joined, that would put McDowell out of position to cover Washington.[2] By the terms of Lincoln's plan, McDowell was not going to McClellan as a reinforcement but as a separate, cooperating army. McClellan could not give McDowell certain orders, and if he did, McDowell was authorized to disobey them.

McClellan was not at all pleased with the kind of assistance he was about to get from McDowell. He wrote Lincoln a long, rambling, disconnected letter, in which he discussed the positions of his and the enemy's troops; the size of the enemy army, larger than his, of course; the health of the soldiers; his need for reinforcements; and the effect of rains on the roads. In between these subjects, he complained about his incomplete authority over McDowell and said that McDowell ought to be sent by water. The letter, almost incoherent in spots, revealed the nervous oppression that always gripped McClellan at a critical moment.[3] He had convinced himself, as he had previously done in the fall of 1861, that the administration was trying to sacrifice him. In a letter to his friend, Gen-

[1] *Ibid.*, VII, 166. Lincoln's instructions of May 17, 1862.
[2] Stanton to McClellan, May 18, 1862, *ibid.*, VII, 168–169.
[3] McClellan to Lincoln, May 21, 1862, McClellan, *Own Story*, 345–

350.

eral Ambrose E. Burnside, he made the incredible statement that his captures of Manassas and Yorktown would be ranked by history as his "brightest chaplets" because he had accomplished them by pure military skill and without having to fight. Of his present situation, where it looked as though he would have to fight, he wrote: "The Government have deliberately placed me in this position. If I win, the greater the glory. If I lose, they will be damned forever, both by God and men." [4]

On the Rappahannock, McDowell was getting his army ready to move to the Peninsula. On May 23, a Friday, Lincoln and several Cabinet members came down to visit the General. McDowell told the President that he could start on Sunday, but recalled that once before, at Manassas, he had initiated a move on the Sabbath and had been widely criticized for it. He also said that some of the troops were worn and needed a little rest. Lincoln reflected a moment and said: "I'll tell you what to do; take *a good ready* and start Monday morning." Lincoln and his party left about dark on Friday to return to Washington. On Sunday McDowell felt he had everything ready to start the movement the next day. In camp was Herman Haupt, director of railroad transportation for the Eastern armies, who had been advising McDowell about supply problems. That morning Haupt received a call to come to McDowell's headquarters. He found the General in a state of great excitement. McDowell had just got an order from Lincoln suspending the movement to join McClellan. [5]

When Lincoln got back to Washington on Saturday, he received some news that startled him. Things were happening in the Valley. The Confederate authorities had found out that McDowell was going to McClellan, and they had decided

[4] McClellan to Burnside, May 21, 1862, *Official Records*, IX, 392.

[5] Haupt, *Reminiscences*, 49–50; *C. C. W., Reports*, 1863, I, 262–269.

to stop the move by sending Jackson down the Valley in an apparent drive against Washington. They had reinforced Jackson, and on the twenty-third he started to move. First, he turned to the west where advanced units of Fremont's army were approaching, and beat them back. Then he turned to the east and defeated a part of Banks' army at Front Royal. The news of Front Royal shook Lincoln but did not affect his decision to send McDowell to McClellan. The President informed McClellan of Jackson's movement and of McDowell's intentions to start forward on Monday.[6] Later in the day, however, the intelligence from the Valley became more ominous. Jackson was driving northward, and Banks was falling back. At a conference with Stanton and Chase at the War Department, Lincoln decided to halt McDowell's movement and to send Chase to the Rappahannock to explain the situation to the General.[7]

Lincoln did not make the decision to hold McDowell near Washington because he was stampeded by fear for the safety of the capital. Undoubtedly he considered that Jackson might ultimately be a threat to Washington, and certainly he thought that Jackson, unless checked, would completely smash up Banks. But Lincoln's motive in suspending McDowell's movement was offensive, not defensive. He wanted to use McDowell to catch and destroy Jackson. The President's plan, made up on the afternoon of the twenty-fourth, was to move McDowell into the Valley from the east and Fremont from the west; he reasoned that Jackson would chase Banks northward a distance and then turn back. If McDowell and Fremont could get to the Valley on time, they could cut off his retreat. At four that afternoon Lincoln telegraphed McClellan that because of Banks' critical condition

[6] Lincoln to McClellan, May 24, 1862, *Official Records*, XI, pt. 1, 30.

[7] Schuckers, *Chase*, 436–437.

he was stopping McDowell's movement to join McClellan and that he was going to try to throw McDowell and Fremont in Jackson's rear.[8] At the same hour Lincoln telegraphed Fremont that Banks must be relieved and ordered the Pathfinder to move to Harrisonburg. A few hours later Lincoln sent Fremont another despatch urging the General to move fast: "Put the utmost speed into it. Do not lose a minute." [9]

Commander in chief Lincoln was acting up to his title. He was designing and directing both strategy and tactics. His plan to capture Jackson was strategic in nature; his order to Fremont to march to a specific point was tactical. He also gave McDowell strategic and tactical instructions. One hour later than he had telegraphed McClellan and Fremont, Lincoln sent McDowell an order suspending the movement to the Peninsula. He informed the General of the plan to catch Jackson and directed him to move to the Valley with 20,000 troops and told him on what route to move. McDowell protested the order, saying that he could never get to the Valley on time and that the proper move was to the Peninsula, but said that he would obey it at once. Lincoln thanked him for his promise of immediate and rapid action; and, referring to McDowell's regret that the march to McClellan had been suspended, the President said: "The change was as painful to me as it can possibly be to you or to any one." [1]

On the next day, Sunday, Lincoln was at the War Department receiving telegrams about the situation in the Valley. The news was bad. Jackson was driving Banks before him, and enemy units were threatening other Union forces in the Valley. The intelligence service could not ascertain the size of the Confederate army. Lincoln, therefore, could not deter-

[8] Lincoln to McClellan, May 24, 1862, *Official Records*, XI, pt. 1, 30.

[9] Lincoln to Fremont, May 24, 1862, two telegrams, *Works of Lincoln*, VII, 178–179.

[1] Lincoln to McDowell, May 24, 1862, two telegrams, *ibid.*, VII, 180–181; McDowell to Lincoln, May 24, *Official Records*, XII, pt. 3, 220–221.

mine whether Jackson's movement was merely a diversion to prevent reinforcements from going to McClellan or was a real offensive against Washington. At two in the afternoon, Lincoln, more worried than he had been the day before, sent McClellan a telegram summarizing the situation as it was then known at Washington: "I think the movement is a general and concerted one. . . . I think the time is near when you must either attack Richmond or give up the job and come to the defence of Washington. Let me hear from you instantly." McClellan replied that the time was very near when he would attack Richmond; and, accurately divining the purpose of Jackson's campaign, he told Lincoln the Confederates were trying to prevent reinforcements from going to the Army of the Potomac.[2] A few hours later Lincoln had more definite information to send McClellan. Despatches came in announcing that Jackson had caught Banks at Winchester that morning and had badly defeated him. The reports stated that Banks was in full retreat toward the Potomac, and that Jackson, with an army of 30,000, was right on his heels. Lincoln again summarized the situation for McClellan. The President did not think Jackson would attack Washington, but he thought Stonewall might cross the Potomac at Harper's Ferry and threaten Maryland. Lincoln told McClellan that he was pushing the movement to get Fremont and McDowell in Jackson's rear. "If McDowell's force was now beyond our reach, we should be utterly helpless," Lincoln wrote. "Apprehension of something like this, and no unwillingness to sustain you, has always been my reason for withholding McDowell's force from you. Please understand this, and do the best you can with the force you have."[3]

McClellan did not understand it at all. He was contemptu-

[2] Lincoln to McClellan, May 25, 1862, *Works of Lincoln*, VII, 183; McClellan to Lincoln, May 25, McClellan, *Own Story*, 367.

[3] Lincoln to McClellan, May 25, 1862, 8:30 p.m., *Works of Lincoln*, VII, 186–188.

ous of Lincoln's handling of the Valley situation. When he received Lincoln's first telegram of May 25, he was writing a letter to his wife. After reading the telegram, he wrote her that the President was "terribly scared" and wanted him to come back and save Washington. "Heaven help a country governed by such counsels," he exclaimed. At ten o'clock that night he got Lincoln's second telegram, and he added to his letter to Mrs. McClellan that they were in a panic at the capital. He was glad they were frightened: "A scare will do them good, and may bring them to their senses." The next day he found out they were not as scared as he had thought. Lincoln had learned that Banks was safely over the Potomac with his army, and the President despatched McClellan that things looked better. McClellan was vastly relieved. He had feared he would be ordered back to Washington, and being in Washington was the worst fate he could think of.[4]

Lincoln was so far from being scared that he was directing with high hopes the movement to close the trap around Jackson. As the President had foreseen, Jackson could not stay long in the northern end of the Valley with Federal forces, McDowell and Fremont, in position to move on his line of communications. Jackson started to retreat fast. Lincoln urged McDowell and Fremont to move after him faster. To McDowell he telegraphed that reports indicated Jackson had stopped at Winchester: "Assuming this, it is for you a question of legs. Put in all the speed you can. I have told Fremont as much, and directed him to drive at them as fast as possible."[5] Much to Lincoln's irritation, Fremont came toward the Valley on a different route from the one Lincoln had ordered him to take. It took Fremont about eight days to move

[4] McClellan to Mrs. McClellan, May 25, 26, 1862, McClellan, *Own Story*, 396–397; Lincoln to McClellan, May 26, *Official Records*, XI, pt. 1, 32.

[5] Lincoln to McDowell, May 28, 1862, *Works of Lincoln*, VII, 198; Lincoln to Fremont, May 28, *ibid.*, VII, 199–200.

seventy miles; McDowell advanced at about the same speed. Jackson, in the meantime, marched fifty miles in two days. Lincoln kept pressing McDowell and Fremont, and also Banks, to get more speed into their movements. The plan to catch Jackson was Lincoln's own, and he desperately wanted it to succeed.[6] "You must be up to time you promised . . . ," he reminded Fremont, and to McDowell he telegraphed: ". . . the game is before you." His final order to the two generals, sent through Stanton, as Jackson was slipping away to safety was: "Do not let the enemy escape you." [7]

McDowell and Fremont came up to Jackson's escape route too late to close it. Jackson not only went through but turned and defeated Fremont and the advance units of McDowell as he went. Lincoln's plan to trap Jackson had failed, and the Confederate plan of using Jackson to prevent McDowell from going to McClellan had succeeded. There will probably always be controversy over Lincoln's management of the Valley campaign. Was there any possibility that his plan to cut Jackson off could have worked? Did he act wisely in suspending McDowell's movement and ordering McDowell to the Valley? The chances of catching Jackson were slim from the beginning. The Union forces were in poor positions from which to start the chase. Fremont was relatively close to the Confederate escape corridor, but he had to march over difficult mountain terrain; McDowell's line of advance to the Valley was longer than Jackson's line of retreat from the Potomac. McDowell and Fremont were slowed by the necessity of maintaining supply lines behind them as they advanced. Jackson, falling back toward his base, did not have to worry about his communications. Still, when all is said that can be, of the diffi-

[6] Lincoln's telegrams to McDowell, Banks, and Fremont, May 29–30, *Works of Lincoln*, VII, 201–204.

[7] Lincoln to Fremont, May 30, 1862, *ibid.*, VII, 205; Lincoln to McDowell, May 30, *ibid.*, VII, 206; Stanton to McDowell and Fremont, June 2, *Official Records*, XII, pt. 3, 321.

culties facing Fremont and McDowell, the fact remains that they could have moved faster than they did. There was a chance—not as great a one as Lincoln thought, but an outside chance—that they could have caught Jackson.

Lincoln was severely criticized by McClellan's friends for halting McDowell's movement to the Peninsula, and many historians of the war have repeated the criticisms. The usual presentation of the case against Lincoln is that the President was panic-stricken by Jackson's advance and thought Washington was about to fall; he needlessly stopped McDowell from reinforcing McClellan and thereby prevented McClellan from capturing Richmond. The weakness in this interpretation of Lincoln's motives is that his despatches reveal little fear for the safety of Washington. He expressed some fear for the safety of Banks, which was reasonable, for he did not want the largest Union army in the Valley cut to pieces. He was apprehensive that Jackson might cross the Potomac and raid Union Maryland. Undoubtedly he thought at times that Jackson might strike for Washington. His two o'clock despatch of May 25 to McClellan, in which he told the General to attack Richmond or return for the defence of the capital, indicates that he had considered the possibility of an attack on the city. But Lincoln's predominant purpose throughout was offensive —to run Jackson down and remove the Confederate threat in the Valley. He did not think Banks and Fremont could do the job alone, so he ordered McDowell to help them.

The question remains: did Lincoln make the best use of McDowell's force? Or put another way, where would McDowell have been of most good to the Union cause—in the Valley or with McClellan? Lincoln, of course, intended that McDowell should appear in both places, first in the Valley to destroy Jackson and then later with McClellan to capture Richmond. As it turned out, McDowell was of no use in either place. He did not catch Jackson, and his army was so beat up by the move to the Valley that he was unable to go to Mc-Clellan. The Confederates thought Richmond was certain to fall if McDowell joined McClellan. To prevent the juncture they had launched Jackson's offensive. The plan succeeded, and it was assumed then and has been since, that the Valley campaign saved Richmond by holding McDowell near Washington. This view rests on the further assumption that if Mc-Clellan had got McDowell he would immediately have captured Richmond. He might have done so. But it can also be assumed, with as much evidence, that McClellan would have sat down and decided that the enemy had also received a reinforcement—larger than his, of course—and that he could not move until he got still more men. Magnifying the size of the enemy as an excuse for inaction was the thing he did best; he did it often, and he might well have done it then. It cannot be said with certainty, therefore, that Lincoln, by sending McDowell to the Valley, prevented McClellan from taking Richmond. From the strategic point of view, Lincoln's handling of the Valley situation was fairly good. He had acted to save Banks' army from destruction, and he had conceived a scheme to catch the invaders that might have succeeded. The most serious criticism of him is not that he kept McDowell from McClellan but that in his instructions to McDowell and Fremont he got too far down on the tactical level. He was too inexperienced to deal with details of tactics. In particular, he showed an unawareness of the problem of logistics and of the effect of hard marching upon troops. He seemed to think that McDowell could go to the Valley, defeat Jackson, and immediately return and be ready for the Peninsula.

In those spring weeks when the Union armies seemed to be stalled on all fronts, Lincoln's patience with the generals wore very thin. He began to have some doubts about the capabilities of the military mind. The constant calls by commanding generals for more troops irritated and distressed him. Every commander from Richmond to Corinth, Lincoln observed, had convinced himself that he faced an enemy army superior in size.[8] The President was also disgusted with the practice of some generals of reporting military intelligence without verifying its accuracy. During the Valley campaign, McDowell sent in a despatch saying that one of his officers had found no Confederates on the east side of the Blue Ridge. Snappishly Lincoln replied: "You say General Geary's scouts report that they find no enemy this side of the Blue Ridge. Neither do I. Have they been to the Blue Ridge looking for them?" [9]

As his misgivings about the abilities of the generals increased, Lincoln tended to exercise more control over tactical movements and arrangements After the failure of the attempt to trap Jackson, Lincoln took direct charge of the defence system in the Valley. He instructed Fremont where to post his army and how to cooperate with Banks if the Confederates came north again. Getting down to fine details, the President told Fremont what precautions to take against a surprise: "By proper scout lookouts, and beacons of smoke by day and fires by night, you can always have timely notice of the enemy's approach. I know not as to you, but by some this has been too much neglected." [1] Fremont protested that he did not have enough men and asked for part of Banks' army. Lincoln replied that if he reinforced Fremont from Banks he would have to reinforce Banks from someplace else, and he wanted all available troops to go to McClellan. The Valley would have to be held by the forces of Banks and Fremont as they were then disposed, said Lincoln. They were placed right, and they could hold their positions. Then came the iron sentence:

[8] Lincoln to Halleck, May 24, 1862, *Works of Lincoln*, VII, 179–180.
[9] Lincoln to McDowell, May 28, 1862, *ibid.*, VII, 197.
[1] Lincoln to Fremont, June 9, 12, 13, 1862, *ibid.*, VII, 214, 218–220.

"I have arranged this, and am very unwilling to have it deranged." [2]

While McDowell and Fremont were chasing after Jackson, McClellan had been inching closer to Richmond. As he got near the capital, he crossed part of his army to the south side of the Chickahominy. He had to do this because Richmond was south of the river. He also had to leave a portion of his force on the north side, to meet McDowell if that officer's movement was resumed and to protect his line of communication to the York. The division of the army was necessary, but it placed between his forces a river subject to sudden freshets and rises. Lincoln worried a lot about the possibility of a flooded Chickahominy isolating the wings of the army from each other.[3] McClellan's troops south of the river were within five miles of Richmond, and those north of it were not much farther off. He was approaching the hour of decision, and approaching it with his customary nervous depression. He telegraphed Lincoln that the Confederates were concentrating "everything" before Richmond for a desperate defence and that it was the "duty" of the government to send him all available troops by *water*. If the government did not do as he wanted, it would be guilty of committing "an irreparable fault." There was a peremptory tone in the despatch that Lincoln noted and did not like but excused. In reply, he observed mildly that neither he nor McClellan could know with certainty that the whole of the enemy was being concentrated on Richmond; the government had intelligence that large rebel forces were still in the Valley. Kindly but emphatically, he let McClellan know where the power to make strategic decisions rested. It rests with me, he said. He would help McClellan all he could, but as commander in chief he had to consider the

[2] Fremont to Lincoln, June 12, 1862, Lincoln MSS., vol. 78; Lincoln to Fremont, June 15, *Works of Lincoln*, VII, 222–224.

[3] Lincoln to McClellan, June 3, 1862, *ibid.*, VII, 210.

needs of other armies and theaters, to exercise a "due regard to all points," as he expressed it.[4]

With McClellan almost at the gates of Richmond, Johnston, the Confederate commander, decided that the time had come for him to attack. On May 31 and June 1, he fell upon McClellan's forces south of the Chickahominy. In the battle of Fair Oaks or Seven Pines, as it is variously called, the Confederates at first drove the Federals back, but McClellan was able to bring help over from the north side and regain the ground he had lost. While the fighting was in progress, Lincoln wrote the General an encouraging note: "Stand well on your guard, hold all your ground, or yield only inch by inch and in good order." [5] McClellan held his ground, but Fair Oaks almost ruined him as a general. It was the first big battle he had fought, and the first time he had seen dead and wounded men in large numbers. The sight unnerved him. He wrote to his wife that he was sickened when he saw the battle-field, with its "mangled corpses" and suffering wounded. "Victory has no charms for me when purchased at such cost," he said. From now on, he was to be terribly conscious of casualties. A little later he told his wife: "Every poor fellow that is killed or wounded almost haunts me." [6] McClellan was revealing another of his weaknesses as a soldier. He loved his men too much. He loved them so much that he did not want to hurt them. Because he over-identified himself with them, they loved him. They sensed that he wanted to care for them, and they idolized him as they did no other commander of the Army of the Potomac. But McClellan's affection for his soldiers was a dangerous emotion. It made him forget the hard fact that soldiers exist to fight and possibly to die. He had no

[4] McClellan to Lincoln, May 28, 1862, McClellan, *Own Story*, 372; Lincoln to McClellan, May 28, *Works of Lincoln*, VII, 198–199.

[5] Lincoln to McClellan, June 1, 1862, *ibid.*, VII, 208.

[6] McClellan to Mrs. McClellan, June 2, 23, 1862, McClellan, *Own Story*, 398, 408.

business wandering around a battlefield crying over the dead. It was his business to win victories, and if men died in the process, that was war. The trouble with McClellan was that he liked to think of war as bloodless strategy, as moves on a gigantic chessboard. Manassas and Yorktown were his brightest chaplets, he had said, and no lives had been lost at those places.

Fair Oaks was proof to McClellan that he had been right in saying the Confederates were concentrating an immense force against him, and he thought the government would now see it his way. He renewed his demands for reinforcements.[7] Lincoln and Stanton were impressed with the strength of the enemy offensive at Fair Oaks and wanted to help McClellan all they could. They notified him that they were sending him McCall's division. The General glowed with gratitude, and flatly promised that he would move and take Richmond the moment McCall arrived and the ground was dry enough to admit the passage of artillery. Three days later he was himself again and asking for still more help. He asked Stanton to detach troops from Halleck and send them to the Peninsula.[8]

With affairs in the Valley quiet, Lincoln decided to send the whole of McDowell's force to McClellan, McCall to go by water and the main body by land. Poor McDowell was going through a hard time at the close of the Valley campaign. McClellan and his friends blamed him for Lincoln's suspension of the movement to the Peninsula, and other critics ridiculed him for his failure to catch Jackson. Some wag in Washington put on a bulletin board a despatch purporting to be from McDowell in which the General said he held Willard's Hotel, a point of great strategic importance, and would defend it to the death but he needed reinforcements.[9] On June 8

[7] McClellan to Lincoln, June 4, 1862, McClellan, *Own Story*, 386; McClellan to Stanton, June 4, *ibid.*, 386–387.

[8] McClellan to Stanton, June 7, 10, 1862, *ibid.*, 387–388.

[9] Heintzelman MS. Journal, June 15, 1862.

Lincoln conferred with McDowell and directed him to resume the move to Richmond that had been interrupted by the Valley campaign. McDowell was eager to go but he never went. First, he was delayed because one of his divisions was so beaten out of shape by its marching in the Valley that he had to spend a lot of time refitting it. Then reports from Fremont and Banks stated that the Confederates were assembling their forces for another offensive, and the government held McDowell back until the Valley seemed secure from danger. When McDowell was finally ready to move, it was late June and too late to aid McClellan. By that time the Peninsula campaign was ended.[1]

On the day that McDowell got his instructions from Lincoln to go to Richmond he telegraphed McClellan he was coming. McClellan's reaction to the news was curious. Now he thought he did not need McDowell, and he was not sure he wanted him. In a sarcastic letter to his wife, McClellan said Lincoln and Stanton were getting quite amiable, but he feared the Greeks bearing gifts. McClellan's chief of staff, writing to his wife, whispered a secret: the Army of the Potomac would take Richmond before McDowell arrived, and McDowell, if he did not get whipped on the way down, would share none of the glory.[2] In a strange mood of confidence, McClellan was ready to operate without McDowell. He told his wife that in a few days he would move on Richmond and capture it. By the use of artillery, he hoped to carry the city with little loss of life. Writing to Lincoln about McDowell's movement, McClellan urged that McDowell come by water. He said that if McDowell were attacked on the way on the land route, it might be difficult for the Army of the Potomac to "rescue" him! He did not want to have to extend his right

[1] McDowell to McClellan, June 8, 1862, McClellan MSS., Ser. 1; *Official Records*, XII, pt. 1, 284–285, 287.

[2] McClellan to Mrs. McClellan, June 9, 1862, McClellan, *Own Story*, 402; R. B. Marcy to Mrs. Marcy, June 9, McClellan MSS., Ser. 2.

to meet McDowell because the move would derange his plans
—his plans to take Richmond, he meant.[3]

McClellan's attitude about McDowell must have puzzled
Lincoln. The explanation of it was that McClellan did not
want to be reinforced by McDowell on the basis of the terms
previously set forth by the President: that McDowell's force
should operate as a separate, cooperating army not completely
under McClellan's control. He wanted McDowell on his terms
and under his command or not at all. In a telegram to Stanton, he said: "If I cannot fully control all his troops I want
none of them, but would prefer to fight the battle with what
I have, and let others be responsible for the results." [4] This
was a remarkable statement for a field commander to address
to the government. He was saying that he wanted to conduct
a vitally important operation completely in his own way and
that, rather than receive aid in a form he did not like, he
would run the risk of defeat. But if he were defeated as a result of doing it his way, the responsibility would not rest on
him but on the government. He had no right to chance defeat because he objected to Lincoln's order, no right to throw
the responsibility of failure upon the government, and certainly no right to prescribe the conditions upon which he
would receive reinforcements. Here, as on other occasions,
McClellan was assuming that he was big enough to treat with
the government as an equal party.

Lincoln was not offended by McClellan's despatch when
Stanton showed it to him. The President probably thought
that McClellan had written it in a moment of stress and had
not meant all that he had said. Instead of rebuking the General, Lincoln wrote him a kindly and encouraging letter. He
told McClellan that McDowell might not come at all. Part of

[3] McClellan to Mrs. McClellan, June 15, 1862, McClellan, *Own
Story*, 405–406; McClellan to Lincoln, June 12, *Official Records*, XI,
pt. 3, 225.

[4] McClellan to Stanton, June 14, 1862, McClellan, *Own Story*, 389.

McDowell's force, he said, was "so out at elbows, and out at toes" that it was unfit for service and would be so for some time. Other reinforcements, however, were being sent on, and McDowell would go as soon as possible. Lincoln must have felt a deep sympathy for the young General so oppressed by responsibility, for he closed the letter with a characteristically humble Lincolnian sentence: "I believe I would come and see you were it not that I fear my presence might divert you and the army from more important matters." [5]

Shortly before Lincoln wrote to McClellan, he had got a first-hand account of the state of affairs in the Army of the Potomac. General Burnside, McClellan's intimate friend and commander of an expedition which had seized some points on the coast of North Carolina, came up from his department to Fortress Monroe on official business. McClellan heard that Burnside was there, and asked "Burn" to come to see him. Burnside got permission from Stanton to go and went up to the front. When he returned to the Fortress, Burnside telegraphed Stanton that he had spent six hours with McClellan and knew all about the latter's situation. Stanton thought Burnside's information was so important that he ordered the General to come to Washington and present it in person. Burnside arrived on June 12.[6] He saw Stanton in the morning and met with Lincoln and the Cabinet that night. Burnside's staff waited up for him. At midnight the General came in, hoarse from answering questions and declaring that if ever there was an honest man on the face of the earth it was Abraham Lincoln.[7]

[5] Lincoln to McClellan, June 15, 1862, *Works of Lincoln*, VII, 220–221.

[6] Burnside to Stanton, June 9, 11, 1862, *Official Records*, IX, 398, 399; Burnside to Stanton, June 11, *ibid.*, LI, pt. 1, 673.

[7] D. R. Larned, Burnside's secretary, to Amelia Larned, June 16, 1862, Larned MSS.

From Fortress Monroe, on his way back to North Carolina, Burnside sent McClellan a summary of the interview. The President had confidence in McClellan and was anxious to grant all McClellan wanted, wrote Burnside. As proof of his words, Lincoln had said that Burnside could do anything McClellan ordered him to do without referring to Washington. This meant that McClellan could draw freely on Burnside for reinforcements. It also meant that Lincoln was trying to strengthen McClellan as much as possible for the final push on Richmond.[8]

McClellan was supposedly putting the last touches on his preparations for the final push. His intelligence service, always inefficient and inaccurate, was performing up to its standards. It gave McClellan a report that 10,000 troops had left Richmond to reinforce Jackson. McClellan sent the information on to Washington. He could not have chosen a more effective way to prevent reinforcements from being sent to him than to magnify the Confederate menace in the Valley. Curiously enough, McClellan thought that the news would strengthen his plea for reinforcements. His interpretation of the meaning of the report was characteristic. He thought it meant that the Confederates were so overwhelmingly strong at Richmond that they could afford to detach troops for service in the Valley. If they were so strong he would need more men to whip them.[9] Lincoln was not quite as ready as McClellan to believe that reinforcements were going to Jackson. He surmised that the Confederates might have put out the rumor to deceive the Federals. But even if the information were true, Lincoln did not think it meant what McClellan thought. The President pointed out to McClellan that it

[8] Burnside to McClellan, June 13, 14, 1863, McClellan MSS., Ser. 1.
[9] McClellan to Stanton, June 18, 1862, two telegrams, *Official Records*, XI, pt. 3, 232, 233.

might mean the Confederates did not intend to make a desperate defence of Richmond. Furthermore, said Lincoln to the General, if 10,000 men have left Richmond, it is as good as an equal reinforcement to you. Lincoln wanted McClellan to provide more definite information of the movements of the enemy and of his own plans: "I could better dispose of things if I knew about what day you can attack Richmond, and would be glad to be informed, if you think you can inform me with safety." [1] McClellan's reply was hardly a model of exactness. He said his move on Richmond might start at any hour, maybe after tomorrow, if Providence permitted, if the weather was right, and after the completion of some necessary preliminaries.[2]

McClellan had nothing more to report on the reinforcements going to Jackson, but intelligence from the Valley indicated the presence of increased Confederate forces. Lincoln was worried and puzzled by the situation. He did not think the Confederates were strong enough to reinforce Jackson in force, but he could not afford to take a chance that they had not done so. Until he could determine the truth of the matter, he had to keep troops in the Valley that otherwise could be sent to McClellan.[3] Lincoln was also worried about the disposition he had made of the forces in the Valley, those at Manassas, and McDowell's army. He wondered whether he had placed them properly to defend Washington and cooperate with each other. In particular, he was beginning to think that McDowell on the Rappahannock was out of position to do anything. Lincoln decided that he needed some military advice about his problems. There was no officer in Washing-

[1] Lincoln to McClellan, June 18, 19, 1862, *Works of Lincoln*, VII, 228–229.

[2] McClellan to Lincoln, June 18, 1862, *Official Records*, XI, pt. 3, 233.

[3] Lincoln to McClellan, June 20, 1862, *Works of Lincoln*, VII, 229.

ton that the President considered capable of giving him any counsel, but he knew where to go. On June 23 he left Washington on a special train for West Point, New York.[4]

He was going to see old General Scott, who had gone to West Point to live after retiring. What Lincoln and Scott talked about has never been fully revealed. Undoubtedly they went over the whole strategic situation in the East and the West, and discussed a number of generals, including McClellan. The big matter they considered was the arrangement of the Union forces south and west of Washington. Lincoln asked Scott to present his views on this subject in writing. In the report he gave Lincoln, the General said that Banks and Fremont were rightly placed and strong enough to stop any enemy threat in the Valley and that the forces at Manassas and in the forts on the Potomac were adequate to halt any thrust from the south. Scott pointed out the truth of what Lincoln had suspected: that McDowell was completely out of position and always had been. If McDowell was supposed to cover Washington, he could do it better if placed closer to the capital. Located where he was, he could cooperate neither with the forces in the Valley nor with McClellan. He was too far away from the Valley, and he could not reach McClellan easily by land because of the absence of railroad communication south of the Rappahannock and because he lacked adequate supply trains. If enough water transport were available, advised Scott, McDowell should be sent to McClellan by the York River route.[5] Lincoln never had a chance to put Scott's recommendations about McDowell into action. Events were about to occur in the Peninsula that would make the question of reinforcing McClellan seem a small matter.

[4] New York *Herald,* June 25, 26, 1862; New York *Times,* June 25, 26; New York *Tribune,* June 25.

[5] Scott to Lincoln, June 24, 1862, *Works of Lincoln,* VII, 233–234.

On June 25, McClellan, lately so apparently full of confidence and offensive spirit, wrote Stanton a dark and bitter letter. He said he had information that the Confederate army in front of Richmond had been reinforced by Jackson, which was true, and by troops from the West, which was false, and that it now numbered 200,000. His estimate was fantastically wrong. The Confederate army numbered about 85,000. McClellan believed that the vast enemy host he had conjured up was about to attack and destroy him, and he morbidly announced that he would die with his troops. Apparently he expected a mass slaughter, a sort of St. Bartholomew's Day of the Army of the Potomac. Again, as he had done in his despatch of June 14 to Stanton, he absolved himself of any responsibility for what might happen: "But if the result of the action . . . is a disaster, the responsibility cannot be thrown on my shoulders; it must rest where it belongs." [6]

McClellan wrote his letter to Stanton about six o'clock in the evening. Earlier in the day he had sent two other despatches describing the dangers confronting him. Lincoln had seen the telegrams, and undoubtedly he was anxious about McClellan's situation. But when the President read the six-o'clock communication, his kindly patience snapped a little. He telegraphed McClellan that he had seen the General's three bulletins: "The later one . . . suggesting the probability of your being overwhelmed by 200,000, and talking of where the responsibility will belong, pains me very much. I give you all I can, and act on the presumption that you will do the best you can with what you have, while you continue, ungenerously I think, to assume that I could give you more if I would." [7]

[6] McClellan to Stanton, June 25, 1862, McClellan, *Own Story*, 392–393.

[7] Lincoln to McClellan, June 26, 1862, *Works of Lincoln*, VII, 234–235.

McClellan would have to do the best he could with what he had. On the day that Lincoln sent his telegram, the Confederates launched an all-out offensive against the Army of the Potomac.

Chapter 6

Failure in the Peninsula

N the fighting at Fair Oaks, Johnston, the Confederate commander, had been badly wounded. He had to give up the command, and Robert E. Lee succeeded to the place. Lee took over at a moment when McClellan's army was within less than five miles of Richmond. During the first weeks of June, Lee was trying to devise a plan to defeat McClellan and relieve the capital from the threat of Union occupation. Lee's cavalry leader brought him a piece of information about the disposition of the Federal army that gave him the inspiration for a scheme not just to beat McClellan but to smash him completely, and perhaps to end the war. Before Fair Oaks, McClellan had had the larger part of his army north of the Chickahominy and the smaller part south. It was the force south that Johnston had attacked. But as McClellan moved closer to Richmond after Fair Oaks, he necessarily had to shift the bulk of his army to the south side. By mid-June, he had about two-thirds of his force south of the river and one-third north. He left one corps of about 30,000 under the command of General Fitz John Porter on the north bank to guard his communications with the York and to make contact with McDowell if the latter should come.

Lee's plan was to augment the size of the Confederate army by bringing Jackson to Richmond and to concentrate his forces north of the Chickahominy for a destructive blow at Porter's corps. Lee thought that if he could wipe out Porter that McClellan would cross the rest of the Federal army to the north side and retreat to the York in order to protect his communications. The Confederate commander intended to attack the Federals constantly as they fell back and cut them to pieces. There was an element of risk in his plan, but it was slight. To make his striking force north of the river large enough to crush the Union right, he had to strip his forces on the south side down to a small number. If, when Lee opened his offensive, McClellan should learn that only a handful of Confederates remained on the south bank, he could go into Richmond almost unopposed. There was little likelihood, however, that McClellan would find this fact out while trying to fight off a smashing attack on his own right. In fact, there was little chance that McClellan would attempt to take Richmond even if he knew he could, for its possession would have been of no value to him. If he got it, he could not have held it, with the enemy on his line of supply to the York, unless he could quickly open a new line on the James. Lee had every military reason to think that his proposed attack would force McClellan to retire to the York and forget all about Richmond. On June 26, confident that he was about to destroy the Union army, Lee hurled his troops on Porter's corps. The first engagement of what would become known as the battle of the Seven Days had started.

In the first day of fighting the Federals stopped the Confederate attack. As the battle started, McClellan was calm and confident. He sent a despatch to the government saying that the enemy was assailing his right but that he was sure he could hold his ground.[1] That night, when he knew the outcome of the battle, he was wildly jubilant. From Porter's headquarters, he telegraphed Stanton: "Victory today complete & against

[1] McClellan to Stanton, June 26, 1862, McClellan, *Own Story*, 410.

great odds. I almost begin to think we are invincible." [2] As a description of what had happened, his telegram was highly misleading. One corps of his army had been attacked, and it had repulsed the enemy. That he should call the action a "complete victory" showed his military immaturity. He should have said to the government: Today the enemy struck our right wing, we repelled the attack, situation not yet fully developed. Such an account would have given Lincoln and Stanton a clear picture of the situation and would have enabled the President to plan intelligent moves to aid McClellan. Lincoln might well have concluded from McClellan's rosy despatches that the General needed no help at all. This would not be the first time that McClellan would raise false hopes by reporting a partial or a minor victory as a complete one.

Lee's plan was not working out as well as he had expected. In the second day of fighting, he dislodged Porter's corps from its position, but he did not smash it or break it up. The Confederates suffered heavy casualties, and McClellan was able to reinforce Porter from the south side. At this point, McClellan's situation was fairly good. He could have menaced Richmond with his left and possibly have forced Lee to draw back for the defence of the city. Or, better yet, he could have massed his army north of the Chickahominy and fought a showdown battle for his communications. He might well have defeated the weakened Confederates and then have taken Richmond. He told one of his corps commanders he was considering such a move.[3] He considered it but he did not do it, because of a typical McClellan reason. He believed that if the Confederates had dared to attack him they must have overwhelming numbers. He was confirmed in this opinion

[2] McClellan to Stanton, June 26, 1862, 9 p.m., McClellan MSS., Ser. 1.

[3] Heintzelman MS. Journal, June 27, 1862.

by a report given him by his intelligence service on the day the attack started stating that Lee had at least 180,000 men.[4]

Everything that McClellan did during the Seven Days was based on the assumption that he faced an enemy that outnumbered him two to one. Believing this, he could not bring himself to fight a decisive battle north of the Chickahominy. Neither did he do what Lee thought he would do, retreat to the York. Instead he destroyed his base on the York, pulled Porter over to the south bank, and started to retreat toward the James where, with the aid of the Navy, he intended to set up a new base. His move compelled Lee to cross the Chickahominy also and made it necessary for the Confederate commander to revise his whole plan of operations. As McClellan started his movement to the James, he informed the War Department of what he was going to do and said he might not be heard from for days, until he reached his new base. He was about to commence one of the most difficult movements in war: to transfer an army from one base to another across a fighting front. He had enough to worry about with his own problems; but often when in a crisis such as the one he was now in, McClellan would offer advice about matters that did not directly concern him. Now he told Stanton that for the better security of Washington all the troops in the Valley and around the capital ought to be put under one commander. The time had come, he said, to bring the best men into the important positions.[5]

Lincoln had anticipated McClellan in forming the Valley and Washington forces into one army. On the day before McClellan advised the step, Lincoln had taken it. But McClellan never would have thought the officer whom the President selected as commander of the new army was one of the best men. This was John Pope, whom McClellan came to hate

---

[4] *Official Records*, XI, pt. 1, 51.
[5] McClellan to Stanton, June 27, 1862, McClellan MSS., Ser. 1.

more than anybody else except Stanton. Pope had served under Halleck in the West, and as commander of a small independent army had won some small victories. He was pugnacious and confident and conceited. Part of the reputation he
had won in the West was the result of his own boasting about
his triumphs and the publicity he got from newspaper reporters attached to his headquarters. But he liked to fight, and
Lincoln, becoming increasingly disgusted because so many
generals did not seem to know what fighting was, had noted
this quality. Pope was from Illinois, and Lincoln had known
him before the war. The General's father had been a district
judge, in whose court Lincoln had practiced for years. When
Lincoln came to Washingon to be inaugurated, Pope had
accompanied him on the train for part of the trip. Pope tried
to use his acquaintance with Lincoln and his Illinois political
connections to get his army rank increased. He offered to
come to Washington and serve as Lincoln's military secretary,
and he got the Republican bosses of the state to bring pressure
on the President to promote him.[6] Pope's efforts to win Lincoln's favor by using political influence did not succeed, but
his record in the West brought him favorably to the President's attention. After the failure of the movement to trap
Jackson, Lincoln had decided to unify the forces in the Washington area into one army. As commander, he selected the
aggressive officer from the West, who was recommended by
victories won by fighting.

   In the latter part of June, Stanton asked Pope to come to
Washington for a few days. The Secretary did not tell Pope
why his presence was desired, but the General must have

   [6] Isaac N. Arnold, *The Life of Abraham Lincoln,* 287–288; Pope to
W. H. Lamon, April 11, 1861, Lincoln MSS., vol. 41; Pope to Lincoln,
April 20, *ibid.,* vol. 43; Governor Richard Yates to Lincoln, May 8,
and Senator Lyman Trumbull to Lincoln, May 9, *ibid.,* vol. 45; Yates,
J. K. Dubois, William Butler, and O. M. Hatch to Lincoln, June 17,
ibid., vol. 48.

known that he would not be called from the field to the capital unless a new command was to be offered to him. Halleck, foreseeing that he might lose Pope and not wanting to, objected to his subordinate making the trip, but Stanton insisted that Pope come. After Pope reached Washington, Halleck received a telegram from Stanton saying that in Lincoln's opinion the exigencies of the service required that Pope have a command in the East.[7] Pope arrived in Washington while Lincoln was at West Point seeing General Scott. The General conferred with Stanton and with Lincoln when the latter returned. He learned that the government planned to unite the forces of McDowell, Banks, and Fremont, and wanted him to command the new army, to be known as the Army of Virginia. The objective of his army, he was told, would be to operate just east of the Valley, threatening the enemy forces there and in western Virginia and thus drawing off troops from the army facing McClellan at Richmond. According to Pope's recollections after the war, he told Lincoln and Stanton the proposed movement was a forlorn hope and asked to be returned to the West, but they persuaded him to accept the assignment as a matter of duty.[8]

On June 26 the order was issued officially creating the Army of Virginia. By the language of the order Pope was to operate so as to protect Washington and western Virginia from "danger or insult," to attack Jackson and threaten Charlottesville, and to "render the most effective aid to relieve General McClellan and capture Richmond." [9] Apparently Lincoln had changed his mind about using Pope's army merely as a diver-

[7] Stanton to Pope, June 19, 1862; Pope to Stanton, June 20; Pope to Halleck, June 20; Halleck to Pope, June 20; Stanton to Halleck, June 27, in *Official Records,* XVII, pt. 2, 17, 18, 20, 41.

[8] Clarence C. Buel and Robert U. Johnson (eds.), *Battles and Leaders of the Civil War,* II, 449, 450, hereafter cited as *Battles and Leaders; C. C. W., Reports,* 1865, supplement, II, 104.

[9] *Works of Lincoln,* VII, 235–236.

sionary force to relieve the pressure on McClellan, or more probably Stanton, who had first explained the plan to Pope, had not fully understood what was in the President's mind. Pope's operation as stated in the order was to be primarily offensive in nature, and his main objective was the capture of Richmond. He was to move his army down through western Virginia and into the Valley, cleaning out the enemy there, and then to turn west against Richmond. At the same time McClellan was to close in on the capital from the east. What Lincoln had in mind, although naturally he did not lay out all the details in the order, was a pincers movement of the Army of the Potomac and the Army of Virginia that would snip off the Confederate army and capital between them. When the two armies were in position to communicate or co-operate with each other, the question of the chief command was to be governed by the Rules and Articles of War, which meant that McClellan, the senior officer, would exercise control over Pope.

While the plans were being drawn for Pope's campaign, the General was enjoying a tremendous personal triumph in official Washington. He impressed people favorably on first acquaintance, and he probably impressed Lincoln. John Pope was a striking military figure. Large in body, he looked good in a uniform. His piercing eyes looked out from a full face. He combed his long, dark hair straight back, and he wore an immense beard that spread down onto his chest. The thing that Pope did best was to talk. He talked about the necessity of offensive war against the enemy, which pleased Lincoln, and about the necessity of freeing the slaves of rebels, which delighted the radicals. Mostly he talked about the merits of John Pope, which seemed to enchant everybody. Pope may have dazzled governmental circles, but he did something that enraged his troops almost to the point of frenzy. Probably no general ever got off to a worse start with an army. Soon after he assumed command, he issued an address to his men. He had come to them from the West, he said, and from an army that always saw the backs of its enemies and that always attacked and that always won. He had heard too much talk in the East about bases of supplies and lines of retreat, and he wanted his soldiers to forget such phrases. "Let us study the probable lines of retreat for our opponents," he urged, "and leave our own to take care of themselves." The Army of Virginia hated Pope after it read this effusion. There was a lot of military nonsense in the address, and Pope was justly ridiculed for writing it. It is probable, however, that he was not the sole author. After the war, he told a friend that many of his papers and orders had been written by Stanton who, speaking with stirring words through Pope, wanted to condemn by implication McClellan's inaction and cautiousness. Undoubtedly Stanton had something to do with composing Pope's tasteless address.[1]

Lincoln's plan to bring the armies of McClellan and Pope together in a great converging movement on Richmond was a fine strategic conception, but it was never to be carried out. On the day that Pope's army was created Lee struck McClellan's right wing, and a few days later McClellan was in retreat to the James. All thoughts of offensive operations had to be abandoned in view of the altered situation in the Peninsula. Pope acted as a military adviser to Lincoln during the first frantic hours of the Seven Days when the President did not know exactly how serious McClellan's reverse was. Pope recalled later that Lincoln spent many hours on a sofa in Stanton's office, waiting for news from the Peninsula and looking depressed and anxious. Pope counseled the President

---

[1] *Official Records*, XII, pt. 3, 473–474; Cox, *Military Reminiscences*, I, 222–223.

not to let McClellan retire to the James, which would carry
the Army of the Potomac farther away from Pope, but to
order him to retreat northward to a point between the Pamunkey and the York, where Pope could reach him with
help. Such advice was useless, of course, even if Lincoln had
been disposed to act on it. McClellan had already started his
retrograde movement, and it was too late to stop him.[2]

Right before or right after McClellan got to the James,
Lincoln called Pope before the Cabinet to discuss the situation of the Army of the Potomac and what could be done to
relieve McClellan. Pope declared that he would do anything
that Lincoln ordered, that he would move directly toward
Richmond even though the enemy was between him and
McClellan. One condition Pope laid down: if he marched to
aid McClellan, the government was to give McClellan peremptory orders to attack the minute he heard Pope was engaged.[3] Pope said he would have to insist on this condition because McClellan was feeble and irresolute and would let the
Army of Virginia be destroyed if left to his own inclinations.
Pope believed the accusation he had thrown at McClellan.
The two men seemed to be instinctive enemies. Almost from
the moment of their first exchange of official despatches, they
despised and distrusted each other. In whatever way the seed
of hatred between them had been planted, it was now sprout-
ing mightily.

As soon as Lincoln learned that McClellan had been attacked and was falling back to a new base, he began to look
for reinforcements that could be sent to the Army of the Potomac. He first thought of Burnside in North Carolina. On
June 28 he telegraphed Burnside: "I think you had better go,
with any reinforcements you can spare, to General McClel-

[2] *C. C. W., Reports,* 1863, I, 280; *ibid.,* 1865, supplement, II,
110–111.

[3] *Ibid.,* 1865, supplement, II, 104–105; *Battles and Leaders,* II,
452–457.

lan." [4] The same day Stanton despatched Halleck that McClellan had met with a reverse and that the President wanted Halleck to send 25,000 men to the East. Just before this, Halleck had started an expedition toward East Tennessee, and Stanton told the General that Lincoln did not want him to detach any troops if it meant weakening the expedition. Halleck replied that he would send the reinforcements but that if he did he would have to give up completely the invasion of East Tennessee.[5] He did not want to lose any part of his army, and he was shrewdly using an argument that he knew would cause Lincoln to withdraw the request to aid McClellan. The response from Washington was immediate and what Halleck had hoped for. Stanton telegraphed the General that the East Tennessee movement must not be abandoned and that Lincoln was displeased because it was proceeding so tardily. The President himself sent Halleck a telegram on the same day that Stanton sent his. Lincoln told Halleck not to detach any of his army if by so doing the advance on Chattanooga would be delayed. Showing the importance he attached to East Tennessee as a part of the general strategic situation Lincoln said: "To take and hold the railroad at or east of Cleveland, in East Tennessee, I think fully as important as the taking and holding of Richmond." [6]

While Lincoln was casting around for reinforcements for McClellan, the Army of the Potomac was moving toward the James. As it fell back, Lee struck it in attack after attack. In no one of the almost daily assaults did he win a decisive victory. The Federal army, even though in full retreat and burdened with a large baggage train, parried every blow that

---

[4] Lincoln to Burnside, June 28, 1862, *Works of Lincoln,* VII, 239; Stanton to Burnside, June 28, *Official Records,* IX, 404–405.

[5] Stanton to Halleck, June 28, 1862, *ibid.,* XI, pt. 3, 271; Halleck to Stanton, June 30, *ibid.,* XI, pt. 3, 279–280.

[6] Stanton to Halleck, and Lincoln to Halleck, June 30, 1862, *Works of Lincoln,* VII, 247–248.

Lee threw. In fact, at Malvern Hill, the last engagement of the Seven Days, McClellan repulsed the Confederates so badly that had he counterattacked he probably would have defeated Lee and could have got Richmond. Instead he retired from the field and to his new base at Harrison's Landing on the James.

He did not counterattack because his state of mind during the whole of the Seven Days made him incapable of thinking in offensive terms. He was oppressed by the idea that he was being attacked by an enemy force twice as large as his and that his whole army might be defeated and slaughtered. His one thought was to get the army to a place of safety—a place where the government could send him huge reinforcements. Midway in the movement to the James, McClellan sent a telegram to Stanton that was surely one of the most extraordinary documents that any government ever received from a general in the field. It was a bitter and recriminatory despatch, full of allusions about treachery in Washington, and it showed that McClellan's mind had become unhinged by events. Several themes ran through the communication: I have lost because my force was too small—I am not responsible for the defeat— you *must* send me large reinforcements at once. He had expressed such sentiments before, but never as sharply and as dramatically as now. His main theme was the accusation that the government had sacrificed the Army of the Potomac:

I feel too earnestly to-night. I have seen too many dead and wounded comrades to feel otherwise than that the government has not sustained this army. If you do not do so now the game is lost.

If I save this army now, I tell you plainly that I owe no thanks to you or to any other persons in Washington.

You have done your best to sacrifice this army.[7]

[7] McClellan to Stanton, June 28, 1862, McClellan, *Own Story*, 424–425.

McClellan was well pleased with his telegram. He told his wife that they would never forgive him in Washington for it, but that he thought it might be the last one he would live to write and he wanted it true. He would have been disappointed if he had known that Stanton and Lincoln did not see the last two sentences. When the telegram arrived at the telegraph office at the War Department, the officials there were horrified by the closing section. The supervisor of military telegrams said he would not permit such a false and improper accusation to be laid before the Secretary, and he took the responsibility of deleting the offending sentences. Not until months later was the complete version published.[8]

Judged by any standards, McClellan's telegram was inept and ill-advised. He did what no general can afford to do: he admitted defeat.[9] What was most surprising was that he admitted defeat when he had not been defeated. Before, after the first encounter of the Seven Days, he had called a partial victory a complete one. Now he called a partial reverse a disaster. He was giving a fine demonstration of his inability to evaluate the reality of events. All that had happened was that his right wing had been whipped and that he was withdrawing under attack to a new base. That was all he needed to tell the government to give it an accurate picture of the situation. His telegram could have caused Lincoln to think that the army was about to be completely destroyed. Lincoln did not conclude that from the despatch, because he discounted some of McClellan's croaking. But he was definitely worried by what was occurring in the Peninsula, and his anxiety was sharpened because he did not know, and could not find out from what McClellan had said, exactly what was happening. He sent the

[8] McClellan to Mrs. McClellan, July 20, 1862, *ibid.*, 452; Bates, *Lincoln in the Telegraph Office*, 109–110.

[9] H. J. Eckenrode and Bryan Conrad, *George B. McClellan: The Man Who Saved the Union*, 98–99.

General a telegram designed to calm McClellan's excited brain. "Save your army, at all events," Lincoln wrote. "Will send reinforcements as fast as we can. Of course they cannot reach you to-day, to-morrow, or next day." Showing that he did not clearly understand from McClellan's despatches what the situation was, Lincoln said: "If you have had a drawn battle or a repulse, it is the price we pay for the enemy not being in Washington. We protected Washington, and the enemy concentrated on you." [1]

As late as June 30, the fifth of the Seven Days, Lincoln had but a vague idea of what McClellan was doing. On the twenty-ninth a reporter arrived in Washington from the Peninsula and told the President he had talked with a paymaster who had said the Federal army had crossed safely to the south side of the Chickahominy. From this intelligence, Lincoln concluded that McClellan might be fighting before Richmond, but he was worried because no news had come through from McClellan himself. [2] Not until July 1, when McClellan was almost to the James, did Lincoln hear directly from the General. Then McClellan, about to fight Malvern Hill, asked for reinforcements so he could resume the offensive. He wanted Lincoln to send him 50,000 more troops. Lincoln replied by telegram. We do not have the men to help you, the President said, and even if we did we could not get them to you in time. He advised McClellan to find a place of security and wait. [3]

In a letter to the General, Lincoln explained more fully the difficulty of sending reinforcements. Outside of the Army of the Potomac, Lincoln pointed out, there were not 75,000 men in the entire Eastern theater. McClellan's idea that the government could find 50,000 men immediately was "simply ab-

[1] Lincoln to McClellan, June 28, 1862, *Works of Lincoln*, VII, 239–240.

[2] Lincoln to W. H. Seward, June 29, 30, 1862, *ibid.*, VII, 243–245.

[3] McClellan to Lincoln, July 1, 1862, *Official Records*, XI, pt. 3, 281; Lincoln to McClellan, July 1, *Works of Lincoln*, VII, 253.

surd." He did not expect McClellan to do the impossible, Lincoln said: "If you think you are not strong enough to take Richmond just now, I do not ask you to try just now. Save the army, material and personal, and I will strengthen it for the offensive again as fast as I can." [4]

Safe at Harrison's Landing on the James, McClellan regained his composure and his confidence. He was very proud of his change of base. It was a movement without parallel in the annals of war, he informed Lincoln, and it was especially memorable because "we have preserved our trains, our guns, our material, and above all, our honor." [5] He sent his chief of staff, General R. B. Marcy, to Washington to explain the magnificent movement to the government and to ask for 100,000 reinforcements! [6] Marcy arrived in the capital on July 3 and conferred with Lincoln and Stanton at the War Department. Eagerly the President asked about McClellan's situation. Marcy replied that with reinforcements McClellan could still take Richmond. Lincoln said: "I will telegraph to Halleck and ask him if he cannot squeeze out 10,000 men for McClellan." The President also said that he would send McClellan 11,000 from Washington, and would try to bring up 10,000 from Burnside, and 10,000 from South Carolina. Marcy sent McClellan an account of the interview, and said that Lincoln showed every evidence of friendship for the General. [7]

McClellan refused to believe that the President was friendly. If Lincoln were, he would send more reinforcements; besides, he did not seem to understand that McClellan

[4] Lincoln to McClellan, July 2, 1862, *ibid.,* VII, 254-255.

[5] McClellan to Lincoln, July 4, 1862, McClellan, *Own Story,* 484-485.

[6] McClellan to Stanton, July 3, 1862, *Official Records,* XI, pt. 3, 291.

[7] Marcy to McClellan, July 4, 1862, McClellan MSS., Ser. 1. Marcy later wrote an account of the conference, copies of which are in *ibid.,* vols. 107, 108.

had temporarily saved the army from destruction by a hugely superior enemy who might strike again at any hour. Feeling very much unappreciated, McClellan asserted that he would save the army without any help from the government and lead it to victory "in spite of all enemies in all directions." [8] His feelings were not soothed any by a letter from Lincoln giving the President's impressions of the meeting with Marcy. Lincoln said that he understood McClellan's situation but that to reinforce the General sufficiently to resume the offensive was impossible. The government could give him about 25,000 men from Washington and the Carolinas now but not another man for over a month. For the moment, therefore, McClellan would have to stand on the defensive. Lincoln added a postscript that he may have meant to be ironic: "If at any time you feel able to take the offensive, you are not restrained from doing so." [9]

Lincoln kept his head better during the Peninsula crisis than did many of the military men. The acts and words of some of them must have confirmed Lincoln's doubts of the infallibility of the military mind. Right after the Army of the Potomac got to Harrison's Landing, Quartermaster General Meigs and another officer went out one night to the Soldiers' Home, where Lincoln often went to escape the summer heat of the city. They woke the President up and urged him to order the army away from the Peninsula immediately before it was slaughtered by the Confederates.[1] They said that there was a chance to get the men to safety, but that all the supplies would have to be destroyed and all the horses killed. Lincoln sent them on their way with a refusal and went back to sleep. Telling the story later, the President said: "Thus often, I who

[8] McClellan to Marcy, July 4, 1862, *ibid.*, Ser. 1.

[9] Lincoln to McClellan, July 4, 1862, *Works of Lincoln*, VII, 259–260.

[1] MS. Diary of M. C. Meigs, July 4, 5, 1862, in Meigs MSS.

am not a specially brave man have had to sustain the sinking courage of these professional fighters in critical times." [2]

Perhaps it was because he thought McClellan's courage needed sustaining that Lincoln decided to go down to Harrison's Landing and see the General. More probably the President wanted to find out on the spot how the officers and men of the army had been affected by the recent reverses. On July 7, accompanied by Assistant Secretary of War Watson, he left on the steamer *Ariel* for the James.[3] He arrived at the Landing late on the afternoon of the next day, and at sundown rode around the lines inspecting the troops. He seemed to be surprised by their good condition and spirits.[4] The next day he called five of the corps generals to a conference aboard the boat that was McClellan's headquarters. He asked each of them two questions: Could the army be removed safely from the Peninsula and was it secure in its present position? He made a written memorandum of their answers. All five said the army was secure, and three said removal from its present position would be ruinous to the cause. Two favored taking the army back to near Washington. After the questioning was over, Lincoln and the officers took a glass of wine together, and the President got ready to go back to Washington.[5] Before he met the generals, Lincoln had asked McClellan about removing the army. The President did not say he thought the army ought to be removed from the James, he merely inquired if it could be removed safely. But McClellan immediately decided Lincoln was about to play "a paltry trick" on him. He did not like the President's manner, McClellan told his wife; Lincoln acted like a man about to do something of

[2] Dennett, *Diary of John Hay*, 176.

[3] Stanton to General John A. Dix, July 7, 1862, *Official Records*, LI, pt. 1, 717.

[4] Heintzelman MS. Journal, July 8, 1862.

[5] *Ibid.*, July 9, 1862; *Works of Lincoln*, VII, 262–266.

which he was ashamed. Lincoln was an old stick and pretty poor timber at that, concluded the General.[6]

While Lincoln was in camp, McClellan handed him the famous document known as the Harrison's Landing letter. Late in June McClellan had asked Lincoln for permission to present in writing his views on the state of military affairs throughout the country. Lincoln had replied that if it would not take too much of McClellan's time he would be glad to have the General's ideas.[7] Probably McClellan had started to work on his proposed paper right away. At any rate, he had it ready when Lincoln came to the Landing. It was cast in the form of a private letter to Lincoln. There was little in it about military topics. McClellan talked mainly about policy, the policy the government should adopt on the issue then dividing the Republican party—should the destruction of slavery be made one of the objectives of the war? The radicals were demanding that Lincoln indorse an emancipation policy. McClellan warned Lincoln that the government must not take up the radical program. We should conduct the war on high Christian principles, he said, and wage it against the armed forces and the government of the enemy but not against the Southern people. The confiscation of property or the forcible abolition of slavery should not be contemplated for a moment. Lincoln should determine upon a conservative policy, advised McClellan, and then select a general in chief to carry it out. "I do not ask for that place for myself," said the General. "I am willing to serve you in such position as you may assign me, and I will do so as faithfully as ever subordinate served superior." McClellan gave his letter to Lincoln on board the *Ariel*. The President read it through and thanked

[6] McClellan to Mrs. McClellan, July 9, 1862, McClellan, *Own Story*, 446; McClellan to Mrs. McClellan, July 10, 17, Myers, *McClellan*, 311, 313.

[7] McClellan to Lincoln, June 20, 1862, *Official Records*, XI, pt. 1, 48; Lincoln to McClellan, June 21, *Works of Lincoln*, VII, 229–230.

McClellan, but gave no indication of his reaction to the proposals in the document.[8] McClellan was well pleased with the letter. He told his wife that if Lincoln made its ideas his own the country would be saved.[9]

Probably no single act of McClellan has been more criticized by historians than his writing of the Harrison's Landing letter. Most of the criticism is unjustified. It has been assumed that he wrote it with an eye to enlisting the support of the Democrats for the presidency, but McClellan intended the letter for the private consideration of Lincoln alone. The General did not make the communication public. It has been charged that McClellan stepped outside his proper military sphere by proffering political advice to the President. Judged by modern standards, McClellan did act improperly, but he has to be judged by Civil War standards. Then there was no particular tradition or rule against generals giving their views on political issues. Nearly every prominent officer at sometime or another told the newspapers or Congress or Lincoln what the policy of the government should be. At almost the same moment that McClellan in the Harrison's Landing letter was urging Lincoln to hold by a conservative policy, Pope in Washington was telling a Congressional committee that the government should adopt a radical policy. Both officers were acting normally—for the Civil War. The Harrison's Landing letter was nothing more than a well-meant piece of advice from an egotistical young general who thought he was much greater than he was. The chief criticism of McClellan should not be that he offered advice to Lincoln but that he was not qualified to offer it. Only generals who win great victories should presume to counsel their political superiors about policy.

[8] McClellan to Lincoln, July 7, 1862, McClellan, *Own Story*, 487–489.

[9] McClellan to Mrs. McClellan, July 8, 1862, *ibid.*, 444–445.

Lincoln returned to Washington in brighter spirits than he had left. He told his secretaries that he had found the army in better condition and in more numbers than he had expected.[1] The President was about to put into effect McClellan's recommendation that the office of general in chief be recreated, but not because McClellan had recommended it. Lincoln had decided on the move before he went to Harrison's Landing, and the man he had in mind for the post was not McClellan but Halleck. Since the removal of McClellan as supreme commander in March, Lincoln had exercised all the functions of the office formerly held by McClellan and Scott. He had passed on the strategic plans proposed by field commanders like McClellan, and he had formulated strategy himself, as in the Valley campaign. Now, because of everything that had happened in the Peninsula campaign—his original doubts about the feasibility of the movement, the troubled issue of reinforcements for McClellan, the reverse that McClellan had just met—he wanted a military man in Washington to tell him what to do about military matters, to make the decisions he found so difficult to make. In particular, he wanted a military man to determine what should be done with McClellan's army. Should it be left in the Peninsula or be returned to Washington? Lincoln felt that it ought to be withdrawn, but he thought that an expert ought to decide the issue.

Lincoln selected Halleck to be general in chief because he thought the General was the best man for the job. Halleck was then the most successful Northern general. The victories in the West, although in reality won by Grant and other generals, were credited to Halleck in popular estimation. He was supposed to have great strategic ability. Lincoln heard Halleck's merits praised by men he respected. Pope, soon after his arrival in Washington, urged Lincoln to call Halleck east to take command of all operations in Virginia. When Lincoln

[1] John G. Nicolay to Therena Bates, July 13, 1862, Nicolay MSS.

visited Scott at West Point, the old General apparently advised the President to make Halleck general in chief. Scott had proposed Halleck for the post in 1861, when it was given to McClellan, and it was natural for him to repeat the recommendation. Stanton, probably influenced by Pope, supported the appointment of Halleck. Lincoln, impressed by Halleck's record and the character of his backers, felt that he was choosing the ablest officer in the country to direct the movements of all the armies.[2]

Lincoln broached the subject of the supreme command to Halleck indirectly. He first asked the General to come to Washington for a flying visit. At the same time he sent a personal messenger to confer with Halleck. The General understood that Lincoln wanted him to take command in Virginia or to give some advice about the military situation in the East. Perhaps Lincoln, at this point, had not absolutely decided to offer the command to Halleck, or, more probably, he wanted to see and talk to Halleck before taking final action. Halleck did not want to go to the capital. He telegraphed Lincoln that if he came all that he could counsel would be to place all the forces in the Eastern theater under one commander.[3] Halleck's balkiness about leaving the West forced Lincoln to bring the matter of the chief command into the open and to make the appointment without first seeing Halleck personally. On July 11 Lincoln issued an order appointing Halleck "to command the whole land forces of the United States, as general-in-chief" and ordering the General to repair to Washington.[4] Halleck had trouble winding up his affairs in the West, and had to keep delaying his departure.

[2] *C. C. W., Reports,* 1865, supplement, II, 111; John T. Morse (ed.), *Diary of Gideon Welles,* I, 108–109, 119; Gideon Welles, *Lincoln and Seward,* 192.

[3] Lincoln to Halleck, July 26, 1862, *Works of Lincoln,* VII, 255, 261–262; Halleck to Lincoln, July 10, Lincoln MSS., vol. 80.

[4] *Works of Lincoln,* VII, 266–267.

Lincoln, becoming more and more nervous about McClellan's situation in the Peninsula, prodded Halleck to hurry. "I am very anxious—almost impatient—to have you here," he wired the General.[5] Halleck finally arrived in the capital about the twenty-third.[6] He came reluctantly and only because he felt he had to obey Lincoln's order. He wanted to stay in the West, and he was sure he would hate Washington and all its politicians.[7]

Henry Wager Halleck would hold the office of general in chief until early in 1864, a longer period than any other general kept the post in the war. He would be subjected to much ridicule, and he would receive but little praise for his work. He was supreme commander in name but rarely in fact. He provided Lincoln with military advice, which was sometimes accepted, but he exercised little actual control over military operations. His tenure of command was an experiment in unified direction of the armies that did not work out well because he disliked responsibility and did not want to direct. He delighted to counsel but he hated to decide. Nevertheless, the experiment was necessary, and for Lincoln it was educational. The government was groping toward a modern command system, and Lincoln learned much from his experience with Halleck. He put many of the lessons into practical effect in 1864 when an efficient command arrangement was finally created. The trial of Halleck prepared the way for Grant.

Halleck had the reputation of being the most unpopular man in Washington.[8] It was a title he worked hard to deserve. Surly and gruff in manner, he had no restraints about insult-

[5] Lincoln to Halleck, July 14, 1862, *Official Records,* XI, pt. 3, 321.

[6] Halleck to Lincoln, July 19, 1862, Lincoln MSS., vol. 80.

[7] Halleck to General W. T. Sherman, July 16, 1862, *Official Records,* XVII, pt. 2, 100; Halleck to McClellan, July 30, McClellan, *Own Story,* 473–474.

[8] John Sherman to W. T. Sherman, January 19, 1864, W. T. Sherman MSS.

ing people, even important governmental officials. He detested politicians and let them know it. To him they were "gassy" wirepullers seeking to interfere in military affairs, and he hoped that they would emulate the mad swine of Gadara and run into the sea.[9] Although he complained about their intervening in army matters, he sometimes injected himself into the making of policy. By 1863 the Federal armies had occupied large areas in the South, and the problem of reconstruction was emerging as a political issue. Halleck decided that the generals, practical men, were the people best qualified to frame a reconstruction plan. He asked a number of them to give him their views, so that he could present a composite scheme to Lincoln. A program drawn up by generals, he said, would be better than the "Utopian theories" of politicians.[1]

Many people disliked Halleck simply because of his appearance and his habits of behavior. In a war in which handsome and impressive generals thrilled an eager public, Halleck had the misfortune to look plain and act ordinary. Forty-seven years of age in 1862, he seemed older. His medium height figure was inclined to fatness, his chin was double, and his hair was receding in front. He slouched when he stood and he stooped when he walked. His large head hung forward from his body, his complexion was olive, and his facial features were flabby. His eyes, as described by various observers, were bulging, fishy, watery, and dull. Because of his eyes, Washington gossips speculated that he was an opium addict. Most people who came in contact with him were irritated by his harsh manner or repelled by his mannerisms, one of which was to sit and scratch his elbows. Some who had business with

[9] Halleck to General John M. Schofield, August 16, 1863, Schofield MSS., in box marked "Halleck"; Halleck to Schofield, November 28, 1862, *Official Records*, XXII, pt. 1, 793–794.

[1] Halleck to W. T. Sherman, August 27, October 1, 1863, Sherman MSS.

him claimed to detect a quality of insincerity or of shiftiness in his character. Although he could be tricky and evasive, he often only seemed to be so because of his foxy demeanor. During an interview, he would hold his head sideways and stare fishily at his visitor. Conversing with Halleck, said one officer, was like talking to somebody over your shoulder.[2]

Before the war, Halleck was considered to be the foremost American authority on the theory of war. He was one of the few officers in the country who could read French well enough to translate the works of the great French writers on warfare into English. He had published several books of translations and several that he had written himself. His scholarly activities had won him the nickname of Old Brains. His best-known volume was *Elements of Military Art and Science,* first published in 1846. It was crammed with facts and definitions, but it said little about the higher art of war. What it did say was banal. One solemn sentence stated: "When war is commenced by attacking a nation in peace, it is called *offensive,* and when undertaken to repel invasion, or the attack of an enemy, it is called *defensive.*"[3] Halleck knew the history and the rules of war, but he did not always know how to apply the rules to American situations. He was always inclined to go by the book, when sometimes he would have done better to throw it away. Nevertheless, his knowledge of war qualified him to be a valuable military adviser to Lincoln. He could provide Lincoln with the kind of technical information that the President did not have and that he needed to solve certain military problems. If Lincoln had wanted only an adviser, he

[2] Army correspondence of Boston *Traveller,* quoted in New York *Tribune,* May 31, 1862, p. 1; Welles, *Diary,* I, 373; Beale, *Diary of Edward Bates,* 293; Wilson, *Under the Old Flag,* I, 98–99; William E. Doster, *Lincoln and Episodes of the Civil War,* 178–179; George H. Gordon, *A War Diary of Events in the War of the Great Rebellion, 1863–1865,* 137; Wallace, *An Autobiography,* II, 570–571.

[3] Henry W. Halleck, *Elements of Military Art and Science . . . ,* 35.

could not have chosen a better one than Halleck. But the President intended Halleck to do more than counsel. He wanted him to command.

When Halleck came to Washington, he meant to command. He had stipulated as the condition of his accepting the office of general in chief that he have full power and responsibility to plan and direct operations.[4] Lincoln readily assented. He was eager to let a trained soldier make the decisions. After Halleck took over, Lincoln avoided exercising the function of control. To generals who inquired what he wanted them to do in a particular situation, he would say: ". . . I wish not to control. That I now leave to General Halleck," or "You must call on General Halleck, who commands, and whose business it is to understand and care for the whole field." [5] At first, Halleck did plan and direct, and care for the whole field. He was a real general in chief until the second battle of Bull Run in August, 1862. The Union army was defeated in that engagement, and apparently Halleck thought that he was to blame for the reverse or that he was blamed for it when he had not been responsible for it. At any rate, after Bull Run, he shrank from using his authority as supreme commander, shrank from taking the responsibility of making decisions. Lincoln described what happened to Halleck by saying that the General broke down, lost his pluck, and became little more than "a first-rate clerk." [6] In military terms, he became a technical adviser to the President and a staff critic of the plans of field generals. Halleck thought his job was a thankless one, and when he gave it up in 1864, he professed to be glad he was getting out. In a letter to a friend, he depicted himself as a mere adviser to Lincoln and Stanton and an executor of their verdicts: "If I disagree with them in opinion, I say so; but

[4] Dennett, *Diary of John Hay*, 167.
[5] Lincoln to McClellan, August 29, 1862, *Works of Lincoln*, VIII, 19; Lincoln to General J. T. Boyle, July 13, *ibid.*, VII, 275–276.
[6] Dennett, *Diary of John Hay*, 167, 176; Beale, *Diary of Bates*, 180.

when they decide, it is my duty faithfully to carry out their decisions." [7] Lincoln kept Halleck on in the position of general in chief after the General abnegated responsibility because he valued Halleck's technical knowledge and respected his character. Sometimes the President got irritated at what he called Halleck's "habitual attitude of demur," but he thought the General was absolutely sincere and had no personal axes to grind. On one occasion, Lincoln said that he was Halleck's friend because nobody else was. [8]

Immediately after Halleck arrived in Washington, Lincoln dumped a problem in his lap. What should be done about McClellan's army? Should it be left in the Peninsula and be reinforced for another move against Richmond or should it be brought back to near Washington and combined with Pope's forces for an advance on the enemy capital from the north? Lincoln had been troubled about the position of the Army of the Potomac ever since the retreat to the James. He feared that the failure of McClellan's campaign meant that Richmond could not be captured by operating against it from the east. He also was worried because the two principal Union armies, McClellan's and Pope's, were widely separated from each other and hence unable to reinforce each other quickly. These were the thoughts in his mind when he had asked McClellan and the corps commanders at Harrison's Landing whether the army was secure in its position and if it could be removed safely. Here was a complex military situation, and Lincoln was not sure he knew enough about military science to decide what should be done. Here was an issue that the learned Halleck ought to be able to resolve easily.

From the Peninsula, McClellan was bombarding Lincoln with requests for reinforcements and arguments why the army

[7] Halleck to W. T. Sherman, February 16, 1864, *Official Records,* XXXII, pt. 2, 407–408.

[8] Noah Brooks, *Washington in Lincoln's Time,* 36–37, 140; Dennett, *Diary of John Hay,* 45.

should not be withdrawn from its present location. The General had divined from Lincoln's questions at the Landing that withdrawal was in the President's mind, and he wanted to get it out.[9] In his private letters to his wife and his friends, he was saying some bitter things about his superior officers. To a Democratic politician in New York he wrote: "I have lost all regard and respect for the majority of the administration & doubt the propriety of my brave men's blood being shed to further the designs of such a set of heartless villains."[1] This was another of his many statements in which he revealed that in some respects he considered himself to be independent of the government. As commander of a field army, he had no right to judge whether or not he would risk lives merely because he disliked the personnel of the administration. It was his duty to risk lives if he could win victories, regardless of what he thought of the characters of Stanton and Lincoln.

McClellan became so worked up as he thought about the stupidity of Lincoln and the treachery of Stanton, whom he blamed for withholding reinforcements from him, that he decided to resign. When he heard that Halleck might be appointed general in chief, he was sure that he would get out. He could not remain a subordinate, he said, in an army he had once commanded. He asked his business friends in New York to look around for a job for him. These men, powers in the Democratic party and well aware of McClellan's future value to the party if he succeeded in the war, were dismayed by his intention to quit. They besought him to stay and urged his wife to use her influence with him to get him to reconsider. They even promised that they would get General Scott to tell Halleck to treat McClellan fairly. Finally, McClellan relieved them by saying that he would remain on as long as

[9] McClellan to Lincoln, July 11, 12, 17, 18, 1862, McClellan, *Own Story*, 490.
[1] McClellan to S. L. M. Barlow, July 15, 1862, McClellan MSS., Ser. 1.

the Army of the Potomac needed him. That could be pretty long, as he could hardly have conceived of its not needing him.[2] Probably he had never seriously considered resigning. When he had first voiced the purpose, he had been fearful that he might be removed.[3] He would have resigned to avert the humiliation of removal but not for any other reason.

Lincoln sent Halleck to Harrison's Landing to consult with McClellan about future operations of the Army of the Potomac and to tell McClellan that if he could not take Richmond with reinforcements of 20,000 that the army would have to be withdrawn from the Peninsula. Halleck left on July 24. The next day Lincoln told a friend that he was satisfied McClellan would never fight and that he had authorized Halleck to remove him if Old Brains thought it necessary. Lincoln said that if by some magic he could reinforce McClellan with 100,000 men today that McClellan would be in ecstasy and would say that he could take Richmond, but that the next day McClellan would have certain information that the enemy army numbered 400,000 and that he could not advance unless he got still more help.[4]

Halleck arrived at McClellan's camp on the afternoon of the twenty-fifth. He told McClellan that he came by Lincoln's authority to find out what the situation of the Army of the Potomac was and what McClellan's plans were. McClellan said that he intended to operate against Richmond on the line of the James, going up the south side and capturing first Petersburg and then Richmond. Halleck replied that the army

---

[2] McClellan to Mrs. McClellan, July 17, 18, 20, 1862, McClellan, *Own Story*, 449–451, 453; McClellan to W. H. Aspinwall, July 19, McClellan MSS., Ser. 1; Aspinwall to McClellan and to Mrs. McClellan, July 24, *ibid.*; J. W. Alsop to McClellan, July 24 and McClellan to Alsop, July 26, *ibid.*

[3] McClellan, *Own Story*, 449.

[4] Pease and Randall, *Diary of Browning*, 563.

would have to be returned to Washington and united with Pope unless McClellan felt that he was strong enough to operate against Richmond with a fair chance of success. To this, McClellan said that he could win if given 30,000 reinforcements. Halleck said that the most Lincoln would send was 20,000 and that if McClellan could not get Richmond with that number the army must be withdrawn. Halleck advised McClellan to lay the whole matter before his officers. McClellan agreed to do so, and Halleck retired to the boat that had brought him down. Immediately McClellan called his generals into council and told them what Halleck had said. They voted to advance against Richmond with the promised 20,000 reinforcements. The next morning McClellan told Halleck of their decision and said he would attack Richmond as soon as the reinforcements arrived. Halleck started for Washington to give Lincoln the news.[5]

All of McClellan's talk to Halleck sounded like action, but, of course, there was to be none. Before Halleck left, McClellan told him that the Confederate army defending Richmond numbered 200,000 and that his own army totalled 90,000. If McClellan really believed these figures, it was absurd for him to talk about attacking Richmond with 20,000 or even 30,000 reinforcements. He undoubtedly did not believe them; but by pretending to, he had his excuse for not doing anything. Right after Halleck got back to Washington, McClellan proved Lincoln to be an accurate prophet. McClellan telegraphed that after thinking the matter over he had decided that he would need an additional 20,000 reinforcements, that is, 40,000 in all. Halleck was on the point of recommending to Lincoln that 20,000 be sent to McClellan. McClellan's telegram changed the picture completely. The government did

[5] Halleck to Stanton, July 27, 1862, *Official Records,* XI, pt. 3, 337–338; Heintzelman MS. Journal, July 26.

not have 40,000 men available. Lincoln made his decision immediately. The army would have to be withdrawn.[6]

Halleck had been accompanied to the Landing by several officers. Among them was General Burnside. As the Seven Days had started Lincoln had telegraphed Burnside to go to McClellan with aid. Burnside had come up to Fortress Monroe with about 8,000 troops, and had stayed there with them while the government was trying to determine what to do with McClellan's army. He had been ordered to go with Halleck to McClellan's camp, and he had sat in at the council of McClellan's officers. Just before or just after Burnside went to the Landing, Lincoln talked to him about removing McClellan from command, and offered the post to Burnside. Burnside was extremely loyal to McClellan and distrustful of his own abilities. He urged Lincoln to retain McClellan. From the evidence, it seems that Lincoln was ready to oust McClellan, but that he did not know whom to put in when Burnside refused the command, and hence kept McClellan.[7] Burnside saved McClellan.

Although the government had quickly decided to remove the army from the James, it did not at first directly inform McClellan of what was contemplated. Halleck led up to it by instructing McClellan to send away his sick and wounded. Halleck's indirect approach was obviously because of security reasons. The government had no desire to advertise the coming withdrawal to the enemy. McClellan probably sensed that the government would decide to remove the army, even before he received the order about the sick and wounded. He was in a wild and vengeful mood. He wrote to a friend that the rascals in Washington would remove him except that they feared his men and public opinion. Well might they fear him,

[6] *C. C. W., Reports,* 1863, I, 452–456.
[7] *Ibid.,* 1863, I, 637–639, 650; Ben: Perley Poore, *Life and Public Services of Ambrose E. Burnside,* 154.

he exclaimed, for they knew that if he succeeded that his foot would be "upon their necks." [8] On August 3, Halleck gave McClellan the government's decision: the army was to be returned to a position south of Washington, and the movement was to start as soon as possible. McClellan was enraged when he got the order. He protested bitterly to Halleck; but Lincoln was behind the order and it stood. "It will not be rescinded. . . . ," Halleck calmly informed McClellan.[9]

Lincoln—and Halleck and Stanton—would have done better to have left the army where it was. It was only twenty-five miles from Richmond and on a supply line that could always be kept open. It was closer to Richmond than it would be until 1864. Seldom if ever in military history has an army that near to an enemy capital retired without the enemy firing a shot at it. Lincoln would have made a wiser decision if he had kept the army on the James and removed McClellan as its commander. He should have replaced McClellan with a general who was not afraid to fight and who had some capacity to estimate the strength of the enemy. He could have given the command to Pope, who was soon to show that he had plenty of defects but who was pugnacious and who might have smashed his way into Richmond. There is no evidence that Lincoln considered keeping the army in the Peninsula and giving it a new leader. He was impressed with Halleck's learned and theoretical talk about the military error and the danger of having the armies of McClellan and Pope separated and the necessity of obeying the textbooks by uniting them. In a technical sense, the two Union armies were separated, which according to the books was bad, and there was an enemy force, the Confederate army at Richmond, between them, which according to the books was worse. Actually the Federal

[8] McClellan to S. L. M. Barlow, July 30, 1862, McClellan MSS., Ser. 1.

[9] Heintzelman MS. Journal, August 4, 1862; McClellan, *Own Story*, 491, 494–498; Halleck to McClellan, August 5, McClellan MSS., Ser. 1.

armies were not separated in a dangerous or strategic sense, because the Federal navy controlled the water lines between Washington and the Peninsula, and some kind of cooperation was always possible.

But McClellan was largely to blame for Lincoln's acceptance of Halleck's theorizing. His exaggeration of the numbers of the enemy made Halleck's arguments look correct. Pope had 40,000 men, McClellan had over 90,000. And by McClellan's estimate, Lee had 200,000. If an enemy army of that size was between the Union forces, then Lincoln had reason to think that the Union armies ought to be brought together. If Lincoln had known, as he would have, had McClellan possessed any ability to judge realities, that the Confederate army numbered not over 75,000, the President might have made a different decision about withdrawing the army. McClellan's weakness of magnifying the size of the enemy caught up with him at last. More than anybody, he was responsible for the collapse of the Peninsula campaign.

Chapter 7

"He Has Got the Slows"

At Harrison's Landing, McClellan was getting ready to remove the army from the Peninsula. By the terms of Halleck's order, the troops were to be taken by water to Acquia Creek, a tributary of the Rappahannock River. From there they could be united with Pope's army, then operating south of the Rappahannock farther west. McClellan had protested strongly against the withdrawal order when he received it, and he continued to protest as he prepared to carry it out. He was going to obey it—unless he saw a chance to make a sudden dash into Richmond, but he was not going to execute it with eagerness or view it with approval. To him the order was nothing more than an attempt by his enemies in Washington to force him to resign. But he intended to foil the scoundrels. He would hold on to his command and compel them to place him on leave of absence. Then when defeat came to the Union cause because of his departure, they would have to call him back to save the country. He was especially bitter about Halleck, but in characteristic fashion he condemned Old Brains not so much for having made a wrong military decision but for not acting like a gentleman. He had received several brusque telegrams from Halleck, and he was deeply pained that anyone should so address George B. McClellan.[1] His angry feelings

[1] McClellan to Mrs. McClellan, August 8, 10, 14, 1862, McClellan, *Own Story*, 464–467.

about the administration were shared by the officers who were his intimates. Fitz John Porter, his closest friend and a man much like McClellan, wrote to a leading Democratic editor that the government's management of affairs in Virginia deserved to result in defeat. Indulging in the kind of loose and dangerous talk that would later help involve him in a court-martial, Porter added: "Would that this army was in Washington to rid us of incumbents ruining our country." [2]

McClellan did not get his withdrawal movement under way until almost mid-August. To Halleck it seemed that McClellan was proceeding with inexcusable slowness. The general in chief sent McClellan some sharp despatches to hurry up. McClellan was evacuating the army slowly, but he was moving about as fast as his abilities and the transportation situation in the Peninsula would let him. He performed any movement, an advance or a withdrawal, sluggishly, and he did have some real trouble in collecting enough water transport to carry the army.[3] Undoubtedly he delayed a little, hoping that he could get the withdrawal order rescinded at the last moment. When he realized that it was final, he moved with more decision and rapidity.[4]

Halleck wanted McClellan to bring the Army of the Potomac to northern Virginia with the utmost speed because Pope was in a situation of great potential danger. After the collapse of McClellan's offensive, Pope had moved his army south of the Rappahannock, threatening the Confederate transportation hub of Gordonsville. At first he encountered slight resistance, but soon he found himself confronting units from Lee's army that had come up from Richmond. After the end

[2] Porter to Manton Marble, August 10, 1862, Marble MSS.

[3] Halleck to McClellan, August 9, 10, 12, 1862, McClellan to Halleck, August 10, McClellan, *Own Story*, 500–503.

[4] McClellan to Halleck, August 12, 1862, *ibid.*, 503; McClellan to Halleck, August 17, McClellan MSS., Ser. 1.

of the Seven Days, Lee had studied closely the disposition of the Federal forces in eastern Virginia. He wanted to know whether the Union government was going to reinforce McClellan for another try at Richmond. He had one almost sure way of determining the intentions of the Federals. He knew that Burnside had come to Fortress Monroe with reinforcements for McClellan and that surplus troops at Washington were being assembled for transportation to the James. If these forces moved to join McClellan, then the Federal government was going to strengthen the Army of the Potomac for another offensive. If they did not, the government was planning to withdraw McClellan and unite him with Pope. When Burnside stayed at the Fortress and the troops at Washington remained where they were, Lee concluded that the Federal authorities were going to remove McClellan from the Peninsula. This was what he wanted them to do. He had no desire to fight in the cramped space between the York and the James. He much preferred northern Virginia, where he would have room to maneuver. As soon as he decided that the Army of the Potomac was to be withdrawn, he sent part of his army, headed by Jackson, north to face Pope. Jackson left in July. Lee moved with the remainder of his forces to join Jackson at about the same time that McClellan was leaving the Peninsula. He hoped to be able to fall on Pope and destroy him before McClellan got to Pope.

Pope suddenly realized that he was facing an enemy army as large as his and one that was increasing. Hurriedly he fell back toward the safety of the Rappahannock line. He knew the peril he would be in if Lee's whole army caught up with him before reinforcements from McClellan could arrive. Halleck knew it too, and that was the reason the general in chief sent McClellan so many urgent, nagging telegrams to hasten his withdrawal. Halleck had another reason for wanting to unite the Union forces. He had some doubts about Pope's ability to command a large army, and he preferred to have McClellan in charge of operations in northern Virginia. He promised McClellan the command of all the forces in Virginia as soon as they were brought together.[5] McClellan received the news of Pope's danger with indifference and Halleck's offer of command with scepticism. He did not think that he could reach the Rappahannock in time to help Pope, and he did not believe that the government would give him an important command unless forced to do so by a disaster to Pope.[6] Halleck sent Burnside to the Peninsula to assure McClellan that the command would be his if he would only get his army to northern Virginia. Burnside was able to convince McClellan that the evacuation movement was not a plot to get rid of him. But McClellan continued to react in egocentric fashion to the joining of his army with Pope's. As he watched his troops crossing the Chickahominy enroute to Fortress Monroe, he turned to Burnside and said: "Look at them, Burn. Did you ever see finer men? Oh, I want to see those men beside of Pope's." [7]

In Washington, Halleck fretted as McClellan moved his army down the Peninsula to ports of embarkation on the coast. But as the Army of the Potomac finally approached Acquia Creek, Old Brains felt easier. Pope had retired behind the Rappahannock beyond Lee's immediate reach, and Burnside had brought his force up to Fredericksburg. Now McClellan was near at hand. Halleck thought that if he could combine all the Union forces at some point on the Rappahannock, the Federals could go over from the defen-

[5] Halleck to McClellan, August 7, 1862, McClellan, *Own Story*, 474–475.

[6] McClellan to Mrs. McClellan, August 10, 11, 17, 21, 23, 1862, *ibid.*, 465–466, 468, 470–471.

[7] D. R. Larned to Amelia Larned, August 18, 1862, Larned MSS. Capitals and punctuation supplied.

sive to the offensive. The danger that Lee would fall on one of the separate Union armies seemed to have passed.

As his anxiety about the Virginia situation lifted, Halleck had time to give some attention to affairs in the West. He had been so busy with McClellan and Pope that he had not thought much about his former department.[8] Now he had to think about it, because Lincoln forcibly brought the subject before him. The President was greatly dissatisfied with what was happening, or, to Lincoln's way of thinking, not happening in Tennessee. Before Halleck had left the West, he had started Buell on an offensive toward Chattanooga, which had as its large objective the liberation of East Tennessee. Buell had moved, but he had not moved very far. He was as slow as McClellan, and he had a long supply line to maintain as he advanced. Lincoln lost his patience as he watched Buell's crawling movement. To him Buell's talk about supply difficulties and the like was only the customary military excuse for inaction. He was getting tired of that kind of talk. He asked Halleck to recommend somebody to take Buell's place. Halleck defended Buell and asked Lincoln to give the General more time. Then Halleck wrote to Buell urging him to act before "the administration," meaning Lincoln and Stanton, forced his removal. When Buell still did not move, Lincoln told Halleck to relieve him from command. Again Halleck was able to persuade the President to delay the decision and to give Buell one more chance.[9] But the chance was a slim one. Buell had to win or go. Lincoln was now judging generals by a single standard—the stern standard of victory. Halleck explained the new criterion to one officer: "The government seems determined to apply the guillotine to all unsuccessful generals. It seems rather hard to do this when the gen-

[8] Halleck to McClellan, August 24, 1862, *Official Records*, XII, pt. 3, 647; Halleck to W. T. Sherman, August 25, *ibid.*, XVII, pt. 2, 186.

[9] Halleck to Buell, August 12, 18, 1862, *ibid.*, XVI, pt. 2, 314–315, 360.

eral is not at fault; but, perhaps, with us now, as in the French Revolution, some harsh measures are required." [1]

On August 24, McClellan, who did not completely measure up to the new standard, arrived at Acquia Creek and reported by telegraph to Halleck. He asked where Pope was and what his own status was. Specifically he inquired whether he was in command of all the forces in Virginia, including Pope's, as Halleck had promised he would be. Halleck, ignoring McClellan's query about command arrangements, replied that he did not know where Pope was or where the enemy army was and that he had been trying all day to ascertain Pope's situation. The explanation of this astonishing state of affairs was that the Confederates had crossed the Rappahannock on the twenty-fourth and moved a force around in Pope's rear. Surprised and excited by the appearance of the enemy, Pope did not immediately inform Halleck what was happening. Then the force in his rear cut his telegraphic communications with Washington, and he could not get any despatches through. Halleck, of course, did not know that Pope's communications had been broken. He knew only that he should be receiving reports from Pope, and he was puzzled that none came. On the twenty-sixth, he still had no word from Pope. Then Old Brains began to worry that Pope might be in trouble. He decided that he needed McClellan's counsel and asked McClellan to come up to Alexandria. [2] McClellan jumped at the invitation. He thought that at Alexandria, where he would be close to Halleck, he would be in a better position than at Acquia Creek to argue his claim for the command of the combined Union forces. He went immediately.

By the time McClellan got to Alexandria, Halleck had found out a little about Pope's situation. Two corps of the

[1] Halleck to General H. G. Wright, August 25, 1862, *ibid.*, XVI, pt. 2, 421.

[2] McClellan to Halleck, August 24, 1862, McClellan, *Own Story*, 508; Halleck to McClellan, August 24, 26, *ibid.*, 508–509.

Army of the Potomac, Porter's and Heintzelman's, had reached Acquia Creek before McClellan got there and with his permission had pushed on to join Pope. They had gone forward because Porter had intercepted an enemy letter indicating that Pope faced a superior enemy army. Porter, before he left, had arranged with Burnside, in command at Falmouth on the Rappahannock, to telegraph to the latter news of important developments on Pope's front. Porter was now drawing close to Pope, and he was able to send Burnside some information about the disposition of Pope's forces. Burnside relayed Porter's despatches to Lincoln, who came to the War Department telegraph office at seven in the morning daily to receive them.[3] From Porter's telegrams, Halleck could determine only that some of Pope's forces were around Warrenton, that the Confederates had hit Pope's field base and communications center at Manassas, and that a battle seemed to be imminent. Irritated at Pope's carelessness in guarding his rear but fearful that Pope might be in danger, Halleck ordered McClellan to push Franklin's corps of the Army of the Potomac, which had come to Alexandria, out toward Manassas.[4]

McClellan, in an apparent mood of subordination and cooperation, prepared to obey Halleck's order. He also directed Sumner's corps to come up from Acquia with the intention of sending it to Pope. Then reverting to form, he began to think of reasons why Franklin and Sumner should not go to Pope. He bombarded Halleck with telegrams detailing the reasons: the corps lacked equipment to fight; they could not get to Pope in time; they ought to be held back to protect Washington or to cover Pope's retreat in case of a defeat. Again he demanded to know what his position was, what and whom he

³ *Official Records*, XII, pt. 2, supplement, 1003; Lincoln to Burnside, August 27, 28, 1862, *Works of Lincoln*, VIII, 18.

⁴ Halleck to McClellan, August 27, 1862, three despatches, McClellan, *Own Story*, 509-510.

was in command of.[5] By this time Halleck was in no condition
to decide anything. Almost in a panic at the absence of direct
word from Pope, he was breaking down under the pressure
of the situation. He did not know exactly what to do with
McClellan's corps, and he did not know exactly how to define
McClellan's status. He thought, sometimes, that Franklin and
Sumner should go to Pope, but he could see, sometimes, merit
in McClellan's argument that they should not. In his instructions to McClellan about the movement of the corps, he wav-
ered between ordering them to go all the way and to go part
of the way. His decision on the issue of McClellan's authority
showed how close he was to the snapping point. "I have no
time for details," he replied to McClellan. "You will, therefore, as ranking general in the field, direct as you deem best;
but at present orders for Pope's army should go through
me." [6] How the question of the command of all the Union
forces in Virginia could be a detail and how McClellan could
have directed Pope's army from Alexandria were mysteries
that not even Halleck's textbooks could have explained.

As Halleck got more panicky, he let McClellan dominate
him more. He shifted responsibility to McClellan that he
should have exercised himself. He bickered petulantly with
McClellan about moving Franklin and Sumner to Pope, and
then yielded completely to McClellan's contention that the
corps should not go too far from Washington. "Dispose of all
troops as you deem best," he wrote wearily.[7] He should never
have given McClellan discretionary authority to control the
movement of reinforcements to Pope. This power he should

[5] McClellan to Halleck, August 27, 1862, four despatches, *ibid.*,
512–513.

[6] Halleck to McClellan, August 27, 1862, *Official Records,* XII,
pt. 3, 691.

[7] McClellan to Halleck, August 28, 29, 1862, several telegrams,
McClellan, *Own Story,* 513–517; Halleck to McClellan, August 29,
Official Records, XII, pt. 3, 722.

have kept in his own hands, even if McClellan had been a perfect subordinate. The situation of the Union forces in Virginia posed a peculiar problem in command. The separated armies of McClellan and Pope had to be combined in the face of any enemy movement against the smaller force, Pope's. Obviously much, if not all, of the larger army would have to be sent to Pope. But should McClellan go with his army and take command of the united forces? And if he did not go, what should be done with him? From the beginning of the crisis, Halleck boggled the answer to these issues. Previously Halleck had told McClellan that he would have control of the combined armies, but that was when Old Brains thought that he could bring the Union forces together before the Confederates struck. When they threatened to attack with Pope and McClellan separated, Halleck was not sure at first what to do with McClellan. He decided to keep McClellan near him, as an adviser or as someone on whom he could unload responsibility, and send McClellan's troops to Pope. Probably this was the best decision under the circumstances. McClellan might not have been able to get to Pope's army before the Confederates attacked. Even if he could have reached the battle area in time, he would have come into a situation largely unfamiliar to him. If a battle was to be fought immediately, Pope, the man on the spot, seemed to be the general to fight it. Halleck should have informed McClellan immediately that in all probability the Army of the Potomac would have to be transferred temporarily to Pope's command and he, as general in chief, should have taken direct and active charge of the transfer movement.

Halleck did neither of these things. He avoided facing up to McClellan. First, he made the absurd decision that McClellan could send orders to Pope's army through him. Then he directed McClellan to send part of the Army of the Potomac toward Pope, but let himself be influenced by McClellan's insistence that the troops be kept near Washington. Finally he caved in completely and permitted McClellan to do as he pleased about reinforcements for Pope. Halleck ranked both Pope and McClellan. He was the only officer who could command both of them or who could unify the tangled Virginia command situation. When he refused to exercise the function of combining the armies, by telling McClellan to dispose of "all troops" as McClellan deemed best, the command system broke down. On August 30, the War Department issued what it thought was a clarifying order for the armies in Virginia: Burnside at Falmouth was in command of his own corps except the part sent to Pope; McClellan was in command of the Army of the Potomac except that part sent to Pope; Pope was in command of the Army of Virginia and all troops temporarily attached to it; Halleck was in command of all of them.[8] The order was hardly clarifying and certainly was not accurate. Two corps of McClellan's army were with Pope and two had moved toward him. If the latter two were under anybody's command, they were under McClellan's, not Pope's. But McClellan claimed he had no control over any troops in his army. Halleck was not in command of anything. It was time for Lincoln to enter the picture.

The President had watched the situation developing on Pope's front with interest and mounting anxiety. Every day he had come to the telegraph office to read Porter's telegrams to Burnside. He also tried to get information from other sources. On August 29, he telegraphed McClellan asking for news of Pope. McClellan, who up to now had avoided going to Washington so that he would not have to meet Lincoln, seized on Lincoln's telegram as an opportunity to get in direct contact with the President. Lincoln had asked for news, but

[8] McClellan, *Own Story*, 520.

McClellan replied with advice. He said that the government should adopt one of two courses: concentrate all available forces to open communications with Pope or "leave Pope to get out of his scrape" and dispose the available troops so as to make Washington secure against attack. He asked what Lincoln wanted him to do and what his orders and authority were. Ignoring this bid for the chief command in Virginia, Lincoln replied that he thought McClellan's first alternative was the correct one but that he did not wish to control what should be done. "That I now leave to Gen. Halleck, aided by your counsels," said the President.[9] Lincoln was shocked by McClellan's statement about letting Pope get out of his own scrape. The President told his secretary that McClellan seemed to want Pope to be defeated. Lincoln thought that maybe McClellan was a little crazy.[1] Lincoln did not say what he thought of Halleck. He must have noticed that the strain of the situation was affecting the General. He may not have known that Old Brains was refusing to exercise the function of command. Lincoln's telegram to McClellan indicated that he had not lost faith in Halleck's ability. It also indicated that he had a definite idea as to what should be done but that he wanted Halleck to do it on his own initiative. Obviously Lincoln did not believe that the situation in Virginia was so critical that he should intervene in it.

On August 30, it seemed that there was no crisis at all. Halleck finally received a despatch from Pope. It was an exultant document. Pope said that on the previous day he had fought a terrific battle with the Confederates and had driven them from the field and that he would renew the attack on the morrow unless the enemy retreated toward the mountains.

[9] Lincoln to McClellan, August 28, 1862, *Works of Lincoln*, VIII, 19; McClellan to Lincoln and Lincoln to McClellan, August 29, McClellan, *Own Story*, 515.

[1] Dennett, *Diary of Hay*, 45.

That night in Washington Lincoln waited for news of a complete victory from Pope.[2] Several times during the war Lincoln was cruelly disappointed by generals who reported victories that turned out to be defeats. Probably he never had his hopes raised higher than when Pope first telegraphed that he had triumphed at the second battle of Manassas—nor had them dashed lower than when Pope followed with the news that he had been defeated and was in retreat. Pope had many of McClellan's faults in reverse. He was aggressive where McClellan was timid, rash where McClellan was cautious. Like McClellan, he could not judge realities. McClellan magnified dangers, Pope minimized or did not see them. Pope's faults brought about his defeat at Bull Run. When he learned that a part of Lee's army was in his rear at Manassas, Pope went after it. The Confederates, under Jackson, fell back slightly to a strong position. Pope prepared to attack them. He realized that probably the rest of Lee's army was coming to join Jackson, but he thought that he could destroy Jackson before Lee arrived. Actually the bulk of the enemy army was on the field, but Pope never found this out. In a two day battle he flung his men against the Confederate lines with no success. There was no basis at all for his telegram to Halleck. When the Union assaults were exhausted, Lee counterattacked on the thirtieth and drove Pope from the field.

August 31 was a Sunday. By morning the news was coming into Washington, from McClellan and Burnside and other sources, that Pope had been defeated. Lincoln came into the room of his secretary, John Hay, and said: "Well, John, we are whipped again, I am afraid." [3] Later in the day the news looked better, but soon it was definitely known that Pope had retreated north of Bull Run and that the Confederates were

---

[2] Pope to Halleck, August 30, 1862, *Official Records,* XII, pt. 3, 741; Dennett, *Diary of Hay,* 46.

[3] Dennett, *Diary of Hay,* 46.

following him. Pope telegraphed Halleck that the army was intact, but he urged that it be withdrawn to the Washington defences. He said that McClellan's officers had not cooperated with him and that they were spreading demoralization through the army. To save the Army of Virginia from attacks from without and intrigue from within, he advised that Halleck order it back to the capital for reorganization.[4] Poor Halleck was demoralized himself by what was happening. Almost pathetically, he turned to McClellan for aid. Late at night on the thirty-first he despatched McClellan asking for the assistance of the latter's "ability and experience." "I am almost entirely tired out," said the general in chief. Eagerly McClellan replied that he wanted to help. He counseled Halleck to order Pope to fall back to the capital defences and asked for an appointment alone with Old Brains in Washington the next day.[5]

McClellan came to Washington and saw Halleck. The general in chief had instructed Pope to retreat to the fortifications around Washington. Old Brains now gave McClellan verbal instructions to assume command of the capital and its defences. McClellan got busy with his duties. Later in the day he received a message to come to Halleck's house to see the President. Lincoln said that he had heard that McClellan's officers were not cooperating with Pope, and asked McClellan if this were true. McClellan replied that the report was false, that whatever his officers thought of Pope they would support him. McClellan said later that Lincoln was "deeply moved." The President's emotion might well have been suppressed anger. McClellan must have sensed that his answer did not satisfy Lincoln, because he agreed to send a telegram to Porter requesting his friends to give their fullest cooperation to

[4] Pope to Halleck, August 31, September 1, 1862, *Official Records*, XII, pt. 2, 80, 82–83.

[5] Halleck to McClellan, August 31, 1862, and McClellan to Halleck, August 31, two telegrams, McClellan, *Own Story*, 525–526.

Pope.[6] Lincoln had become suspicious about McClellan's generals from reading Porter's despatches to Burnside. Porter's telegrams dripped with contempt for Pope. The President had been further aroused by McClellan's callous phrase about abandoning Pope to his scrape. Lincoln thought that maybe McClellan and his officers wanted Pope to be defeated. Lincoln was about to give McClellan the command of all the troops in and around Washington, but first he wanted to be sure that McClellan had not betrayed Pope. McClellan's telegram to Porter satisfied Lincoln for the moment. The next day Pope's troops approached the city. Lincoln verbally directed McClellan to take command of Pope's forces as they entered the fortifications. Later a formal order was issued placing McClellan in command of the fortifications and of all the troops for the defence of the city.[7]

The Cabinet was in session on September 2. The members were discussing Pope's defeat. Stanton, trembling with rage, said that McClellan had been given the command of all the forces in Washington. Most of the members were opposed to the appointment. Lincoln came in while the talk was going on and confirmed that McClellan was in command. He said that he had done what he thought was best, that McClellan was a good organizer and that he could whip the troops into shape for the defence of Washington better than anybody else. The Cabinet did not seem to be convinced, and Lincoln was distressed. He said that all that McClellan was to do was to put the troops into the fortifications and command them if the enemy attacked the city. No field command was being given McClellan, he emphasized. McClellan had the confidence of the army, said Lincoln, and he intended to use

[6] McClellan to Porter, September 1, 1862, *Official Records*, XII, pt. 3, 787–788; *ibid.*, XIX, pt. 2, 36–37; McClellan, *Own Story*, 534.

[7] McClellan, *Own Story*, 534–536.

McClellan's strength with the soldiers *temporarily*—until the army could be reorganized.[8]

Lincoln was determined that McClellan's command should be temporary because he believed the General was incapable of offensive warfare, which was the kind he wanted ultimately from the Army of the Potomac, and because he thought that McClellan and his officers had not supported Pope properly. The President's suspicions on the latter point were revived after he talked to Pope. Pope, in conversation with Lincoln and in his official report, charged that McClellan, Porter, and other officers of McClellan's army were responsible for his defeat at Manassas. He accused McClellan of having held back men and supplies from Washington and Porter and the other officers of having refused to obey his orders. Lincoln read Pope's report at a Cabinet meeting, and said that three of the generals named by Pope, but not McClellan, would be brought before a court of inquiry. Pope wanted his report published, but Lincoln decided that it could not be at present. The President feared that its bitter charges would increase the demoralization of the forces in Washington.[9]

For the same reason of army morale, Lincoln determined that Pope would have to be sacrificed as a commander. The President had no criticism of Pope's generalship, but he knew that Pope could not serve under McClellan. The bad feeling between the two generals and their friends would wreck the organization of the Eastern army. When Pope asked Halleck what his status was, Old Brains replied evasively that

[8] Welles, *Diary*, I, 104–105, September 2, 1862; Chase's diary, September 2, in Schuckers, *Chase*, 444.

[9] *Diary and Correspondence of Salmon P. Chase, Annual Report of American Historical Association*, 1902, II, 65–66; C. C. W., *Reports*, 1865, supplement, II, 189–190; Pope to Lincoln, September 5, 1862, Lincoln MSS., vol. 86; Halleck to Pope, September 5, *Official Records*, XII, pt. 3, 812–813.

the army was being reorganized and that McClellan commanded all troops in the capital. Then on September 5, Halleck, by Lincoln's direction, relieved Pope of command. Halleck told Pope that in the present crisis individual careers had to be sacrificed to the general good of the army.[1] Pope was sent back to the West, where he held minor commands for the rest of the war. He blamed Lincoln for his banishment and thought that the President had treated him unjustly.[2]

Lincoln told a few people why he had given McClellan temporary command of the Washington forces. He also expressed to them his conviction that McClellan and some of his officers had tried to make Pope fail. Lincoln's anger at McClellan and the Army of the Potomac generals who had been with Pope was real, and it increased as he heard more accounts of their actions and words. Herman Haupt, the transportation director, came to Washington after the battle at Manassas and saw Lincoln. Haupt was full of stories about the refusal of McClellan's officers to support Pope. He must have recounted some of them to Lincoln. Perhaps he told Lincoln of the drunk general who on the way to Manassas said: "I don't care for John Pope a pinch of owl dung."[3] Talking with John Hay about McClellan's course during the Manassas campaign, Lincoln said: "He has acted badly in this matter, but we must use what tools we have. There is no man in the Army who can man these fortifications and lick these troops of ours into shape half as well as he. . . . If he can't fight himself, he excels in making others ready to fight." Lincoln said almost the same thing to Secretary of the Navy Welles: "I must have McClellan to reorganize the army and bring it out of chaos,

---

[1] Pope to Halleck, September 3, 1862; Halleck to Pope, September 3; Pope to Halleck, September 5; Halleck to Pope, September 5, in *ibid.*, XII, pt. 3, 808–809, 812–813.

[2] Pope to E. B. Washburne, February 1, 1863, Washburne MSS.; Pope to Stanton, December 25, 1864, Stanton MSS.

[3] Haupt, *Reminiscences*, 82–83.

but there has been a design, a purpose in breaking down Pope, without regard of consequences to the country. It is shocking to see and know this; but there is no remedy at present. McClellan has the army with him." [4] McClellan would have been shocked and unbelieving if he had known what Lincoln was saying about him and why the President had appointed him to command. McClellan assumed that the government had called on him because he was the only man who could save the country.[5]

Months later Porter would be tried before a court-martial on charges of refusing to obey Pope's orders at Manassas. He was found guilty and dismissed from the army. Many years after the war, another military tribunal reheard the case and decided he was innocent. The second decision was correct. Porter did nothing wrong at Manassas, but his telegrams to Burnside, coupled with other evidence, made it seem to Lincoln and others that he had. Neither did McClellan deliberately try to bring about Pope's defeat by holding back Franklin and Sumner. McClellan held them back because he could not act decisively in a crisis. He was not trying to break down Pope as Lincoln thought. He was only acting natural.

Lincoln's plan to use McClellan in a temporary capacity to reorganize the army for active operations under another commander depended on the Confederates remaining quiet during the reorganization period. Lee abruptly upset Lincoln's project. Early in September he crossed his army over the Potomac and moved into western Maryland. The Confederates were on Union soil. Obviously the Army of the Potomac had to move against them, and, at the very least, to repel the invasion. But who should command the army in this important campaign? Lincoln did not think that McClellan

[4] Dennett, *Diary of Hay*, 47, September 5, 1862; Welles, *Diary*, I, 113, September 5; William D. Kelley, *Lincoln and Stanton*, 73.

[5] McClellan to Mrs. McClellan, September 5, 8, 1862, McClellan, *Own Story*, 567–568.

should. The President sent for Burnside and again offered him the command. As he had done before, Burnside declined the appointment and urged McClellan for the command.[6] Burnside's unwillingness to take the command placed Lincoln in a dilemma. Somebody had to lead the army against Lee. Burnside was, in Lincoln's estimation, the only available general, besides McClellan, who could command a large army. He was the only general in the East, again except for McClellan, who had ever exercised independent command. But with Burnside refusing to lead the army, the only alternative was McClellan. It was a bitter alternative for Lincoln, but he took it. McClellan was given the field command of the Army of the Potomac. According to Gideon Welles, Lincoln said that Halleck made the appointment. Welles quoted Lincoln as saying: ". . . I wish you to understand it was not made by me. I put McClellan in command here to defend the city, for he has great powers of organization, and discipline; . . . and there his usefulness ends. He can't go ahead—he can't strike a blow." [7] But Halleck told a Congressional committee that Lincoln and he discussed for days who should command the army in Maryland and that Lincoln made the decision to name McClellan. In Halleck's account, Lincoln went to McClellan's house early one morning and said: "General, you will take command of the forces in the field." [8]

Halleck's story was undoubtedly the correct one. Welles probably misunderstood Lincoln. What the President was saying to Welles was that he had not wanted to give McClellan an active command but had been forced to by the enemy thrust into Maryland and that he doubted that McClellan would win any substantial success against Lee. McClellan had still another version of what happened. He said that he never

[6] Pease and Randall, *Diary of Browning*, 589–590; *C. C. W.*, *Reports*, 1863, I, 650; Poore, *Burnside*, 154.

[7] Welles, *Diary*, I, 124.

[8] *C. C. W.*, *Reports*, 1863, I, 451, 453–454.

received at any time any orders or instructions from Lincoln or Halleck, that of his own initiative he had taken the army to Maryland because he thought it was time to move against Lee, and that had he been defeated he would have been put to death.[9] This was pure romance. He either forgot the conference at his house with Lincoln, or he was lying. It is hard to see how he could have forgotten the meeting. As a matter of fact, Lincoln talked with McClellan several times about the Maryland situation. On one occasion Lincoln proposed to leave Washington and go to McClellan's camp to see the General. Halleck and General Banks, fearing that Confederate cavalry in the vicinity might capture the President, had insisted that he remain in the city and that McClellan come to Washington.[1]

As McClellan moved into western Maryland, he had a wonderful piece of luck. He came into possession of a Confederate document showing the disposition of Lee's army. From it McClellan learned that the Confederate army was not concentrated but widely separated. Lee had advanced into Maryland from the Manassas area, but he knew that he could not maintain a line of supply over the Potomac that close to Washington. He intended to open a supply line through the Valley after he got to Maryland. But he found that a Federal garrison at Harper's Ferry at the head of the Valley, which he had expected would evacuate as he entered Maryland, had remained in its position. The Confederates could have no secure supply line unless the garrison was captured, so Lee sent Jackson to take Harper's Ferry. An order of Lee's regarding Jackson's movement and the arrangement of the other units of the army was captured by Union soldiers and brought to McClellan. McClellan was exultant when he read the order.

[9] *Ibid.*, 1863, I, 438–439; McClellan, *Own Story*, 549, 551.
[1] N. P. Banks to Lincoln, September 12, 1862, and Halleck to Lincoln, September 12, Lincoln MSS., vol. 87.

To one general, he said:."Here is a paper with which if I cannot whip 'Bobbie Lee,' I will be willing to go home." To Lincoln, McClellan wrote that he had the plans of the enemy and was confident of success. He also gave the President the important military information that he had been received enthusiastically by the ladies of Maryland.[2]

McClellan should have been able indeed to whip Lee. All that he had to do was to move forward rapidly and interpose his army between the separate fractions of Lee and Jackson. Then, with his superior force, he could have attacked first one and then the other and destroyed both. He did move forward with what he considered rapidity, but his standards of speed were his own and peculiar. Judged by any objective standards, his advance was slow. It was so slow that it gave Lee time to pull his army together. When Lee realized that McClellan was moving to attack him, he hastily began to concentrate his forces. To delay McClellan until Jackson could return from Harper's Ferry, he stationed part of his army at the pass at South Mountain, through which McClellan would have to go as he marched west. The Confederates resisted McClellan sharply at South Mountain and then retired. They were fighting only a delaying action, but McClellan was in a delirium of joy at his little victory. In despatches to Washington, he described the enemy as retreating in panic before his triumphant army. Completely lost to reality, he told his wife that God had seldom given an army a greater victory than South Mountain.[3] His telegrams to Halleck gave Lincoln the impression that the Confederate army was almost smashed up. "God bless you, and all with you," Lincoln wrote the General. "Destroy the rebel army if possible." The delighted Presi-

[2] John Gibbon, *Personal Recollections of the Civil War*, 73; McClellan to Lincoln, September 13, 1862, *Official Records*, XIX, pt. 2, 281.

[3] McClellan to Halleck, September 15, 1862, three despatches, *Official Records*, XIX, pt. 2, 294–295; McClellan to Mrs. McClellan, *Own Story*, 612.

dent informed a friend that McClellan had won a great victory and was pursuing the flying foe.[4]

McClellan was not pursuing any flying foe. He was moving against an enemy that was retiring in order to concentrate against him. He finally came up to Lee at Antietam Creek. Most of Jackson's corps had rejoined Lee, and the rest were on the way back from Harper's Ferry. McClellan had lost his opportunity to destroy the Confederates in detail. Nevertheless, he was in a favorable position, and Lee was in an unfavorable one. McClellan had superiority in numbers, and the Confederate defensive position was not strong. If McClellan could drive Lee from the field, he might be able to harry the enemy army out of existence before it could reach the safety of Virginia. It was still possible for McClellan to win the great victory of which he had dreamed. McClellan decided to attack the Confederates across Antietam Creek, hitting first their left, then their right, and if the first two attacks succeeded, smashing their center. He launched his offensive on September 17. All through a bloody day, the Federal troops assaulted the Confederate lines. McClellan was nervous during the battle, but he was in what was for him a confident mood. He informed Halleck that he was in the most terrible battle of the war, perhaps of all history, that he had great odds against him, but that he was confident of carrying the day.[5] His attack on his right shoved the Confederates back but did not pierce their lines. His attack on his left was on the point of breaking through the enemy position when the rest of Jackson's troops arrived and held the breach. Undoubtedly at that point, McClellan had victory in his grasp. He had held out of the fighting a reserve of one corps to cover his retreat in case he was defeated. If he had sent this force against the

[4] Lincoln to McClellan, September 15, 1862, and Lincoln to J. K. Dubois, September 15, *Works of Lincoln*, VIII, 34.

[5] McClellan to Halleck, September 17, 1862, *Official Records*, XIX, pt. 2, 312.

weakened Confederate right, he would have swept Lee from the field. He was at the crisis of his career, and he fumbled the moment completely. He did not send in the reserve. He halted the attack for the day. The next day the two armies watched each other, with neither one making a move. On the following day Lee retired from the field and started to move back into Virginia.

McClellan did not try to pursue the Confederates or to impede their retreat. He was more than satisfied to see them leave his front. He considered attacking the Confederates the day after the battle, but he decided it was too dangerous to renew the offensive without "absolute assurance" of success. The whole Union cause in the East rested on his army, he reasoned; and if he attacked and lost, the East would be at Lee's mercy. He was rationalizing his timidity. McClellan had been out of character at Antietam. He had done what he disliked to do: attack the enemy in the open field. He had attacked because he thought he was facing only a part of Lee's army. When he found that his attack was not succeeding and when he saw dead and wounded men falling all around him, he became his usual self again, cautious, fearful, inactive. His reason for not going after Lee was fallacious. Few generals in war are able to attack with absolute assurance of success. He must have known it was fallacious, because it was not the reason he gave the government for failure to move. To Halleck he complained that the troops were fatigued, that his supply trains were inadequate, that he did not have enough men— the familiar McClellan excuses for inaction.[6]

Never did McClellan give a better demonstration of his inability to see the realities of a situation than after Antietam. He really believed that he had won one of the greatest vic-

[6] McClellan's report, *ibid.*, XIX, pt. 1, 65–66; McClellan to Halleck, September 22, 1862, *ibid.*, pt. 2, 342–343; McClellan, *Own Story*, 618–620.

tories of all time. His admirers told him, and he believed them, that his conduct of the battle was a "masterpiece of art." [7] In his fatuous exaltation, he made a supreme mistake. He reported to the government that his victory was "complete." [8] It was not complete in any sense of the word. He should have said that he had attacked the enemy, that he held the field, that the Confederate invasion of Maryland had been repelled. The word complete meant to Lincoln and Halleck, as it would have to any sensible soldier or civilian, that the Confederate army was badly smashed up and that its existence would be ended when McClellan followed up his victory. That was the way Lincoln understood McClellan's despatch. The President happily announced the news of Antietam in a Cabinet meeting. At the end of the meeting, Lincoln, who undoubtedly had a personal fondness for McClellan, said to Postmaster General Blair: "I rejoice in this success for many public reasons but I am also happy on account of McClellan." [9] McClellan's definition of complete was different from Lincoln's, as the General revealed in another telegram to Halleck. As a result of his complete victory, said McClellan, the enemy was driven back to Virginia, and Maryland and Pennsylvania were safe.[1] McClellan thought that his triumph was complete because he had foiled the Confederate offensive. He had done all that he could do; he intended to go no farther. Lincoln naturally concluded that McClellan would follow up such a victory as he had reported with an attack that would end the war in the East.

[7] McClellan to Mrs. McClellan, September 18, 1862, *Own Story*, 612.

[8] McClellan to Halleck, September 19, 1862, *Official Records*, XIX, pt. 2, 330.

[9] Montgomery Blair to McClellan, September 19, 1862, McClellan MSS., Ser. 2. There are no quotation marks around Lincoln's statement in the letter.

[1] McClellan to Halleck, September 19, 1862, *Official Records*, XIX, pt. 2, 330.

McClellan was in such a cock-a-hoop mood at what he thought he had accomplished that he thought of himself as the indispensable man of the Union cause. He was ready to demand that the government meet certain conditions prescribed by him as the price for his continuation in service. He told his wife that he would resign unless Halleck and Stanton were removed from office and he was appointed general in chief. He had saved the country twice, he said, and now it was time for the country to help him a little by removing difficulties from his path.[2] A few days after Antietam, he was enraged when he learned that Lincoln had issued a proclamation freeing slaves in the states in rebellion. For months, Lincoln had considered promulgating such a document. He was waiting for a victory to be won by some general, so that the proclamation would have a favorable public reception. Antietam seemed to be a victory, and after the battle Lincoln issued the Emancipation Proclamation. Ironically, McClellan's report of a complete victory caused Lincoln to announce a policy on slavery that McClellan violently opposed. McClellan and his friends seemed to think that the head of the government had no right to adopt a policy of which they disapproved. Fitz John Porter called Lincoln a political coward who trifled with the lives of thousands of soldiers for political purposes. McClellan said that he would resign, because he would lose his self-respect if he served a government that supported emancipation.[3]

Some of his conservative supporters begged him to indorse the Proclamation. They pointed out that the destruction of slavery was an inevitable result of the war and that he would improve his chances for the presidency by approving emanci-

[2] McClellan to Mrs. McClellan, September 20, 1862, McClellan, *Own Story*, 613–614; Myers, *McClellan*, 362–363.

[3] Porter to Manton Marble, September 30, 1862, Marble MSS.; McClellan to Mrs. McClellan, September 25, McClellan, *Own Story*, 615.

pation.[4] McClellan did not know what course to follow. He invited a group of generals, several of whom had been politicians before the war, to dinner. During the meal, he asked them what he should do about the Proclamation. He said that a number of politicians and officers had urged him to oppose it openly. His guests advised him to make no declaration against it. He agreed that he should not, but he said that some people had told him that the whole army would follow him in opposition to the government's policy. The officers urged him to do nothing to influence the army against the government. McClellan then said that he would issue an order to the soldiers calling their attention to the Emancipation Proclamation and reminding them of their duties as citizens.

A few days later he published the order. He informed the troops that in a democracy the military was subordinate to the civil authority and that the objectives of the war were to be determined by the civil authority. Then came a sentence that must have aroused Lincoln's curiosity: "The remedy for political errors, if any are committed, is to be found only in the action of the people at the polls." [5] Although his enemies interpreted this as a bid for the Democratic presidential nomination, McClellan probably did not mean it that way. He undoubtedly hoped for a Democratic victory that would unseat the Republicans, but in issuing his order he thought that he was only doing his duty as a soldier. The revealing aspect of his action was his notion that he ought to give such an order to the army. In his egotism, he really believed that the army would follow him to a man if he resisted the Proclamation and that the soldiers would not accept it unless he asked them to. McClellan would never have led the army to over-

[4] Frank Blair, Sr., to McClellan, September 30, 1862, McClellan MSS., Ser. 1; Montgomery Blair to McClellan, no date, *ibid.*

[5] Cox, *Military Reminiscences*, I, 355–361; John Cochrane, *War for the Union,* 29–31; *Official Records,* XIX, pt. 2, 395–396.

throw the government, but he showed his weakness of character by believing that he could sway the army in any direction —for or against emancipation, for or against the government. Those people who feared that McClellan might be an American Cromwell need never have worried. He was not the stuff of which dictators are made.

In the weeks after Antietam, the government wanted to know from McClellan what his plans for future operations were. He replied vaguely that he needed time to reorganize the army and that eventually he would move against Lee, probably advancing up the Valley toward Winchester.[6] This was too vague for Lincoln. The President decided to go to McClellan's camp and to find out from the General in a personal conference if and when he intended to take the offensive.[7] Accompanied by a group of civilians and officers, Lincoln arrived October 1 and stayed for several days. To one reporter, the President looked thin, weary, and careworn. He was dressed in black and wore a tall silk hat. The troops cheered him enthusiastically whenever he appeared among them.[8] McClellan thought that Lincoln had come for the purpose of pushing him into a premature advance, and he was ready to be hostile. But he soon decided that the President felt kindly toward him personally. According to McClellan's account of the conversations between him and Lincoln, the President said that he was satisfied with McClellan's generalship and that the only fault he had to find was that McClellan had to have every detail right before he moved.[9]

[6] McClellan to Halleck, September 22, 23, 27, 1862, McClellan, *Own Story,* 624–626; Halleck to McClellan, September 26, *Official Records,* XIX, pt. 2, 359–360.

[7] Dennett, *Diary of Hay,* 218.

[8] Richardson, *Secret Service,* 291.

[9] McClellan, *Own Story,* 627–628, 654–655.

Lincoln said much more than that. He had made the trip to McClellan's headquarters to urge the General to advance, not to utter compliments. He told McClellan that it was necessary for him to strike a blow and chided him for his "overcautiousness." McClellan said that he would move at the earliest opportunity.[1] That Lincoln's feelings about McClellan were not as kindly or flattering as the General believed or affected to believe was evidenced by a story told by one of the civilians who went with the President to McClellan's camp. Early one morning, Lincoln left the tent, and walked with this man, an old Illinois friend, to a slight eminence. Looking out over the spreading expanse of army tents, Lincoln asked his friend if he knew what the sight before them was. The friend, surprised, said that it was the Army of the Potomac. Bitterly Lincoln replied: "So it is called, but that is a mistake; it is only McClellan's bodyguard." [2]

Lincoln knew McClellan too well to rely on any assurance from the General that he would advance at an early date. With McClellan, that might mean months hence or never. Right after the President returned to Washington, on October 6, Halleck transmitted to McClellan an order from Lincoln. The order directed McClellan to cross the Potomac while the roads were good and to fight the Confederates or drive them south. If he crossed the river between the Confederates and Washington and covered the capital as he advanced (that is, if he moved on the eastern side of the Blue Ridge), he would be reinforced by 30,000 men; if he moved up the Valley, by 12,000–15,000. Lincoln advised the first line of operation, but did not order it. McClellan was to report immediately which line he preferred and when he intended

---

[1] Lincoln to McClellan, October 13, 1862, *Works of Lincoln*, VIII, 57; Dennett, *Diary of Hay*, 218.

[2] Nicolay and Hay, *Lincoln*, VI, 175.

to cross the Potomac. McClellan replied that he would move into the Valley and defeat the Confederates at Winchester or compel them to abandon the Valley.[8]

With one of his typical outbursts of preliminary activity, McClellan started his preparations to advance. Then he discovered all kinds of reasons why he would have to delay moving. He did not have enough cavalry, his troops lacked supplies of all kinds, railroads and bridges had to be constructed in his rear and on his line of advance. Some of his excuses were valid. The army was short of some supplies, such as shoes and clothes, and McClellan had difficulty in getting many of his requisitions filled. But his pleas for more time to get ready would have sounded better if he had not advanced similar apologies in the past for his failure to act. Lincoln was getting increasingly impatient with his dallying general. When the President heard that the Confederate cavalry had ridden completely around the Union army, he got angry.[4] He sat down to write McClellan another long letter of advice. The theme of his letter was that McClellan magnified the obstacles facing him and assumed that he could not do what he admitted the enemy was doing all the time. "Should you not claim to be at least his equal in prowess, and act upon the claim?" asked Lincoln. He pointed out that McClellan was nearer to Richmond than the Confederates, most of whom were in the Valley. Why could not McClellan beat them to Richmond by moving east of the Blue Ridge, Lincoln queried, unless he admitted that the rebels could march better than the Union soldiers? "I say 'try'; if we never try, we shall never succeed," the President exhorted. "It is all

[8] Halleck to McClellan, October 6, 1862, *Works of Lincoln,* VIII, 53–54; McClellan to Halleck, October 7, *Official Records,* XIX, pt. 1, 11–12.

[4] John Nicolay to Therena Bates, October 13, 1862, Nicolay MSS.

easy if our troops march as well as the enemy, and it is unmanly to say they cannot do it." [5] Lincoln's letter threw McClellan into a depression. "Lincoln is down on me," he told a friend. He expected to be removed.[6] But he hastened to assure the President that he would move as soon as his men and cavalry were ready and that he would give Lincoln's views "the fullest & most unprejudiced consideration." [7]

The lack of cavalry was now McClellan's main reason for not advancing. He told Halleck that he needed more horses and asked if Lincoln desired him to cross the Potomac now in conformity with the order of October 6 or wait until the horses were secured. Halleck replied that Lincoln had no change to make in his order. But, added Halleck, if McClellan was not in condition to obey the order, he would be able to show his want of ability to execute it. The President did not expect impossibilities, Halleck said, but he was anxious that the good autumn weather should not be wasted in inactivity. Lincoln probably meant, if Halleck presented his thoughts accurately, that McClellan would not have to advance unless he was ready but that any claim of unreadiness would have to be supported by excellent evidence. McClellan interpreted Halleck's despatch to mean that he would not have to move until he judged that his cavalry was of adequate force. He fixed November 1 as the date for an advance.[8] At the same time, he changed his plan of operations. Instead of moving up the Valley, he decided to operate on a line east of the Blue Ridge. This was the line favored by Lincoln, and

[5] Lincoln to McClellan, October 13, 1862, *Works of Lincoln,* VIII, 57–61.

[6] *Battles and Leaders,* III, 105–106.

[7] McClellan to Lincoln, October 17, 1862, McClellan MSS., Ser. 1.

[8] McClellan to Halleck, and Halleck to McClellan, October 21, 1862, McClellan, *Own Story,* 641.

McClellan knew that he could get more reinforcements if he took it.[9]

McClellan was supposedly preparing to cross the Potomac, but most of his despatches to Washington were about the poor quality and inadequate number of his cavalry animals. Lincoln's patience gave way as he read the complaining documents. They sounded like another McClellan excuse for delay. In an acid telegram to the General, Lincoln said: "I have just read your despatches about sore-tongued and fatigued horses. Will you pardon me for asking what the horses of your army have done since the battle of Antietam that fatigues anything?"[1] One of the President's secretaries noted that his chief was getting increasingly critical of McClellan. As the secretary expressed it, Lincoln kept poking sharp sticks under McClellan's ribs.[2] The President had passed the point where he would accept any excuse for delay from McClellan. When the General said that he wanted to fill up some of his old regiments with recruits, Lincoln demanded that McClellan state distinctly if it was his purpose not to go into action until the regiments were enlarged. Hastily McClellan replied that a staff officer had made a mistake in transcribing the despatch.[3]

In his relations with McClellan, Lincoln was exercising functions that he had once wanted Halleck to perform. Old Brains was doing hardly anything. Refusing to accept any responsibility, he cast himself in the role of an interested and informed onlooker. When McClellan asked him for decisions, Halleck answered that he would provide suggestions and advice, but would give no orders. He said that Lincoln had left

[9] *Ibid.*, 643–646; *Official Records*, XIX, pt. 1, 83, 87; McClellan to Halleck, October 22, 1862, McClellan MSS., Ser. 1.

[1] Lincoln to McClellan, October 24 or 25, 1862, *Works of Lincoln*, VIII, 67.

[2] John G. Nicolay to John Hay, October 26, 1862, Nicolay MSS.

[3] Lincoln to McClellan, October 27, 1862, *Works of Lincoln*, VIII, 69–70.

McClellan free to adopt or to disregard the views of the general in chief and that McClellan could do as he pleased.[4]

By the first week in November, McClellan had crossed the Potomac. He made the crossing slowly, and slowly he advanced southward. By November 7, he had most of the army around Warrenton. That night a special courier from Washington arrived in camp with an order from Lincoln dated the fifth relieving McClellan from command and appointing Burnside in his place.[5] McClellan's war career was finished. He never received another assignment to duty.

Lincoln told many people why he removed McClellan. He explained his action more clearly and fully than in the case of any other general that he ousted. One word dominated everything that he said about McClellan—slow. McClellan had been too slow in getting to the field at Antietam, he had been too slow after Antietam, and he had been too slow in crossing the Potomac. When it took McClellan several days to cross a river that Lee had crossed in one, Lincoln said he decided that McClellan would never catch the Confederates, would never get to Richmond.[6] Old Frank Blair came to the White House to plead with Lincoln not to remove McClellan. Lincoln said that he had tried long enough to bore with an auger too dull to take hold. He got up from his chair, stretched, and said: "I said I would remove him if he let Lee's army get away from him, and I must do so. He has got the 'slows,' Mr. Blair."[7] Lincoln relieved McClellan out of a sense of duty to the country, but he did it with some reluctance and a little pain. He considered McClellan to be a good soldier in some respects, and he liked the General personally.

[4] Halleck to McClellan, October 26, 1862, *Official Records,* XIX, pt. 1, 84–85.

[5] *Works of Lincoln,* VIII, 72–73.

[6] Dennett, *Diary of Hay,* 218–219; Richardson, *Secret Service,* 323–324; Pease and Randall, *Diary of Browning,* 590.

[7] Smith, *Blair Family,* II, 144–145.

"He is an admirable engineer," Lincoln was supposed to have said of McClellan, "but he seems to have a special talent for a stationary engine." [8]

Lincoln ended McClellan's military career because he feared that the things McClellan stood for would lose the war and destroy the Union. In November a convention of women met in Washington to discuss ways and means to bring some of the comforts of home to the soldiers. A delegation from the conference called on Lincoln. One of them recalled later that Lincoln's face was rigid and ghastly, and that he seemed to be literally bending under his burdens. They asked him for a word of encouragement. He replied: "I have no word of encouragement to give." He said that the people and the officers of the army had not made up their minds that the country was in a terrible war. The officers, he said, thought that the war could be won by strategy. Hard, tough fighting would win it, he continued, not strategy. The army must be officered by fighting men. [9]

McClellan was not a fighting man. In Lincoln's mind, McClellan stood for strategy, preparation, delay, and at the best, barren victories. Lincoln thought that the country could no longer afford a general like McClellan.

[8] John G. Nicolay to Therena Bates, November 9, 1862, Nicolay MSS.; Arnold, *Lincoln*, 300.

[9] Mary A. Livermore, *My Story of the War*, 555–560.

Chapter 8

Lincoln Chooses New Generals

It was beginning to snow when General C. P. Buckingham, staff officer of the War Department, arrived in camp with the order for McClellan's removal and Burnside's appointment. Buckingham had been instructed by Stanton to see Burnside first and offer him the command. If Burnside refused it, Buckingham was to return to Washington without seeing McClellan. Buckingham got off the special train that had brought him from Washington and went miles through the driving snow to find Burnside. Burnside at first declined the command. He said that he was not competent to direct a large army and that he did not want to displace his friend McClellan. Buckingham replied that if Burnside did not take the command, it would be offered to Joseph Hooker, another corps general, whom Burnside disliked. Burnside then said that he would like to think the matter over and consult with some of his staff officers. After talking with his staff for an hour and a half, Burnside informed Buckingham that he would accept the appointment. Burnside and Buckingham then went to McClellan's headquarters, where they arrived at eleven o'clock that night. Buckingham produced the order of removal. McClellan, always the gentleman, advised Burnside to take the command and said that he would furnish

Burnside with all the information he had about the condition of the army. The snowstorm was getting worse.[1]

People could not help liking Ambrose E. Burnside. His
smile was charming, his manner was hearty, and his ways
were winning. He cast a spell over most people when he met
them. He was a handsome and striking figure of a man. About
six feet in height, he was big in build. His large face was
surrounded by heavy whiskers, which were almost the trade-
mark of his appearance. In his dress, he was studiedly careless and informal. He liked to wear an undress uniform and
a fatigue cap. When he rode before the troops, he wore large
buckskin gauntlets and a loose pistol belt that allowed his
holster to swing at his hip. He seemed dashing and brave, and
he was. He also seemed to be very intelligent, but he was not.
One keen observer said: You have to know Burnside some
time before you realize there is not much behind his showy
front. This was unjust. Burnside was an honest and a humble
man. He was a good subordinate general. But he did not
have the brains to command a large army. He had been right
when he had twice before refused the command because he
doubted his ability.[2]

Why did Lincoln choose a man of incompetence to head
the Army of the Potomac? When he appointed Burnside, Lincoln had no reason to think that the General lacked competence. Burnside had a good record. Early in 1862 he had
commanded a small army operating on the coast of North Carolina, and he had won the objectives of his campaign. Lincoln generally tended to pick as commanders men who had

[1] Stine, *Army of the Potomac*, 241–242; *C. C. W., Reports*, 1863, I,
650; *Battles and Leaders*, III, 106; D. R. Larned to Mrs. A. E. Burnside,
November 9, 1862, Larned MSS.; McClellan, *Own Story*, 651–652.

[2] Cox, *Military Reminiscences*, I, 389–390; Francis Winthrop Palfrey, *The Antietam and Fredericksburg*, 54–55; D. R. Larned to Henry
Larned, December 21, 1861, Larned MSS.; Charles A. Dana, *Recollections of the Civil War*, 138; George Meade, *Life and Letters of George
Gordon Meade*, I, 304.

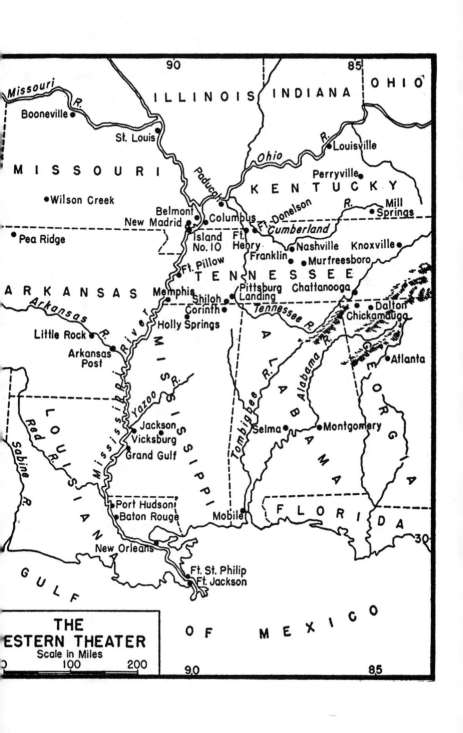

THE
ESTERN THEATER

Scale in Miles

accomplished something in an independent capacity. Burnside had done well in North Carolina, and Lincoln thought well of him for it. When the President had considered displacing McClellan in the summer and right before Antietam, he had offered the command to Burnside. As a corps commander under McClellan, Burnside had the reputation of being a fighting general who handled his men well. Lincoln wanted McClellan's successor to come from the Eastern army. By all odds, Burnside seemed the best choice among the corps generals. The other possibilities were E. V. Sumner, who was old and not in too good health; William B. Franklin, who was dominated by McClellan; and Hooker, who was junior in rank to Burnside and hostile to McClellan. Lincoln did not want to appoint a commander who might be manipulated by McClellan or who would act like McClellan. And for reasons of army morale, he did not want to appoint one who was an open enemy of the idolized "little Mac." Burnside was an ideal compromise. He was known to be a friend to McClellan but not to be under McClellan's control. He had stayed clear of the fight between McClellan and Pope and their supporters, which was another point in his favor. Actually, the once friendly relations between McClellan and Burnside had cooled, although probably Lincoln did not know it. McClellan blamed Burnside for the failure to carry the Confederate right at Antietam; he had refused to see "Burn" the night after the battle and had ignored him most of the time since.[8]

Right before he removed McClellan, Lincoln got rid of another general who had the "slows." Don Carlos Buell got the ax late in October. In September, the Confederate army at Chattanooga suddenly invaded Kentucky. Buell, in order to protect Kentucky and his base at Louisville, had to leave Tennessee and march back to the Ohio River. His retrograde

[8] D. R. Larned to Henry Larned, October 4, 1862, Larned MSS.

movement, coming after his slow advance on Chattanooga and his failure to take it, angered Lincoln and Stanton. The Secretary induced Lincoln to approve an order relieving Buell from command and appointing General George H. Thomas, then serving under Buell, as his successor. A special courier started west with the order, with instructions not to deliver it if Buell was about to fight the Confederates or had won a victory. Halleck, who still believed in Buell, persuaded the President that Buell should be given a chance to fight the Kentucky campaign. Halleck then telegraphed the courier, who was on his way to Buell's army, not to deliver the order, but the messenger did not receive the telegrams. He reached Buell's headquarters and gave the order to Buell, who promptly turned over the command to Thomas. Thomas did not want to take it. He informed Halleck that Buell was ready to attack the enemy and should be retained in command. Halleck replied that the removal order had not been made by him or on his advice and was now suspended by Lincoln's authority.[4]

Buell now had a chance to save himself, but he muffed his opportunity. In October he fought a drawn battle with the Confederates at Perryville. After the battle, the Confederates retired to Tennessee. Buell followed them slowly for a distance and then announced that he would go back to Nashville and prepare to resume his advance on Chattanooga. To Lincoln, the escape of the enemy army and Buell's apparent purpose to move against Chattanooga only after a long period of reorganization seemed like Antietam repeated. He thought that Buell should strike immediately for Chattanooga or Knox-

[4] Order of September 24, 1862, *Official Records*, XVI, pt. 2, 538–539; Halleck to Buell, September 27, *ibid.*, 549; Halleck, to Colonel J. C. McKibben, the courier, September 27, 29, *ibid.*, 549, 554; Buell to Halleck, September 29, and Thomas to Halleck, September 29, *ibid.*, 555; Halleck to Thomas, September 29, and to Buell and Thomas, September 29, *ibid.*, 555; Stanton to David Tod, October 30, *ibid.*, 652.

ville.[5] The President sent Buell an order, through Halleck, that the Federal army must enter East Tennessee before the end of autumn and that it ought to move while the roads were passable. Expressing Lincoln's thoughts accurately, Halleck said: "He does not understand why we cannot march as the enemy marches, live as he lives, and fight as he fights, unless we admit the inferiority of our troops and our generals." [6] Why can't we do what the enemy can do? This was the question Lincoln had asked McClellan in his letter of October 13, using much the same words that he now addressed to Buell. The President was determined to get the answer to the question. His patience was worn out with generals who never fought because they never finished preparing. Such generals he intended to remove from the army.

Buell wanted to prepare some more before he fought. He insisted that the best way to secure East Tennessee was to operate on a line from Nashville. He was right. A Federal army in East Tennessee would have supply difficulties unless it controlled a railroad to the outside. The railroad from Nashville to Chattanooga was the logical line of advance for Buell's army. The trouble with Buell was that he did not seem to sense any need for any celerity in movement on any line. Halleck told Buell that neither the country nor the government could stand repeated delay in both the Eastern and Western theaters.[7] Buell was not impressed. He did not offer to attempt an advance on one of the lines suggested by Lincoln and Halleck. He said only that he was going back to Nashville and start all over again—after he was prepared. Lincoln thought that the country could not afford to wait for

[5] Buell to Halleck, October 16, 1862, *ibid.,* XVI, pt. 2, 619; Halleck to Buell, October 18, *ibid.,* 623.

[6] Halleck to Buell, October 19, 1862, *Works of Lincoln,* VIII, 63–64.

[7] Halleck to Buell, October 23, 1862, *Official Records,* XVI, pt. 2, 638.

Buell. On October 23, orders were prepared relieving Buell and appointing General William S. Rosecrans as commander of the Department of the Cumberland. Rosecrans was serving under Grant at Corinth and did not reach Louisville to assume the command until the thirtieth.[8]

William S. Rosecrans was a graduate of West Point, and for twelve years he had been an officer in the regular army. Like so many officers before the war, he had resigned from the army to take a civilian job that paid more money. When the war started, he secured a commission and served first under McClellan in western Virginia and later under Pope and Halleck in the West. After Halleck went to Washington, Rosecrans transferred to Grant's army. As a subordinate officer in Grant's department, Rosecrans led the Union forces in the minor battles of Iuka and Corinth. He had a semi-independent status in these engagements, which were considered Union victories, and his actions in them probably brought him to the attention of Lincoln, always on the alert to find a general who could do something in an independent capacity.

After the President decided to remove Buell, the question of who should succeed the General came up at a Cabinet meeting. Secretary of the Treasury Chase proposed Rosecrans, like Chase a resident of Ohio; Halleck also indorsed Rosecrans. Stanton, who disliked Rosecrans personally, put forward the name of Thomas, whom he admired. Lincoln decided on Rosecrans. He may have thought that Thomas, having declined the command once, would again; or he may have felt that it was unwise to replace Buell, a native of Kentucky, with another Southern-born general, Thomas of Virginia. "Let

[8] Halleck to Rosecrans, October 23, 24, 1862, *ibid.*, XVI, pt. 2, 639, 640–642; Buell to Halleck, October 29, *ibid.*, 651; Rosecrans' proclamation on taking command, *ibid.*, 655.

the Virginian wait," Lincoln was supposed to have said.[9] He undoubtedly did not say it. He probably chose Rosecrans over Thomas because he thought Rosecrans had had more command experience than Thomas. And Rosecrans was supposed to be what Lincoln was looking for then in commanders, a fighting general.

Old Rosy, as the troops called Rosecrans, was a fascinating personality. He was tall and strongly built. His hair and whiskers were blond, and his complexion florid. He had what one observer called "an intensified Roman nose." In his speech, he was rapid, excited, and dogmatic. He could get quickly and terribly angry at his generals and staff officers, and just as quickly he would become all smiles and stroke the recipients of his irritation with caressing gestures.[1] He had enough quirks in his character to make him interesting. He was a hard worker and wanted officers on his staff who would work. He preferred "sandy fellows" because they were "quick and sharp" and more industrious than brunettes. He could not judge between what was important and what was not. He would spend as much time discussing a small matter with a sergeant as a big one with a major general. He was a convert to Catholicism, and an ardent one. He carried a cross on his watch seal and a rosary in his watch pocket. He loved to discuss religion, and frequently kept his staff up until four in the morning for as long as ten nights running to talk about spiritual matters. After a night of such conversation, the commanding general would often sleep until noon. Rosecrans liked to swear but squared this with his religion by saying he never

[9] Piatt, *Memories of the Men Who Saved the Union*, 81; Freeman Cleaves, *Rock of Chickamauga: The Life of General George H. Thomas*, 117–118; *Official Records*, XXIII, pt. 2, 552.

[1] Dennett, *Diary of Hay*, 188; Ford, *Memoirs of a Volunteer*, 175–177; Cox, *Military Reminiscences*, I, 111–112; Richardson, *Secret Service*, 335–336.

used the name of God. He had a distinction, which he delighted to expound on, between profanity and blasphemy. He was a heavy consumer of whiskey, but he never produced a rationalization for his drinking.[2] As a general, Rosecrans had a good strategic sense and aggressive instincts. But he lacked the balance and poise that a great commander should possess. At a critical moment, he was likely to be overcome by excitement and lose control of himself and the situation. This weakness would destroy him at the crisis of his career.

In the same period when he removed McClellan and Buell, Lincoln changed commanders in another important theater of the war. He appointed General Nathaniel P. Banks to command the Department of the Gulf, with headquarters in New Orleans. Banks succeeded Benjamin F. Butler. Lincoln had been deeply interested in New Orleans as a base for operations on the Mississippi line ever since the naval officer, Porter, had suggested to him in 1861 that the city could be taken. The President had instructed McClellan to confer with the Navy and to draw up a plan for a combined land and naval attack on New Orleans. The plan was formulated while McClellan was general in chief, but the movement against the city was made after he left the office. In the spring of 1862, a naval expedition, accompanied by a small army commanded by Butler, sailed to the Gulf and up the Mississippi, and forced the surrender of New Orleans. Lincoln had expected that the expedition would be able to ascend the Mississippi and clear the river all the way to Vicksburg and above. But the Vicksburg defences turned out to be too strong for the Navy to deal with, and Butler's army was too small to give the Navy any assistance. The Federals had

2 W[illiam] O. B[ickham], *Rosecrans' Campaign with the Fourteenth Army Corps*, 28–29, 143; Theodore C. Smith, *Life and Letters of James A. Garfield*, 271–274; General John Palmer to Lyman Trumbull, January 11, 1863, Trumbull MSS.

New Orleans and a strip of territory around it, but that was all. They had a base, but they could not go far beyond it.

Even if the Federal army had been larger, it could not have done much because of the lack of competence of its commander. Butler was a Massachusetts politician who had received a commission because he was an important Democrat. He was ingenious, resourceful, and colorful, but he was no field general. His chief military talent was in administration. He managed occupied New Orleans sternly, and on the whole, efficiently. In the process, he offended many people, especially the foreign consuls, most of whom he regarded and treated as Confederate agents. The governments of various European countries protested bitterly to Washington at Butler's treatment of their representatives, and Lincoln would have had to remove him to prevent an international incident, if for no other reason. But Lincoln had a military reason for displacing Butler. The President decided to send additional forces to Louisiana. He wanted to make the army in the Gulf Department strong enough to go up the river to Vicksburg and to occupy a larger area of Louisiana. Rightly he distrusted Butler's ability to command an expedition of the magnitude of the one he had in mind. Why he thought Banks could command it is a mystery. Banks was no better than Butler. He was another Massachusetts politician turned warrior. It was true that Banks had had combat experience in the Eastern theater and had exercised an independent command in the Valley, but he had shown no great skill in anything that he had done. He was a willing, aggressive fighter but a poor handler of troops; he had not demonstrated that he possessed the ability to manage a large department. The appointment of Banks was a case of Lincoln misreading his man.

Lincoln told Halleck what he wanted Banks to do in Louisiana. Halleck put the instructions in military form for

Banks. The document showed Lincoln's increasing stature as a strategist. The President regarded the opening of the Mississippi as the first and most important of all the Federal military operations, said Halleck, and Banks was not to lose a moment in accomplishing this objective. Specifically, Banks was to move up the Mississippi toward Vicksburg; another expedition would descend the river to cooperate with him. Together they were to reduce Vicksburg and other Confederate strong points. After the Mississippi line was secured, Lincoln hoped that Banks would be able to move into north Louisiana along Red River, and ultimately advance into Texas.[8]

Banks talked confidently to Lincoln about getting his expedition off for Louisiana at an early date. Weeks went by, and he was still in Washington. Then Lincoln was shown a requisition signed by Banks calling for a tremendous amount of supplies and a large number of horses. It was almost more than Lincoln could stand. Here was a civilian general acting like the worst of the professionals: delaying action until he could accumulate more than enough of everything. Lincoln sat down and wrote a positive letter to the man who was often called, for his initials, Nothing Positive Banks.

In the letter, Lincoln showed that he knew why the Federals lacked the mobility of the Confederates, why Federal armies had the weakness in movement that he had complained of to McClellan and Buell. The Federal armies moved more slowly than the enemy because every Federal commander insisted on gathering huge supplies before he advanced; then he had to get horses and wagons to haul the supplies; then he had to get forage for the horses; then he had to get extra-duty men to take care of the supplies and the animals. The Federal armies were bogged down in the plenitude

[8] Halleck to Banks, November 9, 1862, *Official Records*, XV, 590–591.

of their own supplies. "My dear general," said Lincoln to Banks, "this expanding and piling up of *impedimenta* has been, so far, almost our ruin, and will be our final ruin if it is not abandoned." The requisition could not be filled in a shorter period than two months, said Lincoln, and it would take another month to find enough vessels to carry the supplies and to put the supplies aboard. Go back to your original plan, he exhorted, and get off to Louisiana right away: "You would be better off anywhere, and especially where you are going, for not having a thousand wagons doing nothing but hauling forage to feed the animals that draw them and taking at least two thousand men to care for the wagons and animals, who otherwise might be two thousand good soldiers." Banks weakly replied in a letter that was a measure of the man that the requisition had been drawn up by officers who had not understood his instructions and had been signed by him without close examination.[4]

Lincoln was planning other moves to secure control of the Mississippi line. Halleck had told Banks that a land and naval expedition would come down the river to aid the Army of the Gulf in attacking Vicksburg. This second offensive had been designed largely by the President; Halleck knew little about it. Lincoln's strategic thinking about the necessity of occupying the Mississippi line was excellent, but his strategic plan would produce no results because he selected incompetent commanders to lead both expeditions. The army coming down the river was to be commanded by General John A. McClernand, who was as poor a general as Banks. McClernand was an Illinois politician, a prominent Democrat, turned general. At the beginning of the war, Lincoln had given McClernand a commission in order to draw him and his political followers to the support of the war effort. McCler-

---

[4] Lincoln to Banks, November 22, 1862, *Works of Lincoln*, VIII, 81–83; Banks to Lincoln, November 24, Lincoln MSS., vol. 93.

nand had served in the West under Grant. He was brave and aggressive, but he did not know how to handle troops in the field. He was vain, intriguing, and extremely ambitious. He wrote frequent unofficial letters to Lincoln in which he criticized Grant and other of his superior officers and claimed most of the credit for the victories in the West. Always, he pressed Lincoln to give him an independent command.[5]

In September, he came to Washington on leave. He laid before Lincoln a plan to capture Vicksburg and occupy the whole river line. An army, to be commanded by him, would descend the Mississippi and seize Vicksburg and other points.[6] McClernand claimed that he could go to the Middle West and raise among his political supporters a force large enough to accomplish the objective of his proposed expedition. He was asking for an independent command, and he asked at an opportune moment and put his proposition in a form that tempted Lincoln. The President was planning to send Banks to Louisiana and up the river against Vicksburg and to despatch a naval squadron under Admiral Porter downstream to operate against the Confederate fortress. Now here was McClernand, supposedly a successful general and fresh from triumphs in the West, offering to raise a new army for service on the Mississippi and an army made up of Democrats, the people that Lincoln anxiously wanted to attract to the support of the war.

McClernand's plan looked good to the President politically and militarily. If McClernand could enlist his levies, Lincoln saw the possibility of a great pincers movement by Banks and McClernand on Vicksburg. The President told Porter that a land force would accompany the naval expedition and that

[5] McClernand to Lincoln, January 28, February 8, March 31, June 20, 1862, Lincoln MSS., vols. 67, 68, 72, 78; McClernand to Lincoln, February 27, Nicolay MSS.

[6] McClernand to Lincoln, September 28, 1862, *Official Records*, XVII, pt. 2, 849–853.

McClernand would command it. According to Porter's later account, Lincoln said that McClernand was a better general than Grant. Porter habitually exaggerated what people said, and he undoubtedly exaggerated Lincoln's statement. But the President did believe that McClernand was an able officer. He told Secretary Chase that McClernand was brave and capable, albeit too desirous to be independent of everybody else.[7]

Lincoln decided in late October to give McClernand the command of the river expedition. An order was drawn authorizing McClernand to raise a special force to operate against Vicksburg. Stanton composed the order; Halleck was not consulted. The order stated that McClernand was to gather his force and take it to Memphis or some other point on the river. Memphis was in Grant's department. So, presumably, was Vicksburg. In loose and vague language, the order directed that when a sufficient force not required by operations in Grant's command was organized, an expedition under McClernand could be started against Vicksburg. Lincoln indorsed on the order that he was deeply interested in McClernand's project and wanted it pushed forward.[8] For some reason, Lincoln and Stanton told Halleck nothing about McClernand's proposed movement. As late as December, the general in chief knew only that a special expedition on the Mississippi was being prepared, but he did not know who its commander was or what instructions had been given him.[9]

The organization of the McClernand offensive was a wretched mistake and a prize example of poor military planning. Stanton's order embodied everything that was wrong in a military directive. The President and the Secretary of War had planned an important strategic movement, had prepared

[7] Welles, *Diary*, I, 386–387; Porter, *Incidents and Anecdotes*, 122–123; *Diary of Chase, American Historical Association Rept.*, 97, 103.

[8] Order of October 21, 1862, *Official Records*, XVII, pt. 2, 282, 502.

[9] Halleck to General S. R. Curtis, December 12, 1862, *ibid.*, XVII, pt. 2, 402.

an army to execute it, and had named a commander to lead the army without even telling the general in chief what they were doing. Now they were going to send their expedition into the department of another commander without telling him what their plans were or what his authority, if any, over the expedition was. Grant first learned of McClernand's proposed movement from rumors in newspaper stories. Nobody could have told from reading Stanton's sloppy order whether McClernand was under Grant's command or was independent. McClernand understood that he had an independent command, but the order could be interpreted to mean that he was subject to Grant's control. To increase the chances for confusion, the government could not decide whose department Vicksburg was in. Grant's department included west Tennessee and north Mississippi, and he thought that Vicksburg was in his province.[1] But Halleck, in transmitting to Banks Lincoln's instructions for operating on the Mississippi line, told Banks that for the present the limits between his department and Grant's were being left undefined. Halleck authorized Banks to take command of everything as far up the river as he ascended, which meant Vicksburg and other points in Grant's department.[2]

The most surprising feature in Lincoln's strategic plan to seize the Mississippi line, and the part of it most open to criticism, was his failure to make any use of Grant. The best general in the West was left doing nothing but guarding communication lines near the river. Why Lincoln passed over Grant and selected two incompetents to accomplish one of the most important objectives of Union strategy is hard to explain. There may be significance in the fact that he chose two civilian generals with political backgrounds for the Mississippi mission. Perhaps he was looking ahead to the problem

[1] *Ibid.*, XVII, pt. 2, 278.
[2] *Ibid.*, XV, 590–591.

of establishing military government for occupied areas along the river, and judged that civilian generals would make better administrators than professionals; or he may have felt that officers accustomed to making political appeals would be able to raise large numbers of troops from among the freed slaves. Maybe he was so disgusted by the excuses for inaction presented by professional soldiers that he decided as an experiment to entrust the direction of a big campaign to a couple of amateurs. This would explain why he told Halleck nothing about McClernand's expedition. He knew that Halleck, the epitome of professionalism, would object to an officer of McClernand's type leading an important offensive. More probably, the autumn of 1862 was simply a period when Lincoln's powers of human evaluation were not as sharp as usual. It was his bad time, his time to pick poor generals.

One of Lincoln's new generals, Burnside, was in a state of nervous depression for days after his appointment. Convinced that he was not competent to head a large army, Burnside fretted, drove himself to long hours of work, went almost without sleep, and became physically ill.[3] He knew that he had been put in command because the government wanted offensive action during the autumn months and that he would be expected to produce a plan for an advance on Richmond. So he prepared one immediately and sent it to Halleck. He proposed to stop operating on the line east of the Blue Ridge, the line McClellan had adopted at Lincoln's strong suggestion, and to shift the army eastward to Fredericksburg on the Rappahannock and to move from there against Richmond.[4]

Halleck did not like Burnside's scheme, and he knew that Lincoln would not like it. Old Brains decided that he had

[3] D. R. Larned to H. L. Larned, November 22, 1862, Larned MSS.; General John Cochrane to Lincoln, November 14, Lincoln MSS., vol. 92; Howard, *Autobiography*, I, 314.

[4] Burnside to Halleck, November 7, 1862, *Official Records*, XIX, pt. 2, 552–554.

better go down to Burnside's headquarters at Warrenton and discuss strategic moves personally with "Burn." Halleck arrived on November 12 and returned to Washington the next day. What was said and determined in the long hours of conference between Halleck and Burnside is something of a mystery. In their reports, they gave contradictory accounts of the conversations. Halleck understood from Burnside's written plan that Burnside intended to move down the north bank of the Rappahannock to Falmouth and cross to Fredericksburg on the south side, although Burnside had not said specifically which bank he intended to advance on. The general in chief urged Burnside to continue operations on the Blue Ridge line; Burnside stubbornly insisted on going to the Rappahannock. According to Halleck, Burnside then agreed to modify his original plan and move down the south bank. Halleck refused to approve the changed plan but said he would submit it to Lincoln. In Burnside's account, he said that he wanted to go down the north bank to Falmouth and that Halleck disapproved, but offered to lay the plan before Lincoln for a decision. At some point in the discussion, the two generals misunderstood each other completely. Burnside admitted that he had said to Halleck that he might cross part of the army at the upper fords of the Rappahannock and march it down the south bank. Halleck may not have heard Burnside clearly, or he may have been so tired that he did not grasp what Burnside was saying.

At any rate, Halleck went back to Washington and informed Lincoln that Burnside proposed to take the army to Fredericksburg and then to strike for Richmond.[5] Lincoln was not enthusiastic about Burnside's scheme. As Halleck described Lincoln's reaction, he assented to the plan but did not approve it. Halleck telegraphed Burnside that the President

---

[5] Halleck's report, *ibid.*, XXI, 46–47; Burnside's report, *ibid.*, 83–85; C. C. W., *Reports*, 1863, I, 674.

consented to the movement to Fredericksburg but that Lincoln thought that it would succeed only if Burnside moved rapidly.[6]

Lincoln's diagnosis of Burnside's plan was exactly and completely right. Burnside would have to move fast to win. His best, almost his only, chance to accomplish his objective was to get across the Rappahannock and to be on the way to Richmond before the Confederate army, a part of it then in the Valley and a part east of the Blue Ridge, could shift east to confront him. But Burnside's movement was not conducted rapidly, although most of the fault for its slowness was not the General's. Burnside started his advance promptly enough. He marched down the north side of the river to Falmouth. He could have seized Fredericksburg immediately, and should have done so, but he did not want to cross the river until he got pontoon bridges to establish a secure connection between his troops on both banks.

Burnside expected to find bridges waiting for him at Falmouth. He had told Halleck that he would need pontoons, and Old Brains had issued directions to send a large number of them to Falmouth. But they were not there when Burnside arrived and were not delivered until eight days later. Burnside foolishly held back his crossing until the bridges came. The delay was sufficient to give Lee time to move his army to Fredericksburg. Halleck was largely to blame for the failure to have the pontoons ready. He made little effort to follow up his directions and to find out if they were being executed. He probably did not think the bridges were very important. Understanding as he did that Burnside intended to move along the south side of the river, he naturally concluded that Burnside would have no urgent need for pon-

---

[6] Halleck to Burnside, November 14, 1862, *Official Records,* XIX, pt. 2, 579.

toons at Falmouth.[7] The whole episode showed that there was something badly wrong with the command system or with the humans running it. If the general in chief and a field general who was only a few miles from Washington could not get together on a simple matter like bridges, they were not likely to be able to plan and carry out a campaign of any magnitude.

Lincoln was distressed as he watched what seemed to him the slow progress of Burnside. The President undoubtedly did not know about the delay in the delivery of the bridges. He saw only that Burnside seemed to be as slow as McClellan. Almost a month had passed since Burnside had assumed command, and the Union army was still on the north side of the Rappahannock. Worse than that, Lee had been given time to move to Fredericksburg and was now in position to dispute any attempted crossing of the river by Burnside. Lincoln's new generals did not seem to be any better than the old ones. The President confided to a friend that he had removed McClellan and Buell because of their slowness, but that he had had great fears that he would not find successors who were faster. ". . . I am sorry to add," he said, "that I have seen little since to relieve those fears." [8]

When Lincoln was dissatisfied with a general, he liked to see the officer personally, if that was possible, so that in face to face discussion he could find out what was wrong. So now, perturbed by Burnside's inaction, he decided to have an interview with the General. He asked Burnside to meet him at Acquia Creek. Lincoln made the trip down by water. Probably he went to see Burnside instead of asking Burnside to come to him because he did not want to take the General too

[7] *Ibid.*, XXI, 148–149, 793–795, 799–800.

[8] Lincoln to Carl Schurz, November 24, 1862, *Works of Lincoln*, VIII, 85.

far away from his army. He and Burnside met on November 26, and on the next day Burnside went to Washington to confer further with the President and Halleck.[9]

What was said and determined at these conferences was never fully revealed. At Washington, Lincoln submitted in writing to Halleck and Burnside a proposed plan of operations for Burnside's army. The President grasped the essential fact in Burnside's situation: that the enemy army at Fredericksburg could make Burnside's crossing of the river dangerous if not impossible. Lincoln proposed to protect the crossing by having two subordinate forces operate on the Confederate line of communications south of the Rappahannock at the same time that Burnside attacked at Fredericksburg. One force was to be moved up the river to a point on the south bank and another was to be moved up the Pamunkey River, which was south of the Rappahannock. Lincoln's plan was a bold one, and it would have employed sea power, the one weapon in which at that time the Union was clearly superior to the South. But Halleck and Burnside ruled the plan out because they said it would take too much time to raise and put in position the Pamunkey force.[1]

Later Burnside's friends, but not Burnside, would say that he advised Lincoln that the army ought to go into winter quarters without undertaking an advance but that the President urged him to start an early offensive.[2] There is no evidence for this claim on behalf of Burnside's intelligence. Undoubtedly Lincoln did tell, but not order, Burnside to cross the Rappahannock and attack the enemy if the weather was

[9] Lincoln to Burnside, November 25, 1862, *ibid.*, VIII, 87; Burnside to Lincoln, November 25, *Official Records*, XXI, 798; D. R. Larned to Amelia Larned, November 27, Larned MSS.; John G. Nicolay to Therena Bates, November 27, Nicolay MSS.

[1] Lincoln to Halleck, November 27, 1862, *Works of Lincoln*, VIII, 88–90.

[2] Poore, *Burnside*, 186.

good and if the General thought he had a fair chance to succeed. Burnside had informed Lincoln that he thought he could force a crossing at Fredericksburg but that the attempt would be "somewhat risky."[3] After Burnside rejected Lincoln's plan, the President probably told the General to use his own judgment about when and where to attack.

Burnside determined to cross at Fredericksburg early in December and fight a decisive battle with the Confederate army. His decision was bad. Even if he got his army over the river, he would have to attack the Confederates on grounds of their choosing and where they had nearly every advantage. The terrain around Fredericksburg was a natural defensive position, and the Confederates had increased its strength with field fortifications. So strong was the Confederate line that Lee did not seriously oppose Burnside's crossing. The Confederate commander wanted the Union army to get across and dash itself to pieces in attacks on his works. Burnside was walking into a military trap. He crossed his army, and on December 13 fought the bloody battle of Fredericksburg. His one slim chance of victory was to break the Confederate line at some point with an assault in depth. But he did not commit his troops in massive numbers at any point. Rather he sent them in in what almost might be called piecemeal attacks. Every Union attack was repulsed with heavy losses. At the end of the day, over 12,000 Union troops were killed, wounded, or missing.

Before the battle, Burnside was in a state of nervous depression. He seemed to doubt himself and his plan. He knew that others doubted him. Many of his officers, notably Hooker, openly criticized his generalship.[4] After the battle, he broke down almost completely. One general found him in

[3] *Works of Lincoln*, VIII, 88.
[4] Howard, *Autobiography*, I, 321; MS. notes by D. R. Larned, Burnside's secretary, December 13, 1862, Larned MSS.

his tent convulsed by agony. "Oh! oh those men! oh, those men!" he cried. He pointed over the river: "Those men over there! I am thinking of them all the time." [5] He talked wildly about leading his old corps in a suicidal charge, but his officers talked him out of the idea. He convinced himself that his principal officers were opposed to him and had disobeyed his orders. He could whip the enemy if he had reliable generals, he declared, but lacking them he would have to give up and retire to the north side of the Rappahannock. He cried when he gave the order to recross the river.[6]

Lincoln's thoughts and actions during the battle are not known. He undoubtedly followed its course with his usual anxious interest. Maybe he did not expect too much from Burnside's movement. After the battle, he told a friend that he was troubled about the army and did not know what would become of it: it had fought the enemy over the river, had gained nothing, and could not advance or stay where it was. His chief worry was whether Burnside could withdraw to the north bank in the face of a victorious foe. When Halleck assured him that Burnside could retire safely, Lincoln said: "What you say gives me a great many grains of comfort." [7] Even though Lincoln had fretted about Burnside's ability to recross, he asked the General to state formally his reasons for withdrawing. Burnside replied that he could not carry the enemy positions and that he had to attack or retire. He said that for the failure of the attack he was responsible.[8]

Burnside was willing to shoulder all public responsibility for the defeat. A few days after the battle, he heard that the

[5] *Battles and Leaders,* III, 138.

[6] MS. notes by D. R. Larned, December 14, 15, 1862, and D. R. Larned to Henry Larned, December 16, Larned MSS.; General W. B. Franklin to G. B. McClellan, December 23, 1862, McClellan MSS., Ser. 1.

[7] Pease and Randall, *Diary of Browning,* I, 596, December 15, 1862; Haupt, *Reminiscences,* 176–177.

[8] Halleck to Burnside, December 16, 1862, and Burnside to Halleck, December 16, 17, *Official Records,* XXI, 65–67.

government was being criticized for making him fight at Fredericksburg against his will. He telegraphed Lincoln for permission to come to Washington, and Lincoln granted it.[9] Burnside arrived in the capital at ten o'clock on a Saturday night. He went to a hotel, and sent his secretary to the White House to inquire if Lincoln would see him then or the next morning. The secretary found Lincoln in bed but unable to sleep because of dyspepsia. The President said he would pull on his "breeches" and see Burnside at once.[1] Burnside then went to the White House. He told Lincoln that he would publish a letter taking all the blame for Fredericksburg. Lincoln was relieved and pleased. He said that Burnside was the first general he had found who was willing to relieve him of a particle of responsibility.[2]

Most of Burnside's officers would have agreed that he was responsible for the disaster at Fredericksburg and that he ought to bear the blame. In fact, they thought he should be removed from command. They had believed he was incompetent when he was appointed; now they were bitterly convinced he was too dangerous to be retained. Several of them were so inflamed against Burnside that they went directly to Lincoln with criticism of their superior. First, Generals Franklin and W. F. Smith wrote to Lincoln, saying that the present plan of operating on the Fredericksburg line was impractical and proposing that the army move on the James River line, essentially a return to the Peninsula scheme. Lincoln replied politely that he had read their letter hastily and would submit it to his military advisers, but that he disliked the idea of going to the James.[3]

[9] Burnside to Lincoln, December 19, 20, 1862, Lincoln MSS., vol. 96; Lincoln to Burnside, December 19, *Official Records*, XXI, 866.

[1] D. R. Larned to Amelia Larned, December 23, 1862, Larned MSS.

[2] Henry W. Raymond (ed.), "Excerpts from the Journal of Henry J. Raymond," *Scribner's Monthly*, XIX, 1879, 424.

[3] W. B. Franklin and W. F. Smith to Lincoln, December 20, 1862,

The President must have been mildly astonished that two of Burnside's subordinates would communicate directly with him over their chief's head about proposed movements, but more startling developments were to come. On December 30, Generals John Newton and John Cochrane arrived in Washington on leave. They had come to tell somebody in authority that Burnside was getting ready to cross the Rappahannock again and that the officers and soldiers had no confidence in the commander and that his movement ought to be stopped. They looked first for certain Congressional leaders to unfold their story to, and when they could not find them, they decided to talk to Lincoln. Late in the afternoon they went to the White House. They told Lincoln that the army distrusted Burnside's ability and that his proposed move would result in another defeat. Lincoln asked sharply if they were trying to get Burnside removed. They replied hastily that they had no such thought in mind, which, of course, was not true.[4] If conditions in the army were as bad as they described them, then the only remedy was to get rid of Burnside.

Lincoln was shocked by the visit of Newton and Cochrane and impressed by what they had said. Without consulting Halleck or Stanton, he telegraphed Burnside: "I have good reason for saying you must not make a general movement of the army without letting me know." Burnside replied that he had rescinded the orders for his advance and was coming to Washington to see the President.[5]

Burnside met Lincoln on New Year's morning. The President said that some officers, whose names he would not divulge, had told him that Burnside's proposed move over the Rappahannock would result in disaster and that none of the

---

Official Records, XXI, 868–870; Lincoln to Franklin and Smith, December 22, *Works of Lincoln*, VIII, 150–151.

[4] *C. C. W., Reports*, 1863, I, 730–746.

[5] Lincoln to Burnside, December 30, 1862, *Works of Lincoln*, VIII, 154; Burnside to Lincoln, December 30, *Official Records*, XII, 900.

leading generals had any faith in it. Burnside explained his plan, which was simply to cross at some point above or below Fredericksburg. Lincoln expressed misgivings that the scheme would succeed, and sent for Halleck and Stanton to come to the White House to join the conference.[6]

Before they arrived, Burnside said that he did not have the confidence of his prominent officers and ought to be relieved and that Halleck and Stanton did not have the confidence of the army and the country and ought to be removed. Later in the day, Burnside put his opinion of Halleck and Stanton in a letter and probably on the next day handed the letter to Lincoln, who read it and returned it to Burnside. Apparently Burnside gave the document to the President in the presence of Halleck and Stanton and then told them that he had asked for their removal, although Halleck later denied that any such scene had taken place.[7]

Lincoln's refusal to receive formally Burnside's letter meant that he did not agree with the General's opinion of Stanton or Halleck or that if he did, he was not ready to remove them. The President almost got rid of Halleck, however, without meaning to. Lincoln wanted Old Brains to go to Burnside's headquarters to examine the places where Burnside proposed to cross, and then to say categorically that he approved or disapproved of Burnside's plan. In a sharp letter to Halleck, Lincoln said: "Your military skill is useless to me if you do not do this." Halleck was willing to advise Burnside, but he refused to say definitely what Burnside should do. He

[6] *C. C. W., Reports,* 1863, I, 717–718.

[7] Burnside to Lincoln, January 1, 1863, *Official Records,* XXI, 941–942; Halleck to W. B. Franklin, June 5, 1863, *ibid.,* 1011; Burnside to Lincoln, January 5, 1863, *ibid.,* 945, and the same letter in *Works of Lincoln,* VIII, 177–178. In the letter of January 5, Burnside referred to his giving the letter of January 1 to Lincoln and his denunciation of Halleck and Stanton. The editor of the *Official Records* stated that this section of the letter of January 5 was not in the document received by Lincoln, although it was included in Burnside's copy.

objected to the tone of Lincoln's letter and to the President's idea that he should order a general in the field to advance at a particular time and place. He asked to be relieved. Lincoln then withdrew his letter, and Halleck withdrew his application for relief.[8]

The conferences between Lincoln, Burnside, Halleck, and Stanton went on for two days, but no decision was reached as to what movement Burnside should make. Burnside returned to camp determined to try another crossing of the Rappahannock, but he wanted distinct authorization from someone in Washington to make the move. He wrote Lincoln that his officers were opposed to his plan but that he was going to execute it, and offered to resign his commission if the President did not approve his movement. Burnside also asked Halleck to give him general directions as to the advisability of an advance over the river.[9] Halleck replied in a letter that was a masterpiece of evasion of responsibility. He said that he advised a crossing some place and at some time, as early as possible, with all or part of the army, if the movement could be made on favorable terms. Burnside would have to decide himself the time, place, and character of the crossing. On Halleck's letter, Lincoln indorsed that he approved the general in chief's views. "Be cautious," said Lincoln, "and do not understand that the government or country is driving you." The President added, in words that must have interested Burnside, that he did not *yet* see how he could profit by changing the command of the Army of the Potomac.[1] Undoubtedly Lincoln realized that he would soon have to relieve Burnside, and he probably thought that Halleck's

[8] Lincoln to Halleck, January 1, 1863, and Halleck to Stanton, January 1, *Works of Lincoln*, VIII, 165–166.

[9] Burnside to Lincoln, January 5, 1863, *ibid.*, VIII, 177–178; Burnside to Halleck, January 5, *Official Records*, XXI, 945.

[1] Halleck to Burnside, January 7, 1863, *Works of Lincoln*, VIII, 179–181; *C. C. W., Reports*, 1863, I, 718–719.

wishy-washy instructions would restrain Burnside from doing anything rash.

Burnside did attempt an advance, but his move got bogged down in a torrential rain and had to be called off. It became known scornfully in the army as "the mud march." Hooker and several other generals openly criticized the movement before and after it was made. Their statements maddened Burnside. He had taken more than he could stand from his generals. He prepared an order dismissing from the service Hooker, Newton, and Cochrane, and relieving from duty a number of other prominent officers.[2] Henry J. Raymond, the publisher of the New York *Times,* was in camp, and Burnside showed him the order. Raymond asked what Burnside would do if Hooker resisted the order. Burnside replied with satisfaction that he would swing Hooker before sundown. The astonished and alarmed Raymond rushed to Washington to tell Lincoln what Burnside proposed to do. The President said sadly that he would stop Burnside from issuing the order but that he feared he would have to relieve Burnside and appoint the intriguing Hooker to the command. Hooker, said Lincoln, was stronger with the country than any other general.[3]

Burnside, of course, had no authority to dismiss an officer from the service. That power rested with the President. An aide of Burnside's suggested that he show the order to Lincoln before making it public. Burnside agreed and went to Washington on January 24. He gave Lincoln the order and his resignation and said that the President could accept either one, but that he could not go on as things were. Lincoln said that he would have to discuss the matter with his advisers. Burnside went back to his camp and returned to Washington

[2] *Official Records,* XXI, 998–999.

[3] "Journal of Henry J. Raymond," *Scribner's Monthly,* XIX, 1880, 703–706.

the next day to get Lincoln's decision. He saw Lincoln right after breakfast. The President said that he had decided to relieve Burnside from command and appoint Hooker in his place. But Lincoln refused to hear of Burnside's giving up his commission. He said: "General, I cannot accept your resignation; we need you, and I cannot accept your resignation." Burnside agreed to stay in the army and take another assignment. The General then made a final trip to Falmouth to deliver to Hooker Lincoln's order making the change in commanders.[4]

Lincoln undoubtedly relieved Burnside with feelings of deep personal regret. He liked Burnside's honesty and humility. Probably Lincoln did not blame Burnside too much for Fredericksburg. But after Fredericksburg, he knew that he would have to remove the General to prevent a breakdown in the administration of the Army of the Potomac. Burnside was destroying the morale and unity of the officers and the army. In fact, Burnside as commander was destroying himself. He was on the point of a breakdown when he was removed. Had he been retained in command, a personal tragedy would have resulted.

One of Lincoln's new generals had failed. By the President's standards, Burnside had been guilty of the McClellan sins of hesitation and slowness. For a while Lincoln thought that another of his appointees, Rosecrans, was going to be no better than Buell. Rosecrans had assumed command in the West late in October, but all during November he made no move toward Chattanooga. He was preparing to advance, he told the government, but could not go forward until he got

[4] Burnside to Lincoln, January 23, 24, 1863, *Official Records*, XXI, 998; *C. C. W., Reports*, 1863, I, 719–722; D. R. Larned to Mrs. A. E. Burnside, January 28, Larned MSS.; the order of removal, January 25, *Works of Lincoln*, VIII, 204; Pease and Randall, *Diary of Browning*, 619.

his supply difficulties straightened out—the old Buell reason for delay. Early in December, Halleck wrote Rosecrans that Lincoln was exceedingly impatient at his failure to move and had twice asked Halleck to name a new commander for the West. "If you remain one more week at Nashville," said Halleck, "I cannot prevent your removal." Rosecrans was enraged by Halleck's communication. To his staff he declared that he would not budge until he was ready, and he wrote to Halleck that he could not be affected by threats of removal.[5]

Halleck replied in a conciliatory letter in which he tried to explain to Rosecrans why Lincoln wanted an offensive in Tennessee. The President had said to him time and again, Halleck wrote, that there were imperative reasons why the enemy must be driven over the Tennessee River at the earliest moment. Lincoln had not told him what the reasons were, but Old Brains knew. The government feared that the friends of the South in England would make an attempt at the January meeting of Parliament to force the government to intervene in the war on the side of the Confederacy. If at that time the Confederates were in possession of middle Tennessee, the supporters of intervention would have an argument that the South was gaining in the war and that England ought to get in on the winning side. Federal possession of middle Tennessee, said Halleck, might be the turning point in Northern foreign relations. Referring to Lincoln's feelings about the possibility of foreign entrance into the war, Halleck said: "You can hardly conceive his great anxiety about it."[6]

Late in December, Rosecrans finally moved forward. Hal-

[5] Halleck to Rosecrans, December 4, 1862, *Official Records,* XX, pt. 2, 117–118; Rosecrans to Halleck, December 4, *ibid.,* 118; Bickham, *Rosecrans' Campaign with the Fourteenth Army Corps,* 120.

[6] Halleck to Rosecrans, December 5, 1862, *Official Records,* XX, pt. 2, 123–124.

leck's urgent presentation of Lincoln's views probably influenced him to start, although at the time he advanced he
felt that he had solved his supply problems. At the same time,
the Confederate army moved out from its lines in middle
Tennessee in an offensive aimed at Nashville. The two armies
met on the last day of the month and fought the battle of
Stone's River. The Confederates attacked Rosecrans' right
wing and bent it back but could not break it. On New Year's
day, while Burnside was discussing his troubles with Lincoln
in Washington, the two armies faced each other with neither
making a move. On the second, the Confederates assaulted
the Federal left and were repulsed. The Confederates then
withdrew from the field and retreated to their original position.

Rosecrans reported the battle to Washington as a Federal
victory.[7] In a sense it was, but only in a very narrow sense.
Rosecrans had made the enemy fall back, but he had not destroyed the enemy army or gained any important territory.
But his despatches announcing a Confederate retreat sounded
wonderful to Lincoln. "God bless you and all with you," the
President telegraphed to Rosecrans.[8] After Fredericksburg
and during the first days of January, when Burnside was going to pieces, Lincoln needed some good military news. So
did the country. Stone's River raised popular morale and
strengthened the government at home and abroad. Lincoln
was profoundly grateful to Rosecrans. Months later, when
he did not feel as kindly toward the General as he did in
January, Lincoln would write to Rosecrans: "I can never forget whilst I remember anything that about the end of last year
and beginning of this, you gave us a hard-earned victory,
which, had there been a defeat instead, the nation could

---

[7] Rosecrans to Halleck, January 3, 5, 1863, *ibid.*, XX, pt. 1, 184–185.
[8] Lincoln to Rosecrans, January 5, 1863, *Works of Lincoln*, VIII,
173–174.

scarcely have lived over." [9] Eventually Lincoln realized the partial nature of Rosecrans' victory, but at the moment he was well satisfied with this new general. Rosecrans was a little slow, but he was not as slow as Buell or McClellan and he would fight.

[9] Lincoln to Rosecrans, August 31, 1863, *ibid.,* IX, 107.

Chapter 9

"Give Us Victories"

LINCOLN did not ask advice from anybody when he chose a successor to Burnside. He appointed Joseph Hooker without consulting Stanton, Halleck, or the Cabinet.[1] Certain writers who lived in the war period and who knew Lincoln and some later historians claimed that the President put before the Cabinet the question of who should command the Army of the Potomac. According to their story, the choice was between three of the corps commanders: Hooker, John Reynolds, and George G. Meade. Stanton, supported by Halleck, was for Reynolds, and Chase was for Hooker. Stanton won out. The appointment was offered to Reynolds, who declined it. Chase then exerted enough pressure to get the command for Hooker, who had promised to back Chase for the presidency.[2] There is little evidence to support the tale. The contemporaries of Lincoln who originated it were not sufficiently in his confidence to know what happened. The only basis for it was that Hooker was close to Chase and the radical Republicans. Lincoln alone selected Hooker, and

[1] Halleck to W. B. Franklin, May 29, 1863, *Official Records*, XXI, 1008–1009; Nicolay and Hay, *Lincoln*, VI, 264–272.

[2] C. P. Benjamin, in *Battles and Leaders*, III, 239–240; Ward Hill Lamon, *Recollections of Abraham Lincoln, 1847–1865*, 192–193; John Bigelow, Jr., *The Campaign of Chancellorsville*, 7; Walter H. Hebert, *Fighting Joe Hooker*, 166.

he chose Hooker for purely military reasons. The President thought that the man who replaced Burnside ought to be one of the senior corps generals. Sumner was too old and was retiring from the service. Franklin was being relieved from duty with the Eastern army because he and Burnside had got in a bitter quarrel about who was responsible for Fredericksburg. This left only Hooker and Meade. Hooker ranked Meade and had a greater reputation.

Lincoln summoned Hooker to Washington for an interview on January 26, the day after Burnside was relieved and Hooker appointed. Hooker, in a later account of the meeting, said that he told Lincoln he could not command the army efficiently unless the President stood between him and Halleck to ward off the latter's enmity. Halleck was his foe, he said, and did not want him to succeed. Hooker detested Halleck, and, as with all of his opinions, made no secret of it.[3] Halleck had a like opinion of Hooker. The bad feeling between the two men dated back to when they had lived in California before the war. Halleck claimed that he knew "things" about Hooker's conduct in California that Hooker was afraid to have revealed and that Hooker, to lessen the effect of anything Halleck might divulge, tried to convince Lincoln that Old Brains was his personal enemy.[4]

Lincoln may or may not have agreed to protect Hooker from Halleck, but he did permit the General, during his tenure of command, an unusual freedom of control from the general in chief. From the time that he assumed command and until mid-June, Hooker reported directly to Lincoln and received all his instructions from the President. Halleck was not informed of what movements Hooker was planning or of what had occurred in those that he executed.[5] But Halleck

[3] *C. C. W., Reports*, 1865, I, 111–112, 175–176.
[4] Halleck to W. T. Sherman, September 16, 1864, Sherman MSS.
[5] Halleck's statement in *Official Records*, XXV, pt. 1, 156.

himself was largely to blame for his lack of authority over Hooker. Ever since Second Manassas, he had increasingly refused to exercise the functions of his office. He had sorely disappointed Lincoln by refusing to assume responsibility in the Burnside crisis. Lincoln probably did not think it was worth while to ask Halleck to make any decisions about what Hooker should do.

Whatever Hooker may have told Lincoln about Halleck on the twenty-sixth, the President told Hooker something about himself that he needed to know. Hooker was a military intriguer of a high order, and he had long angled to get the command of the Army of the Potomac. He had intrigued for it when McClellan was in power, and he had intrigued against Burnside. Lincoln knew this side of Hooker's character and did not like it. "Hooker talks badly," said Lincoln in describing the General's part in undermining Burnside. Hooker had also talked badly about something that came close to Lincoln. In the popular demoralization that followed Fredericksburg, many people, including army officers, said openly that the country needed a dictator. Hooker said it louder than most and gave the impression that he would be ready to take the position. His foolish mouthings had been reported to Lincoln.[6]

The President decided that his new commander needed some sound advice in written form. Probably at the close of their interview, he handed Hooker a letter. It was one of the best of his war letters. He said that he was giving Hooker the command for what he considered good reasons: that Hooker was skillful, confident, and had not mixed in politics (the latter was not true). But, said Lincoln, "I think it best for you to know that there are some things in regard to which I am not quite satisfied with you." Hooker was too ambitious,

[6] "Journal of Henry J. Raymond," *Scribner's Monthly*, XIX, 1880, 422, 704.

Lincoln continued, and his ambition had led him to assail
Burnside and to do "a great wrong" to a brother officer. Pro-
phetically Lincoln said: "I much fear that the spirit you have
aided to infuse into the army, of criticizing their commander
and withholding confidence from him, will now turn upon
you." The President said that he had heard Hooker's talk
about the country's needing a dictator and that he was not
too alarmed about it. "Only those generals who gain successes
can set up dictators," he pointed out. "What I now ask of you
is military success, and I will risk the dictatorship." Possibly
with a thought of Fredericksburg in mind, he ended the letter by advising Hooker to be careful in his operations: "Be-
ware of rashness, but with energy and sleepless vigilance go
forward and give us victories." Hooker's reactions to Lincoln's letter at the time he got it are not known. Months later,
he read it with great emotion to a newspaper correspondent,
and said it was the kind of letter a father might write to
his son.[7]

Joseph Hooker was forty-four years old when he assumed
command of the Army of the Potomac. He was a graduate of
West Point and had served in the Mexican War. He resigned
from the army in 1853 and went to California to live. When
the war started, he came to Washington and secured a commission in the Eastern army. He made a brilliant record as
a regimental, division, and corps commander. Because of
his dashing aggressiveness, the newspapers pinned the name
"Fighting Joe" on him. He had the kind of personality the
press liked. He was nervous, excitable, and talkative. He
liked to tell reporters what he thought of other officers—and
of Joe Hooker. In appearance, he was tall and statuesque; he
had wavy light brown hair, blue eyes, and a florid complexion. Some people said his floridity was caused by heavy drink-

[7] Lincoln to Hooker, January 26, 1863, *Works of Lincoln,* VIII,
206–207; Brooks, *Washington in Lincoln's Time,* 52–53.

ing. He had the reputation of being a sot. Hooker did like to drink, but the truth seems to be that he became easily affected by small amounts.[8]

As a general, Hooker did not have the ability to command and fight a large army. He was a good organizer and administrator. He had sound strategic sense and could devise excellent strategic plans. Up to a certain point, he could execute his plans. But at the critical moment in an operation something happened to Hooker. He stopped, hesitated, drew back. In plain words, he lost his nerve. He lacked the iron resolution required in a great battle captain. As a subordinate commander, he fought his troops well. That was because they fought under his eye. As commander of the Army of the Potomac, he would complain that all the corps were not where he could see them in a battle. His strategic talent was limited to his field of vision. He had difficulty in coordinating the movements of bodies of troops whose positions he could judge only by reports. In military parlance, he could not make war on the map.[9]

Burnside and Hooker were not Lincoln's only problems in the first months of 1863. He also had to deal with two of his political generals who had been relieved of their commands and who now wanted new assignments. They were Butler and Fremont, both darlings of the radical Republicans and both leaders of political groups whose support of the war Lincoln wanted to keep. The squat, squinty Butler, who, as one observer said, looked like a cross-eyed cuttlefish,[1] came East to visit his family in Massachusetts after being relieved in Louisiana. On his way home, he received a message from Lincoln asking him to come immediately to Washington. The Presi-

[8] Dennett, *Diary of Hay,* 86; Hebert, *Hooker,* 23–24; William F. G. Shanks, *Personal Recollections of Distinguished Generals,* 187–191.

[9] Bigelow, *Chancellorsville,* 6–7, 481–482; William Roscoe Livermore, *The Story of the Civil War,* I, 114–115.

[1] Wallace, *Autobiography,* II, 674.

dent said that he had an important and honorable service for Butler to perform.[2] Butler willingly complied, because he wanted to find out in Washington why he had been removed from the Gulf command. When he met Lincoln, he learned that the President wanted him to go back to Louisiana and raise an army from the hordes of Negroes soon to be freed by the Emancipation Proclamation. Butler objected that this would make him a mere recruiting agent. He said he wanted his former command restored. Lincoln hesitated, but said he would do it if Banks could be taken care of satisfactorily. Lincoln did not definitely promise Butler the command, nor did Butler say definitely he would accept it if offered. Butler left to go to his family.

Many years after the war, Butler would say that during the interview Lincoln offered him Grant's command on the Mississippi.[3] His statement was false by all the evidence of the contemporary documents. Lincoln had too high an opinion of Grant as a fighting general to displace him with an untried officer. The President had no intention of giving Butler a field command any place. He did want to employ Butler's abilities as an organizer and propagandist to bring the manpower resources of the colored population of the Gulf area into the war effort. Lincoln explained his purpose clearly in a letter to Stanton. Butler should return to Louisiana, said the President, but Banks must not be hurt by the arrangement. Lincoln proposed that after the Mississippi was opened Banks should head an expedition into Texas and Butler should concentrate on recruiting activities. Lincoln said the same thing in a letter to Banks. Gently he told Banks that he was placing Butler in command over him but that Banks would get to invade Texas. The government must get some

[2] Lincoln to Butler, December 29, 1862, *Works of Lincoln,* VIII, 154.

[3] Benjamin F. Butler, *Butler's Book,* 549–551.

good out of the Emancipation Proclamation, said Lincoln, and for that purpose there was no man like Butler and no place like Louisiana.[4]

Lincoln never sent the letter to Banks. There was no need to send it. Butler refused to go to Louisiana unless he had command of an army and the opportunity for field service. He declined the command on the terms proposed by Lincoln. He said that the offer was sufficient vindication for his removal and that he would continue to support the administration.[5] Lincoln quietly dropped the matter.

Lincoln believed that there was a place in the military setup for Butler, but he doubted that there was one for Fremont. After his experience with the Pathfinder in Missouri and Virginia, Lincoln was convinced that Fremont was incapable of holding an important command. Fremont wanted a command, but his radical Republican backers were much more active than he in demanding one of Lincoln. In March, George W. Julian, a radical leader, went to the White House to urge the President to assign Fremont to active service. Lincoln pointed out that Fremont held one of the highest ranks in the army and that to give him a command commensurate with his rank a general commanding one of the biggest departments would have to be removed. Lincoln said that Fremont's situation reminded him of the old man who told his son to take a wife. The son asked: "Whose wife shall I take?" Julian said the appointment of Fremont to a command would stir the country. The President replied that it would please Fremont's friends and displease the conservatives and that was all that he could see in

[4] Lincoln to Stanton, January 23, 1863, *Works of Lincoln*, VIII, 203; Lincoln to Banks, January 23, Paul M. Angle (ed.), *New Letters and Papers of Lincoln*, 312–313.

[5] Butler to S. P. Chase, February 28, 1863, Jessie A. Marshall (ed.), *Private and Official Correspondence of General Benjamin F. Butler during the Period of the Civil War*, III, 21–27.

the stirring argument.[6] The best offer that Fremont's supporters could pry out of Lincoln was one to place the General in command of a school of instruction for colored soldiers in Virginia. Fremont declined the offer and told his friends to say to Lincoln that he did not want to embarrass the President by asking that a department be created for him. His humility must have surprised and pleased Lincoln.[7]

Lincoln had used the political generals at the beginning of the war to unify Northern opinion. Now he would not give them places unless they could demonstrate real ability. To a politician friend who demanded important commands for Butler and Fremont, Lincoln wrote that he could not give them places without removing good fighting generals like Grant. In firm words that showed his confidence in himself, Lincoln said: "I am compelled to take a more impartial and unprejudiced view of things. Without claiming to be your superior, which I do not, my position enables me to understand my duty in all these matters better than you possibly can, and I hope you do not yet doubt my integrity." [8]

From his position of understanding Lincoln studied the actions of two other civilian generals, Banks and McClernand, from whom just a few months before he had expected great things when he sent them to open the Mississippi. Banks had floundered around in minor operations in Louisiana and had done nothing to accomplish the objective Lincoln had set for him. McClernand had got ready to go against Vicksburg but found that Grant had anticipated him in launching an offensive against the river fortress. In his foolish ambition, Mc-

[6] George W. Julian, *Political Recollections, 1840–1872*, 229–230.

[7] Fremont to Stanton, March 17, 31, 1863, Stanton MSS.; Stanton to Fremont, March 21, Stanton MS. Letterbook, I, in *ibid.;* Lincoln to Charles Sumner, June 1, *Works of Lincoln*, VIII, 288–289; Fremont to Sumner, June 9, Lincoln MSS., vol. 113.

[8] Lincoln to I. N. Arnold, May 26, 1863, Gilbert A. Tracy (ed.), *Uncollected Letters of Abraham Lincoln*, 224–226.

Clernand tried to destroy Grant, the most successful Union general in the West and an officer whom Lincoln valued, and ended by destroying himself.

While McClernand was raising troops for his secret expedition and sending them down to Memphis, Grant was working out a plan of his own to take Vicksburg. He submitted it to Halleck and got it approved. Grant proposed to move with the main part of his army from near Memphis straight south into Mississippi and then to wheel westward against Vicksburg. At the same time, he would send a corps under General W. T. Sherman down the Mississippi to land north of Vicksburg and attack the defences above the city. Sherman's attack was expected to divert attention from Grant's movement. Halleck privately authorized Grant to make use of any troops in his department, which meant any part of McClernand's force that was in west Tennessee. By this time Halleck had found out something about McClernand's expedition; and he was determined, to judge from his actions, to stop it, or rather to persuade Lincoln to stop it. Halleck thought Grant had faults as a soldier, but the vision of McClernand leading an important movement horrified Halleck's military soul.

McClernand was enraged when he heard that Sherman was heading an expedition that he considered his own private property. He telegraphed Lincoln and Stanton that he believed he had been superseded. Stanton, replying for Lincoln, said that he had not been but that the operations against Vicksburg were in Grant's department and that McClernand's force would be a corps in Grant's army assigned to operations on the Mississippi under Grant's general supervision. The War Department issued orders stating that by the direction of Lincoln the troops in Grant's department were to be organized into three corps, of which McClernand's was one.[9]

[9] McClernand to Lincoln and Stanton, December 17, 1862, *Official Records*, XVII, pt. 2, 420; Stanton to McClernand, December 18, *ibid.*,

The President had wrecked McClernand's hopes of having an independent command, but he tried to preserve a semi-independent status for the General. Halleck told Grant that it was Lincoln's "wish" that McClernand have the immediate command of the operations against Vicksburg—under Grant's direction.[1]

McClernand now came down to Memphis, only to find that his troops had been taken to Vicksburg by Sherman. In a cold fury, he wrote Lincoln that accident or intention had conspired to thwart the President's authority in appointing him commander of the Mississippi expedition but that with Lincoln's support he would overcome his enemies.[2] Nobody had thwarted Lincoln's authority. The change in command arrangements on the Mississippi was done by his direction. Grant's announced intention to move on Vicksburg broke open the secrecy surrounding the McClernand expedition and forced Lincoln and Stanton to define McClernand's status in relation to Grant. Halleck had a chance to point out to Lincoln the danger, and the absurdity, of putting a relatively untried officer in command of an important movement and sending him to operate independently in the department of the best general the government had in the region. Halleck convinced Lincoln that Grant should direct the movement against Vicksburg, but the President was easily persuaded. Lincoln had had a high opinion of Grant since the river campaign of 1862. Now he easily realized that the victor of Henry and Donelson was the logical man to lead the offensive against Vicksburg and that all troops on the Mississippi line, including McClernand's, should be unified under a single command.

420; orders of December 18, *ibid.*, 432–433; Grant to McClernand, December 18, *ibid.*, 425.

[1] Halleck to Grant, December 18, 1862, *ibid.*, pt. 1, 476.

[2] McClernand to Lincoln, December 29, 1862, Lincoln MSS., vol. 97.

Halleck played a decisive part in destroying the independent McClernand expedition, but Old Brains was partially to blame for its ever having been conceived. When he came to Washington to be general in chief, Halleck had left Grant in west Tennessee and north Mississippi with nothing to do but guard railroad communications along the river. After he assumed the chief command, he largely ignored Grant. He planned no important movement for Grant's army, nor, so far as the record shows, did he try to impress on Lincoln that Grant was a fine general. Only when McClernand threatened to become the leading actor on the Mississippi did Halleck spring forward as Grant's champion.

Grant's first attempt to take Vicksburg failed. He moved south from near Memphis into north Mississippi, establishing field bases of supply as he went. The Confederates gave him so much trouble with his line of supply, destroying one of his bases completely, that he decided to go back to Memphis to reorganize. Sherman came down the Mississippi on transports and debarked north of Vicksburg. He assaulted the Confederate defences but found them too strong to carry. Not knowing what had happened to Grant or where Grant was, Sherman determined to retire up the river and await directions from his superior. Before he could pull back, McClernand arrived, bursting with wrath and importance. McClernand ranked Sherman, and, asserting his rank and his instructions from Lincoln, he took command of Sherman's forces. McClernand announced that he was going to go up the river and capture Arkansas Post, a Confederate fort situated where the Arkansas River flowed into the Mississippi. How the seizure of the fort would further the opening of the Mississippi did not figure in McClernand's thinking. He was angry and wanted glory. He would show his enemies and Lincoln what kind of man he was.

Before he went up river, he wrote Lincoln a letter in which

he demanded the removal of Halleck. He accused the general in chief of contempt of superior authority, because he had deprived McClernand of the command of the Vicksburg expedition in violation of Lincoln's wishes, and of gross incompetency, because disaster had attended his exercise of the supreme command. McClernand urged Lincoln to assume the functions of the general in chief: "It will be impossible that you should do worse; I am confident that you will do better." [3] Lincoln must have wondered if McClernand was patronizing him.

When Grant got back to Memphis he learned that Sherman's offensive had failed also and that McClernand had gone chasing off to Arkansas Post with all of Sherman's force. Not impressed by McClernand's capture of the place, Grant telegraphed him that his move was not approved. Grant was ready to call any bluff by McClernand that he had secret instructions from a higher authority. Unless you are acting on authority not derived from me, he told McClernand, get immediately in position where you can operate against Vicksburg. Grant knew that he had the power to control McClernand, and he meant to control him. Halleck, speaking for Lincoln, authorized Grant to relieve McClernand from the command of the river expedition if necessary or to take command of it himself. Grant decided to assume personal control of the operations against Vicksburg on the river line.[4] He also decided to abandon his original plan of moving part of the army southward through Mississippi and to transport his entire force by water down the river to some point above Vicksburg from which he could operate directly against the city.

It is often said that Grant gave up his first plan because the

[3] McClernand to Lincoln, January 7, 1863, *ibid.*, vol. 100.

[4] Grant to McClernand, January 11, 1863, *Official Records*, XVII, pt. 2, 553–554; Halleck to Grant, January 12, *ibid.*, 555; Grant to General J. B. McPherson, January 13, *ibid.*, 557.

Confederates had so thoroughly disrupted his supply line, and this may be true. But it is just as probable that he changed plans because of the problem of McClernand. If Grant stayed in Mississippi, McClernand, by virtue of his rank and his relationship with Lincoln, would command all troops on the river and might cart them off to other Arkansas Posts. Grant could have relieved McClernand, but he knew that Lincoln would be displeased if he did. He remembered that it was Lincoln's "wish" that McClernand have the immediate command on the river. The only device that Grant could adopt to control McClernand and to observe Lincoln's desire was to go to the Mississippi line himself and take command of everything. Grant's decision stamped him as a greater and smarter general than McClellan. McClellan would never have accepted McClernand or have tried to understand why Lincoln had given him a command. Grant realized that the President must have had some reason for entrusting the river expedition to McClernand. He could not imagine what it was, but out of deference to Lincoln he was willing to put up with McClernand, for the time being, and try to make some use of him.

McClernand sullenly obeyed Grant's order to return his force to near Vicksburg. In a letter to Grant that was almost insubordinate, he said that he accepted the responsibility for going to Arkansas Post and that the officer who in the present strait of the country refused to take responsibility was unworthy of public trust. He sent a copy of the letter to Lincoln, and said that his success at Arkansas Post was gall and wormwood to the West Pointers who had been persecuting him for months. Unaware that Grant was coming to the Mississippi, he asked Lincoln to make him independent of Grant's control.[5]

[5] McClernand to Grant, January 16, 1863, *ibid.*, XVII, pt. 2, 566–567; McClernand to Lincoln, January 16, Lincoln MSS., vol. 100.

Before he received McClernand's communication, Lincoln answered the General's letter demanding the removal of Halleck. Lincoln wrote to McClernand just a few days before he relieved Burnside from command. He was wearied and saddened by the intrigues and jealousies of the officers of the Eastern army, and he did not want to see a single other military feud get started. He gave McClernand wise advice which might have saved the General's career and made him a useful officer—if he had taken it. "I have too many *family* controversies, so to speak, already on my hands to voluntarily, or so long as I can avoid it, take up another," Lincoln wrote. "You are now doing well—well for the country, and well for yourself—much better than you could possibly be if you engaged in open war with General Halleck. Allow me to beg that, for your sake, for my sake, and for the country's sake, you give your whole attention to the better work." [6]

McClernand was not willing to do the better work. He wanted to engage in war, not against Halleck now, but against Grant. He exploded with rage when he read an order by Grant in which Grant announced that he was assuming command on the Mississippi. McClernand wrote Grant demanding to know whether he was relieved from command of the river expedition or restricted to the command of a single corps. Calmly Grant replied that he was taking command of operations on the Mississippi by authority from Halleck and that McClernand was limited to a corps command. [7] McClernand answered with a despatch that was probably intended to provoke Grant to the point where he would engage in open controversy with McClernand. Then Lincoln would have to intervene and settle the issue of authority. McClernand said

[6] Lincoln to McClernand, January 22, 1863, Lincoln MSS., vol. 101, and in *Works of Lincoln*, VIII, 201. In the published version the word "family" is not underlined.

[7] McClernand to Grant, January 30, 1863, and Grant to McClernand, January 31, *Official Records*, XXIV, pt. 1, 12–13.

that he acquiesced in Grant's order because he wanted to avoid a conflict of authority in the presence of the enemy but that he protested the competency and justice of the order and wanted his protest sent to the President. He referred to himself as the author and actual promoter of the river expedition.[8] Grant must have been angered by the despatch, but he swallowed its insulting tone. For the present, he was determined not to quarrel with the President's appointee.

During the winter and early spring months of 1863, Grant made one attempt after another to get into Vicksburg. Each one failed. He tried to dig a canal across the peninsula opposite Vicksburg so that the Navy could pass its transports safely past the Confederate batteries. His plan was to march his troops down the west bank of the river, have them picked up by the Navy and crossed to the east side, and then to move against Vicksburg from the south. The canal did not fill with enough water to carry the ships. He tried to operate against Vicksburg from the north, moving down through the maze of swamps, bayous, and small rivers above the town. He got bogged down in the soft ground of the terrain and ran into strong Confederate defences. He considered a scheme to move the Navy through various waterways in Louisiana down to the Red River, from which it could enter the Mississippi and ascend the river and transport the army to the east side below Vicksburg. In order to secure a continuous water connection to the Red, another canal had to be dug. It was partially completed, but it too was unserviceable.

Grant said later that he had little faith that any of these attempts would succeed. He said that he had worked out a plan to take Vicksburg that would have to wait until spring for execution. In the meantime, he had to keep the army busy. If he took it back to Memphis for the winter, the North-

[8] McClernand to Grant, February 1, 1863, *ibid.*, XXIV, pt. 1, 13–14.

ern public would interpret the move as a defeat and popular morale would be depressed. If he held his forces near Vicksburg doing nothing, the Confederates might figure out the real move he had in mind. So Grant kept his men digging canals and fighting in swamps to deceive the enemy.

Lincoln watched Grant's various moves with interest and approval. Always fascinated by engineering projects, Lincoln followed eagerly the progress of Grant's first canal. Grant must have been surprised when he received a despatch from Halleck instructing him to devote particular attention to the canal because Lincoln attached great importance to it.[9] Perhaps Grant was flattered that the President was watching his campaign so closely. But he must also have realized that a commander in chief who would notice such a strategic detail would demand a strict accounting for failure and could not be fooled by false excuses.

Lincoln had little fear that Grant would fail. He told a friend that he considered Grant to be the rising general of the war.[1] And he was determined that the Mississippi line should be secured. He intended to bring all the resources he could command to the aid of Grant. Halleck, writing to a general in Missouri to urge him to send surplus troops to the Mississippi, said that Lincoln had "repeatedly ordered" that all available troops west of the river be despatched to Grant.[2] To Grant, Halleck wrote that the government would do everything possible to assist him. The eyes and hopes of the entire country were directed to Grant's army, said Halleck. Using a phrase that Lincoln often employed about important strategic objectives in the West, Halleck said that the opening

[9] Halleck to Grant, January 25, 1863, *ibid.,* XXIV, pt. 1, 10.

[1] Colonel S. Noble to Lyman Trumbull, February 24, 1863, Trumbull MSS.

[2] Halleck to S. R. Curtis, February 17, 1863, *Official Records,* XXII, pt. 2, 113.

of the Mississippi would be of more advantage to the Union cause than the capture of twenty Richmonds.[3]

Lincoln might think that Grant was the rising general of the war, but he wanted to know more about the General's character and generalship. Not everybody in the government admired Grant. Some believed the stories of drunkenness that followed Grant through the war. At intervals during the Vicksburg campaign, Lincoln received accounts charging that Grant was monumentally drunk at some critical moment. McClernand sent one such report to the President.[4] Lincoln wanted to check these accusations and to get a reliable evaluation of Grant as a soldier. Unfortunately, Grant was too far away for Lincoln to employ his favorite technique of a personal interview. He would have to see Grant through the eyes of others. In March, an observer was sent to Grant's headquarters, instructed to stay for months, if necessary, and to make daily reports of Grant's operations. He was Charles A. Dana, late of the New York *Tribune*. Stanton selected Dana for the job, and Dana's reports were made to the War Department. But obviously Stanton would not have sent a civilian official to Grant's army to study the General every day without Lincoln's knowledge and approval. The President may even have suggested the idea of employing Dana.

Ostensibly Dana went as a special commissioner of the Department to investigate the paymaster service in the West. Actually he was to provide the Department with information that would enable the government to measure Grant's abilities.[5] Dana stayed with Grant until July. Every day he des-

[3] Halleck to Grant, March 20, 1863, *ibid.,* XXIV, pt. 1, 22.

[4] McClernand to Lincoln, March 15, 1863, Lincoln MSS., vol. 106; Murat Halstead to S. P. Chase, April 1, and Chase to Lincoln, enclosing Halstead's letter, April 4, *ibid.,* vol. 108.

[5] Dana, *Recollections,* 21; James Harrison Wilson, *Life of Charles A. Dana,* 200–201; Stanton to Dana, March 30, 1863, *Official Records,* XXIV, pt. 1, 67.

patched to Washington a well-written summary of affairs in Grant's army. Nearly every report he wrote was highly favorable to Grant. Dana too believed that Grant was the rising man.[6]

Other observers came in April to look at Grant. They were Adjutant General Lorenzo Thomas; Congressman E. B. Washburne, a personal friend of Grant's; and Governor Richard Yates of Illinois. After the war, Admiral Porter, who commanded the naval squadron assisting Grant in the operations against Vicksburg, said that Thomas told him he had authority from Lincoln to remove Grant. According to Porter, Thomas stated that there had been complaints about Grant and that Lincoln had sent him to investigate them; Thomas approved Grant's course and saved Grant's job. Either Thomas or Porter recounted a confused and false story. There is nothing in the contemporary documents to indicate that Lincoln considered relieving Grant. And even if he had considered it, he would never have authorized Thomas to make the removal on his own judgment. The power to remove generals Lincoln reserved for himself. Lincoln undoubtedly instructed Thomas to make some sort of inquiry into Grant's generalship, probably to report on Grant's administrative abilities, which were thought in some quarters to be poor, and Thomas may have turned in a favorable report, which is as much as he had to do with saving Grant.[7]

As April opened, Lincoln hopefully expected victory on the Mississippi line. He thought that Grant and Banks should combine their forces for action against some common point. If Banks could not come up and unite with Grant near Vicksburg, Lincoln believed that Grant should go down river and aid Banks in taking Port Hudson, the second important

[6] For examples of Dana's reports, see Dana to Stanton, April 12, 25, 27, May 23, 24, 26, 1863, in Dana MSS.

[7] Porter, *Incidents and Anecdotes*, 181–183; Washburne to Lincoln, April 30, May 1, 1863, Lincoln MSS., vol. 109.

fortress in the Confederate river defences. Whichever course the generals followed, he wanted them to do it fast. Halleck informed Grant that the President was getting impatient about the Mississippi operations.[8] Banks, however, acted as though he had never been instructed to operate on the river. He marched his army off on a barren expedition into central Louisiana, from where he calmly wrote Lincoln that he might move to Shreveport or back to the Mississippi.[9]

Grant, on the other hand, moved straight toward his objective. He put into execution his real plan to seize Vicksburg. This was to have the Navy run past the Vicksburg batteries and proceed to a point below the city; if the ships made the passage safely, Grant would march the army down the west side of the river and meet the Navy, which would transport the troops to the east bank. Then Grant intended to move rapidly northward against Vicksburg. He hoped to capture it before the Confederates could readjust their defences to his offensive. At the least, he would have placed his army on relatively dry terrain where he could maneuver. In mid-April, the fleet ran by the batteries. The army moved down the Louisiana side of the river to about fifty miles below Vicksburg where the Navy crossed it to the Mississippi side. Grant was over the river and ready to strike for Vicksburg by April 30.

Lincoln watched the first phase of Grant's movement with approval. He had thought from the beginning of the Vicksburg campaign that Grant ought to operate south of the city. That was why he had been so interested in the digging of Grant's first canal. When Grant got below Vicksburg, Lincoln expected that the General would continue down the river and join Banks. He thought that Grant was making a mistake by

[8] Halleck to Grant, April 2, 1863, *Official Records*, XXIV, pt. 1, 25.
[9] Banks to Lincoln, April 17, May 10, 1863, Lincoln MSS., vols. 108, 110.

turning to the north alone, but said nothing.[1] Halleck also believed that Grant should combine with Banks and said so to Grant. But Grant replied that Banks was so far away that a junction of the two armies could not be made without delaying operations against Vicksburg. "I could not lose the time," said Grant. Such words coming from a general must have sounded strange—and wonderful—to Lincoln.[2]

Grant told Halleck he had asked Banks to help him take Vicksburg, after which he would assist Banks capture Port Hudson. Halleck approved the arrangement, but Banks would not agree to it. He decided to attack Port Hudson, and demanded that Grant come to join him.[3] Halleck was angry when he heard that Banks had gone to Port Hudson. Rightly Halleck considered that Banks was violating the spirit and the letter of Lincoln's instructions, and he told Banks so in blunt terms. He also informed the General that Lincoln was greatly disappointed that he and Grant were not acting in conjunction. Halleck might be angry and the President disappointed, but there was little they could do about Banks. By the time he got to Port Hudson, Grant was knocking at the doors of Vicksburg, and it was too late to combine the armies.[4] The government was fortunate that Banks did not join Grant. He ranked Grant and would have commanded the operations against Vicksburg unless Lincoln had arbitrarily placed Grant in control. Banks's magnificent incompetency would have nullified the abilities of even Grant.

After he crossed to the east side of the Mississippi, Grant

[1] Lincoln to Grant, July 13, 1863, *Works of Lincoln,* IX, 26.

[2] Halleck to Grant, May 11, 1863, Stanton MSS.; Grant to Halleck, May 15, *Official Records,* XXIV, pt. 1, 36.

[3] Banks to Grant, May 12, *Official Records,* XXIV, pt. 3, 298–299; Banks to Grant, May 13, two despatches, *ibid.,* 303–304.

[4] Halleck to Banks, May 23, June 3, 4, 18, 27, 1863, *ibid.,* XXVI, pt. 1, 500–501, 534, 535, 603; Banks to Halleck, June 4, 18, *ibid.,* 535–536, 564–565; Halleck to Grant, June 2, *ibid.,* XXIV, pt. 1, 40.

advanced swiftly toward Vicksburg. He defeated the enemy forces that tried to intercept him before he reached the city and closed in on the fortress itself. He attempted to storm the strong field fortifications surrounding Vicksburg, but his attack was repulsed. He then decided to take the place by siege operations. Lincoln was well pleased with Grant's offensive. Grant did not have Vicksburg, but he was almost certain to get it. His campaign had been bold, imaginative, and aggressive. Lincoln said it was "one of the most brilliant in the world." [5]

Soon after the siege started, Grant, with Lincoln's approval, settled the McClernand problem. Ever since he had assumed command of the Vicksburg expedition, Grant had had trouble with McClernand. McClernand was insubordinate and incompetent, but Grant hesitated to relieve the President's friend or to criticize him to Washington. As it turned out, Grant did not have to make any official criticism of McClernand or ask for permission to relieve him. Dana did both for him. In nearly every one of his despatches, Dana bitterly criticized McClernand and advised that he be removed. Dana practically ruined McClernand with the War Department. Stanton informed his agent that Grant had full power to remove any officer and would be supported by the government in whatever he did. In fact, said Stanton, the government would hold Grant responsible for failing to remove an inefficient officer.[6]

The hint could hardly have been stronger, and Grant was eager to act on it. He almost relieved McClernand after the attempt to storm the Vicksburg fortifications, when McClernand falsely reported that he had effected a lodgment in the enemy works, but decided to hold up action until the

[5] Lincoln to I. N. Arnold, May 26, 1863, Tracy, *Uncollected Letters of Lincoln*, 224–226.

[6] Stanton to C. A. Dana, May 5, 1863, *Official Records*, XXIV, pt. 1, 84.

siege was ended.[7] McClernand, however, forced Grant's hand. He knew that Grant and other officers had criticized his part in the attack on the forts. Their strictures, he believed, showed only how jealous the West Pointers were of him and how determined they were to run him out of the army. He was convinced that he alone was responsible for the victories of the river campaign.[8] The criticisms irritated him, and Grant's growing prestige enraged him. Grant, and not he, was emerging as the hero of the West. In his frustration, he did something that he must have known would provoke an open fight with Grant, something that could have been done only by a stupendous egotist who was lost to reason because of fury. He issued a congratulatory address to his corps that was clearly insubordinate and certain to create profound dissension in the army. He said that he and his corps had done most of the fighting in the recent movements and deserved most of the credit for the success of the campaign. He did not send the address to Grant, but it appeared in the newspapers.

When Grant saw it, he was astonished and probably delighted. He now had a reason for removing McClernand that nobody could question. Grant moved promptly. He asked McClernand if the newspaper versions of the address were a true copy. Defiantly McClernand replied that they were and that he would stand on the truth of the statements in the address. Grant then relieved him from command of his corps. McClernand said that having been appointed by Lincoln he denied Grant's right to remove him but would forbear at present making an issue of authority.[9]

[7] Dana to Stanton, May 23, 24, 1863, Dana MSS.; Grant to Halleck, May 24, *Official Records*, XXIV, pt. 1, 37.

[8] McClernand to Grant, June 4, 1863, *Official Records*, XXIV, pt. 1, 165–166; McClernand to Lincoln, May 29, Lincoln MSS., vol. 112.

[9] Grant to McClernand, June 17, 1863, and McClernand to Grant, June 18, *Official Records*, XXIV, pt. 1, 102–103; Grant to Halleck, June 19, *ibid.*, 43.

McClernand retired to Illinois, from where he bombarded Lincoln with demands that he be restored to his command. He described his removal as "an atrocious act of usurpation, oppression, and injustice," and claimed that Grant had been motivated by personal hostility, jealousy, and West Point prejudice.[1] Lincoln sympathized with McClernand's feelings and was pained by his downfall, but he had no intention of mixing in the controversy between him and Grant. He would not intervene in it, he wrote McClernand, because he could do nothing without doing harm. If he forced McClernand upon Grant, Grant would be forced to resign. "Better leave it where the law of the case has placed it," he advised McClernand.[2] McClernand did not want to rest his case, but Lincoln had closed it and closed also McClernand's military career. McClernand remained on inactive status until near the end of the war when he finally received a minor assignment. Another of Lincoln's political generals had been tried, used for what he was worth, and discarded.

During the winter months of 1863, "Fighting Joe" Hooker was reorganizing the Army of the Potomac and getting ready for the spring campaign. As he looked at his 120,000 troops, magnificently trained and equipped, Hooker almost burst with confidence and pride. "If the enemy does not run," he said, "God help them." To a party of officers in his tent, he said: "My plans are perfect, and when I start to carry them out, may God have mercy on General Lee, for I will have none."

As a matter of fact, his plans were not perfect. He had several in mind, but he was not sure which one to adopt. His military problem was difficult. He had to cross a river in the

[1] McClernand to Lincoln, June 23, August 3, 1863, Lincoln MSS., vols. 115, 119.

[2] Lincoln to McClernand, August 12, 1863, *Works of Lincoln*, IX, 71–73.

face of a powerful enemy and to cross it at a point where he could fight on favorable ground after he got over. First he had to decide where he could cross. Lee's army was in and around Fredericksburg behind field fortifications that stretched above and below the town. Obviously an attempted crossing at Fredericksburg would be a repetition of Burnside's debacle. It is possible that Hooker considered attacking the Confederates directly in his front and abandoned the idea because he thought their position was too strong. It is almost certain that he considered crossing the Rappahannock below Fredericksburg with the purpose of turning Lee's right and discarded the plan because the river was too wide to bridge at this point and because Lee could move easily to meet him.[3] Hooker usually shrouded his plans behind such a curtain of secrecy that they cannot be determined from the records.

Early in April, before Hooker had decided on a definite plan of operations, Lincoln came to Falmouth to see the General. The President probably made the trip chiefly for the purpose of finding out if Hooker had a plan, and if so, what it was. He was accompanied by Mrs. Lincoln, his son Tad, and a group of assorted civilians. The party left Washington on the fourth in a snowstorm and traveled by boat to Acquia Creek and from there by train to Falmouth.[4] For the most part, Lincoln enjoyed his several days stay in camp. He reviewed the troops, rode among the soldiers and talked to them, and relaxed at evening dinners. Only one thing disturbed him. He thought that Fighting Joe was too boastful. Hooker said he had the finest army on the planet. He sprinkled his conversation with the phrase: "When I get to Richmond." Lincoln said to a friend: "That is the most depressing

[3] Bigelow, *Chancellorsville*, 106–112.
[4] Lincoln to Hooker, April 3, 1863, *Works of Lincoln*, VIII, 243; Beale, *Diary of Bates*, 287–288.

thing about Hooker. It seems to me that he is overconfident." [5] Before he left for Washington, Lincoln sent for Hooker and Darius N. Couch, the senior corps commander. He said to them, possibly with a thought of the failure of McClellan and Burnside to commit their reserves at Antietam and Fredericksburg: "Gentlemen, in your next battle *put in all your men*." [6]

Lincoln discussed plans of operations with Hooker at Falmouth, but apparently he and the General did not decide on one specific scheme. Hooker was still not sure where he wanted to cross the Rappahannock. But immediately after Lincoln returned to Washington, Hooker submitted to him a written plan. General Daniel Butterfield, Hooker's chief of staff, carried it to the capital. Hooker said that he now believed he had more chance of defeating Lee by crossing above Fredericksburg and turning the enemy left, a statement that shows he had previously considered crossing below. He proposed to send his cavalry to Lee's rear to destroy the Confederate supply lines and to establish itself on Lee's line of communications with Richmond. Hooker would then cross with his infantry, and Lee would retreat. Fighting Joe hoped that he could trap the Confederates between his infantry and cavalry, but he feared they would retire so fast that they would escape him. If they fell back into northwestern Virginia, he would follow and harry them. [7]

Lincoln approved Hooker's plan. In his written indorsement of it, the President said that the primary objective of Hooker's army was the destruction of the enemy army and not the capture of Richmond. Lincoln liked Hooker's idea of turning the Confederate position instead of attacking it in

[5] Brooks, *Washington in Lincoln's Time*, 47–52.

[6] *Battles and Leaders*, III, 120.

[7] Hooker to Lincoln, April 11, 1863, *Official Records*, XXV, pt. 2, 199–200; Julia A. Butterfield (ed.), *A Biographical Memorial of General Daniel Butterfield*, 153–159.

front. He said that Hooker should "fret" Lee at various points, and then: "If he weakens himself, then pitch into him." [8]

Hooker set his plan in action. He sent a cavalry force under General George Stoneman up the Rappahannock to cross the fords and come down in Lee's rear. Stoneman moved slowly, and before he could get over the river the April rains of Virginia started. He had to halt his movement. At a time when the cavalry was supposed to be south of the Rappahannock, Hooker had to inform Lincoln that it had not crossed. Lincoln was depressed by the news and a little disgusted. He wrote Hooker that Stoneman had been out for three days, two of which had been fair, and had moved twenty-five miles. He still had sixty to go, Lincoln pointed out, and a river to cross and the enemy to encounter. "By arithmetic, how many days will it take him to do it?" the President asked. "I do not know that any better can be done, but I greatly fear it is another failure already. Write me often. I am very anxious." [9] Hooker wrote immediately to try to explain what had happened to Stoneman, but apparently Lincoln was not satisfied. He asked Hooker to meet him on the nineteenth at Acquia Creek.[1] What was said and decided at this conference does not appear in the records. Undoubtedly Lincoln and Hooker discussed the effect of the rains on the General's plan. Hooker seems to have thought that if the rains would stop, he could still use Stoneman and execute his design.

But the rains still came. They came for most of the rest of the month. The derangement of Hooker's plan by the weather illustrates one of the worst difficulties Civil War generals labored under when they planned campaigns. At that time

[8] *Works of Lincoln*, VIII, 243–244.

[9] Hooker to Lincoln, April 15, 1863, *Official Records*, XXV, pt. 2, 213; Lincoln to Hooker, April 15, *Works of Lincoln*, VIII, 249.

[1] Hooker to Lincoln, April 17, 1863, *Official Records*, XXV, pt. 2, 220; Stanton to Hooker, April 18, *ibid.*, 227.

there was no scientific method of weather prediction. Generals starting a movement could never know that the elements would not wreck their best laid plans. Quack predictors claimed that they could foretell the weather, and one of them showed up at the White House at the time Stoneman was stopped by the rains. His name was Francis L. Capen, and he described himself as "A Certified Practical Meteorologist & Expert in Computing the Changes in the Weather." He asked Lincoln to recommend him for a job in the War Department and said he could provide information that would save the government thousands of lives and dollars. He gave his written credentials to Lincoln on April 25. Three days later Lincoln indorsed on Capen's application: "It seems to me Mr. Capen knows nothing about the weather, in advance. He told me three days ago that it would not rain again till the 30th of April or 1st of May. It is raining now and has been for ten hours. I can not spare any more time to Mr. Capen." [2]

With the weather continuing adverse and the cavalry stalled north of the Rappahannock, Hooker decided to modify his plan. He informed Lincoln that he was working on a scheme to cross the river by stratagem and that in a few days he would be ready to "spring" on the enemy.[3] Hooker's new plan, which he sent to Lincoln on April 27, was superior to the ones he had previously designed. In fact, it bore the marks of brilliance, and it demonstrated Hooker's great ability for strategic planning. He still proposed to turn Lee's left. To accomplish his purpose, he was going to threaten to cross at Fredericksburg and above the town. While these demonstrations were in progress, he would send three corps thirty miles

[2] F. L. Capen to Lincoln, April 25, 1863, and Lincoln's indorsement, April 28, Lincoln MSS., vol. 109.

[3] Hooker to Lincoln, April 21, 1863, two despatches, *Official Records*, XXV, pt. 2, 236–238.

up the Rappahannock beyond the left of Lee. They would cross the river and its southern tributary, the Rapidan, and sweep down the south bank. As they neared Fredericksburg, they would uncover a ford above the town over which the demonstrating troops above the town could pass to join them. A powerful force would be in position to move on Lee's communications south of Fredericksburg. Lee would have to fight for his communications or retreat. If he fought, Hooker could move on him from two directions with two striking forces: the force west of Fredericksburg and the one directly across the river from the town. Hooker would have Lee in a vise. Not only had Hooker devised a plan to cross an army without loss over a river defended by a strong foe (one of the most difficult operations in war), but he had also arranged to force the enemy to fight on extremely disadvantageous ground.[4]

Hooker described his plan to Lincoln in a letter written on the day that he began his crossing. He had thought out the plan several days before, but he delayed informing Lincoln of it until the last moment for reasons of security. Hooker was always reluctant to reveal his military purposes because he believed people could not keep secrets. He was more secretive than usual about his new plan. He concealed it from his staff officers, and probably did not tell his corps generals about it until the movement started.[5] In his letter to the President, Hooker said that he appreciated how anxious Lincoln was to know what the army was going to do and that he wanted to relieve Lincoln's anxiety as much as possible. Therefore, he was divulging the outline of his scheme to Lincoln alone. Hooker sent his letter to Washington by a staff

[4] Hooker to Lincoln, April 27, 1863, Lincoln MSS., vol. 109.
[5] Hooker to General J. J. Peck, April 26, 1863, *Official Records,* XXV, pt. 2, 256–257.

officer and enclosed some maps and newspapers for Lincoln. The President was pleased by the letter and quite ready to keep Hooker's secret. In characteristic humble words, he thanked Hooker for his communication and added: "While I am anxious, please do not suppose that I am impatient, or waste a moment's thought on me, to your own hindrance, or discomfort." Forgotten and ignored in the strategic planning of Lincoln and Hooker was Halleck. The general in chief did not know that Hooker had crossed the Rappahannock until an officer in Washington told him.[6]

By April 30, Hooker had crossed his turning force over the Rappahannock. He was in an ecstasy of pride as he contemplated his achievement. He boasted to the reporters at his headquarters: "The rebel army is now the legitimate property of the Army of the Potomac. They may as well pack up their haversacks and make for Richmond." He issued a congratulatory address to the troops in which he said that the enemy must now "ingloriously fly" or fight on ground where certain destruction awaited him.[7] Hooker's words boded ill for his success. He seemed to want the enemy to retreat without fighting. He was about to demonstrate the fatal flaw in his character. He was about to lose his nerve.

On May 1 he moved eastward toward Fredericksburg. All that he had to do to defeat Lee was to continue on, uncover the ford above the town, and crush the Confederates between his superior forces. But he was no longer the bragging, confident Fighting Joe. He looked tired, his thoughts seemed far away, and he readily took suggestions from others. He avoided responsibility. He said to General G. K. Warren of his staff: "My God, Warren, I know nothing of this ground," and asked

[6] Lincoln to Hooker, April 28, 1863, Angle, *New Letters and Papers of Lincoln*, 323; Heintzelman MS. Journal, May 1.

[7] Swinton, *Campaigns of the Army of the Potomac*, 275; address of April 30, 1863, *Official Records*, XXV, pt. 1, 171.

Warren to post the troops.[8] Later his enemies would charge that he was drunk, but he was cold sober. He had stopped drinking after he assumed the command. The sudden shutting off of his familiar stimulant was bad for Hooker. He depended on whiskey to brace his courage. He would have been in better shape if he had had a few drinks.

As he advanced eastward, Hooker encountered his first opposition. Lee, deceived until then as to where Hooker would cross, suddenly realized that the Federals were approaching his line of communications. He rushed troops from Fredericksburg west to meet the threat and boldly attacked Hooker's advance units. Lee's move completely demoralized Hooker. The enemy was supposed to fly, and here he was attacking. Hooker stopped, he hesitated, and then he fell back and took up a defensive position around the little settlement of Chancellorsville. He waited for Lee to attack him. He gave up the initiative he had so brilliantly secured, and he gave up victory.

Lee came up to Chancellorsville, and taking Hooker's measure, decided to attack the Union army. He sent Jackson on a wide march that brought him out on Hooker's right. Jackson was to turn the Union right, while Lee attacked the Federal front. Lee's plan was for the two attacking forces to drive straight through and join, destroying Hooker's army between them. The Confederates delivered their assault on May 2. They forced Hooker back with both attacks, but they did not break his lines and they did not succeed in uniting their forces. In fact, Hooker was in an excellent position at the end of the day. He was between the separate parts of the Confederate army with a superior force. If he had had the nerve to counterattack, he might still have won the victory.

[8] MS. Journal of Captain Ulric Dahlgren, May 1, 1863, in John A. Dahlgren MSS., punctuation supplied.

Instead, when the Confederates renewed their attacks the next day he shortened his lines by retiring toward the river and permitted Lee to unite his forces. Hooker was now crowded back against the river but his position was strong defensively. Most of his corps generals wanted him to hold on to it or even to go over to the offensive.

But Hooker was more uncertain of himself and the situation than at the beginning of the battle. On the third, while he was standing on the porch of a house which he had made his headquarters, a Confederate solid shot struck one of the pillars, throwing it against Hooker. He fell to the ground senseless. His staff revived him, and he rode to the rear. It is doubtful that he was capable of exercising the command after the accident. His head and side had been injured. He suffered great pain and slept much. When he was awake, he seemed to be in almost a daze. In one of his waking moments, he ordered Couch to return the army to the north side of the river. The crossing was made on the night of May 5–6. Even then most of the corps commanders wanted to stay and fight.[9]

Lincoln was in agony during the fighting at Chancellorsville. He knew that a battle was going on, but he did not know how it was going. Hooker had told Lincoln that for security reasons he would send no despatches unless there was something decisive to report.[1] Until May 3 Lincoln received no official despatches from the battlefield. On the third, Butterfield, then at Falmouth, although he knew Hooker would not approve his action, decided that the commander in chief ought to know that a battle was in progress. He sent Lincoln two telegrams saying merely that Hooker and Lee were fighting. Hooker himself telegraphed Lincoln on the third. In a triumph of ambiguity, he said that the battle had resulted "in

[9] Bigelow, *Chancellorsville*, 363–365; *C. C. W., Reports*, 1865, I, 31–32, 128; *Battles and Leaders*, III, 169–171.

[1] J. G. Nicolay to Therena Bates, May 4, 1863, Nicolay MSS.

no success to us," and criticized the part of his army at Fredericksburg for not coming to his aid and making his success complete.[2] Lincoln could not tell from the despatches of Hooker and Butterfield how the battle had resulted. Secretary of the Navy Welles saw the President at the War Department on the afternoon of the fourth waiting for more bulletins. Lincoln said that he had a feverish anxiety to learn what had happened but could get no reliable reports. On the next day, he still had no definite news. Welles noted that he was trying to be encouraged and to inspire others with hope and not succeeding very well in either attempt.[3]

On the sixth, Lincoln received a telegram from Butterfield that did not clarify the situation too much. Butterfield, writing for Hooker, said that the army held a strong position but that circumstances which in time would be fully explained made it expedient to retire to the north side of the river. Among the circumstances was the danger to Hooker's communications if the Confederates crossed the river on the Federal right flank. Holding out a hope of victory which he must have known was false, Butterfield said that Hooker hoped the enemy would attack him in his formidable line south of the river. Lincoln misunderstood Butterfield's reference to the right flank. The General had said that Hooker's line of communications would be endangered if the enemy crossed the river on the Federal right. Lincoln thought that Butterfield meant the Federal right flank south of the river was in danger of being turned. The President happily telegraphed Hooker that a heavy rain which had fallen on the fifth and the disruption of Confederate communications by Hooker's cavalry, which had finally got in the enemy rear, would stop any move by Lee in the immediate future against Hooker's right. The

[2] Daniel Butterfield to Lincoln, May 3, 1863, *Official Records*, XXV, pt. 2, 377–378; Hooker to Lincoln, May 3, *ibid.*, 379; Lincoln to Butterfield, May 3, *ibid.*, 378.

[3] Welles, *Diary*, I, 291, 293.

securing of the Union right, Lincoln thought, put a new face on Hooker's situation.[4]

Lincoln sent his cheerful telegram to Hooker during the noon-hour on the sixth. Early in the afternoon another telegram from Butterfield arrived. It announced that the army had retired to the north side of the Rappahannock. A reporter friend saw Lincoln right after he got the despatch. He recalled that the President came into a room at the White House holding the telegram, a picture of despair, his face the color of the French gray wallpaper of the room. Lincoln walked back and forth with his hands clasped behind him. He kept saying: "My God, my God, what will the country say! What will the country say!"[5]

Lincoln's despair was not as great as the reporter thought. But he was badly shaken by the news from the Rappahannock. Give us victories, he had asked of Hooker. And now, with things looking better in the West and a victory in the East likely to end the war, Hooker had failed. Lincoln decided that he had better talk to Hooker and find out why he had been defeated and how badly. At four on the afternoon of the sixth, Lincoln, accompanied by Halleck, left Washington for Hooker's camp.[6]

[4] Butterfield to Lincoln, May 5, 1863, *Official Records*, XXV, pt. 2, 421–422; Lincoln to Hooker, May 6, *ibid.*, 434.

[5] Butterfield to Lincoln, May 6, 1863, *ibid.*, XXV, pt. 2, 434; Brooks, *Washington in Lincoln's Time*, 56–58.

[6] Stanton to Hooker, May 6, 1863, *Official Records*, XXV, pt. 2, 435.

Chapter 10

"Is That All?"

L INCOLN arrived at Hooker's camp on May 7. He and Halleck spent several hours talking to Hooker and his officers and then returned to Washington. One thing that the President wanted to inquire into was the condition and morale of the army after its latest defeat. He summoned the corps commanders to a conference at Hooker's headquarters. He told them that he had come to find out the state of affairs in the army. Much to their surprise and disappointment, he said nothing about the recent operations, nor did he ask their opinion of Hooker's conduct of the battle of Chancellorsville.[1] Many of the corps generals were so disgusted with Hooker's incompetence that they hoped Lincoln would give them an opportunity to advise his removal. After the conference, several of them proposed sending a delegation to Lincoln to ask him to relieve Hooker and appoint Meade to the command. They did not carry out their plan, largely because Meade was reluctant to go along with it, but some officers went to Lincoln individually and told him that Hooker should be relieved. Couch informed the President that he would not serve any longer under Hooker.[2]

[1] General G. G. Meade to Mrs. Meade, May 8, 1863, in Meade, *Life and Letters of Meade*, I, 373; J. G. Nicolay to Therena Bates, May 10, Nicolay MSS.

[2] Meade to Mrs. Meade, May 10, 20, 1863, Meade, *Life and Letters of Meade*, I, 373, 379; General H. W. Slocum to W. H. Seward, Novem-

What Lincoln discussed with Hooker is not completely known. He undoubtedly asked the General to account for Chancellorsville; and Hooker must have convinced Lincoln that he had conducted the battle satisfactorily, for the President told the corps generals that he blamed no one for the defeat. Lincoln queried Hooker about his plans for future operations. As was his frequent habit when having a personal conference with a general, he expressed his own thoughts in a letter which he handed to the officer. He gave Hooker such a letter. What did Hooker propose to do next? he asked. Lincoln suggested that the extended communications of the Confederates, now stretched west of Fredericksburg, were vulnerable to Federal attack. He wanted nothing done in rashness, said Lincoln, but an early movement would help to dispel the bad moral effect of the recent one. "Have you already in your mind a plan wholly or partially formed?" he asked. "If you have, prosecute it without interference from me. If you have not, please inform me, so that I, incompetent as I may be, can try and assist in the formation of some plan for the army." [3]

Hooker replied to Lincoln in a letter written on the day that he received the President's communication. The General may have given his letter to Lincoln personally or despatched it to Washington after the President left camp. Hooker said that he wanted to continue operations on the Rappahannock line and would launch a movement as soon as he judged the army was in condition to fight. Employing odd phraseology, Hooker said that he had decided in his mind on a plan of operations if Lincoln wished to have a plan made. He probably meant that he would reveal the plan to Lincoln if the latter desired him to. His projected move had

ber 14, 1863, Lincoln MSS., vol. 132; Heintzelman MS. Journal, May 13, 1863.

[3] Lincoln to Hooker, May 7, 1863, *Works of Lincoln*, VIII, 264–265.

one great merit, Hooker asserted: the operations of all the corps would be under his personal supervision, that is, within his field of vision.[4] He disclosed in this statement his greatest strategic weakness, the one that unfitted him to command a large army. He could not envision the position of troops he could not see; he could not make war on the map.

A week later Hooker wrote to Lincoln again. He said that although the Confederates had received reinforcements and now outnumbered him, he hoped to start an offensive across the Rappahannock the next day. He warned Lincoln not to speak of his proposed move to anybody. His statement about the comparative size of the armies was false and reminiscent of McClellan at his worst. A telegram that he received from Lincoln on the day that he wrote the President started a train of events reminiscent of Burnside after Fredericksburg. Lincoln, who probably had not received Hooker's letter, asked the General to come up to Washington that night. Canceling his plan to advance, Hooker started immediately.[5]

He conferred with Lincoln that night and the next day. The President, as usual, gave Hooker a letter. Lincoln wrote that he was not anxious for Hooker to undertake an early movement. Referring to his letter of May 7, in which he had suggested that Hooker hit the extended enemy communications, Lincoln said the conditions prevailing then no longer existed: the Confederates had reestablished their communications and regained their original positions. He did not think that Hooker could accomplish much by attempting soon another crossing of the river: "I therefore shall not complain if you do no more for a time than to keep the enemy at bay and out of other mischief by menaces and occasional cavalry raids, if practicable, and to put your own army in good condition

[4] Hooker to Lincoln, May 7, 1863, *Official Records*, XXV, pt. 2, 438.

[5] Hooker to Lincoln, May 13, 1863, *ibid.*, XXV, pt. 2, 473; Lincoln to Hooker, and Hooker to Lincoln, May 13, *ibid.*, 474.

again." Toward the end of the letter, Lincoln said something that must have shaken Hooker. The President said he had some "painful intimations" that some of the corps and division generals were not giving Hooker their full confidence. This would be ruinous if true, Lincoln observed, and he thought that the truth should be ascertained.[6]

As he read this section of the letter, Hooker must have remembered how Burnside, on the eve of a move over the Rappahannock, had been called to Washington and informed that some of his officers distrusted his ability. He might also have recalled Lincoln's prediction that the seeds of intrigue he had helped sow in the army when Burnside was in command would some day sprout trouble for him. Hooker asked Lincoln which officers had criticized him, but the President would not tell him. With an air of bravado that must have irritated Lincoln, Hooker told the President to get the views of every general who came to Washington.[7]

Lincoln had received his first painful intimations about the feelings of Hooker's officers at Falmouth from Couch and other generals. Apparently he was not too disturbed then, thinking that the complaints represented the normal reactions of some officers after a defeat. In the weeks after Chancellorsville, however, a number of officers seem to have written to Lincoln or to have come to Washington to see him, all of them denouncing Hooker and asking his removal. In addition, prominent civilians who had visited the army came to Lincoln to relate that the generals distrusted Hooker.[8] Lincoln was impressed by the reports, and troubled. He knew how much the bad relations between Burnside and his officers had hurt the army, and he wanted no repetition of the performance with Hooker.

[6] Lincoln to Hooker, May 14, 1863, *Works of Lincoln*, VIII, 274–275.
[7] *C. C. W., Reports*, 1865, I, 151.
[8] G. H. Boker to J. W. Forney, May 20, 1863, Lincoln MSS., vol. 111; Heintzelman MS. Journal, May 14, 1863.

The criticisms of Hooker by military men caused Lincoln to revise his opinion of the General's conduct of Chancellorsville. Although at first he had not been inclined to blame Hooker for the defeat, he now had serious doubts of Fighting Joe's ability to direct a large operation. The plain import of the letter he gave the General in Washington was that he wanted Hooker to do nothing for the present but stand on the defensive. The present would last until Lincoln could find a new commander. He was looking for one in the latter part of May. He offered the command to Couch, the senior corps general, who refused it on grounds of health and recommended Meade or Reynolds. Reynolds, hearing that he was being spoken of for the command, went to Washington to see Lincoln. He denounced Hooker as an incompetent, but he too declined to take the command. Lincoln was getting impatient with generals who said Hooker was unfit to exercise responsibility but who would not take any themselves. He told Reynolds that he meant to keep Hooker a while. He said that he was not going to throw the gun away because it had missed fire once, but that he would pick the lock and try it again.[9]

While Lincoln was having trouble with his principal general in the East, one of his principal Western generals was acting in a way that distressed him. This was Rosecrans, who had aroused Lincoln's gratitude and admiration after Stone's River. The President had marked Rosecrans down as a general with a future. But Stone's River seemed to have taken something out of Rosecrans. He lost much of his confidence and aggressiveness. After the battle, he settled down where it had been fought and built extensive fortifications. He called upon the government to furnish him more men and supplies

---

[9] Richard Meade Bache, *Life of General George Meade* . . . , 281; Francis A. Walker, *History of the Second Army Corps in the Army of the Potomac*, 253–255; Meade, *Life and Letters of Meade*, I, 385.

and to allow him ample time for preparation before he attempted another forward move. His plaintive despatches irritated Stanton and Halleck. He sent more telegrams to Washington, said Halleck, than all the other generals in the field combined.[1] He convinced himself that Stanton and Halleck were trying to push him into a premature offensive and were at the same time withholding from him the supplies and reinforcements that he needed. Like some other generals in the war, he tended to break down under the responsibility and tension of command.

Believing as he did that the government was not supporting him properly, it was easy for him to proceed to the suspicion that somebody in Washington wanted him to fail. He decided that Stanton was the villain. His anger at Stanton and his anxiety about his next move made him explosively touchy. When Halleck informed him that there was a vacant major generalcy in the regular army and that Stanton had said it would be awarded to the officer who first won an important victory, Rosecrans almost burst with rage. He wrote to Halleck that he felt degraded to see the government auctioneering commissions and that any officer who fought a battle to secure the promotion would come by it basely. Halleck tried to calm him by saying that the government wanted only to reward merit, but Rosecrans was not to be calmed. He now believed that Stanton was trying to bribe him into action before he was ready.[2] Rosecrans had some cause to be angry. Halleck's letter did give the impression that the commission would be knocked down to the earliest bidder. Nevertheless, Rosecrans should have ignored the whole business. It was not worth his time. Halleck sent similar letters to other generals,

[1] Rosecrans to Halleck, January 30, February 1, 2, 1863, *Official Records*, XXIII, pt. 2, 31, 33–34; Halleck to Rosecrans, February 1, April 20, *ibid.*, 31, 255–256.

[2] Halleck to Rosecrans, March 1, 13, 1863, *ibid.*, XXIII, pt. 2, 95, 138; Rosecrans to Halleck, March 6, *ibid.*, 111.

including Grant. Grant was too busy to bother getting in a controversy with Halleck about what was good military taste. He went ahead with his work and eventually won the commission.

Rosecrans took his resentments and frustrations directly to Lincoln. He wrote the President that after Stone's River Stanton had promised to give him anything he asked for. But, said Rosecrans, nearly all of his requests for men and supplies had been rejected. He had asked that his commission be dated back to December, 1861, which would have ranked him above Grant, and this too had been refused. Lincoln replied with the kind of patient, wise letter that he wrote to so many hypersensitive officers during the war. Stanton's promise was pretty broad, said Lincoln, but it accorded with the kindly feelings that the authorities had for Rosecrans. "Still the promise must have a reasonable construction," Lincoln cautioned. "We know you will not purposely make an unreasonable request, nor persist in one after it shall appear to be such." Seeking to disabuse Rosecrans of the notion that he was the victim of official persecution, Lincoln said: "I know not a single enemy of yours here." The President said that Rosecrans's commission could not be dated back without doing injustice to others. He tried to make the General see that the issue of rank was not important: "Truth to speak, I do not appreciate this matter of rank on paper as you officers do. The world will not forget that you fought the battle of Stone's River, and it will never care a fig whether you rank General Grant on paper, or he so ranks you." [3]

Rosecrans continued to believe that Stanton and Halleck were his enemies. He denounced them openly to the reporters at his headquarters.[4] But toward Lincoln he manifested

[3] Rosecrans to Lincoln, March 16, 1863, *ibid.*, XXIII, pt. 2, 146–147; Lincoln to Rosecrans, March 17, *Works of Lincoln*, VIII, 226–229.

[4] Henry Villard, *Memoirs of Henry Villard, Journalist and Financier*, II, 66–68.

only feelings of great respect and friendship. He refused to allow his name to be used against Lincoln as a presidential possibility. Some of the Eastern radicals decided that Rosecrans would be a good candidate to put forward against Lincoln in 1864 for the Republican nomination. They wanted to know whether he would be interested in a political venture and whether he was sound on the slavery issue. They sent an agent to the General to find out. Rosecrans listened to this man and told him to tell his friends that they were wrong to oppose Lincoln. "He is in his right place," said Rosecrans.[5]

Lincoln was not as satisfied with Rosecrans as the General was with him. He thought that Rosecrans was much too slow in completing his preparations to move against Chattanooga. After Grant closed in on Vicksburg, Lincoln became more impatient with Rosecrans. The President feared that unless Rosecrans went after the Confederates, they would detach troops from East Tennessee to Mississippi and break Grant's siege. He urged Rosecrans to help Grant by taking the offensive. Rosecrans said that he would but did nothing. Halleck, who handled much of the western army correspondence for Lincoln, warned Rosecrans that unless he moved soon part of his army would be taken away and given to Grant.[6]

Rosecrans replied to the pressure from Washington with a strange letter. When Lincoln saw it, he must have wondered if Rosecrans was becoming unbalanced. The General said that he was preparing to strike a telling blow, but that he had submitted the question of an early advance to a council of his generals and they had voted against it. Therefore, said Rosecrans, he would wait until the fate of Vicksburg was settled before he moved forward. A good maxim of war, he informed

[5] Smith, *Garfield*, I, 297–298; James A. Gilmore, *Personal Recollections of Abraham Lincoln and the Civil War*, 100–103, 123, 145–147.

[6] Lincoln to Rosecrans, May 28, 1863, *Works of Lincoln*, VIII, 284; Rosecrans to Lincoln, May 28, *Official Records*, XXIII, pt. 2, 369; Halleck to Rosecrans, June 2, *ibid.*, XXIV, pt. 3, 376.

Halleck, the master of maxims, was never to risk two great battles at the same time.

Old Brains threw the maxims right back at him. Rightly Halleck pointed out that the axiom about not dissipating strength in several endeavors applied to one army but not to two. There was another good maxim to remember, said Halleck: councils of war never fight.[7] Although Halleck thought Rosecrans was wrong, he said that he would not order him to fight if Rosecrans thought he was not ready. At this point Lincoln stepped into the picture. The President had no intention of letting Rosecrans fix his own time to advance. A few days after Rosecrans informed Washington that he would not move, Halleck telegraphed him that the government wanted to know if he was going to advance immediately and demanded a yes or no answer. Rosecrans realized he would have to act. He replied that if immediately meant tonight or tomorrow, no; if it meant about five days hence, yes. On June 24 he moved forward.[8] The fate of Vicksburg was as yet unsettled.

Lincoln had told General Reynolds that he thought he could repair Hooker militarily and use him. The President soon got a chance to test his idea. Early in June, Lee started the offensive that carried him into Pennsylvania and culminated in the battle of Gettysburg. He moved westward from Fredericksburg along the south side of the Rappahannock to the Valley and then swung rapidly northward through the Valley into Maryland and Pennsylvania, using the Valley as his line of communications. As he put his movement into the first phase of its execution, his army was strung out for one hun-

[7] Rosecrans to Halleck, June 11, 1863, *Official Records*, XXIII, pt. 1, 8; Halleck to Rosecrans, June 12, *ibid.*, 8.

[8] Halleck to Rosecrans, June 16, 1863, and Rosecrans to Halleck, June 16, 24, *ibid.*, XXIII, pt. 1, 10.

dred miles, from Fredericksburg to the Valley. Hooker knew that Lee was moving, and he reasoned that Lee intended to cross the upper Potomac or to get between the Union army and Washington. Hooker knew also the general disposition of the enemy forces. He proposed to Lincoln that the best way to meet the Confederate offensive was for him to cross the Rappahannock and attack the rear of Lee's army at Fredericksburg. Later he could return and deal with the advance forces of the Confederates in the Valley or east of it. He asked if this plan met Lincoln's approval and if it accorded with his instructions always to keep Washington covered.[9]

Hooker's plan was completely wrong. His proper course was to place his army in a position from where he could move to encounter the enemy offensive as soon as its direction was developed. In effect, Hooker was proposing that he should avoid meeting the main part of the Confederate army in order to snap up its rear unit. He wanted to abandon what should have been his major objective to attain a minor objective. All through the Gettysburg campaign, he would give every evidence that he was afraid to come to grips with the army that had defeated him at Chancellorsville. Lincoln saw the wrongness in Hooker's plan immediately. He telegraphed Hooker not to cross to the south side of the Rappahannock if Lee crossed north and not to attack the force at Fredericksburg. The President said that while Hooker was assailing the Confederates in their entrenchments Lee would move into an advantageous position north of the river. In homely language, Lincoln gave Hooker some excellent strategic advice: "In one word, I would not take any risk of being entangled upon the river, like an ox jumped half over a fence and liable to be torn by dogs front and rear without a fair chance to gore one way or kick the other." If Lee came to the north side of

[9] Hooker to Lincoln, June 5, 1863, *ibid.*, XXVII, pt. 1, 30.

the river, said Lincoln, stay there and fight him or act on the defensive. The President concluded by saying that he was only offering suggestions to Hooker, not giving orders, and that he wanted to be guided by the judgment of Hooker and Halleck. In fact, said Lincoln, he had turned over Hooker's despatch to Halleck to answer.[1] To Hooker, already shaken by the responsibility of having to counter the Confederate offensive, the news that his hated enemy would have some influence over his movements must have been a bad blow.

A few days later, Lincoln received another telegram from Hooker. Instead of taking Lincoln's sound advice, Hooker proposed an even more fantastic movement than to attack Fredericksburg. Now he wanted to ignore Lee altogether and march into Richmond. He thought that the government should be able to collect a sufficient force to halt Lee's northward move, and then later he could advance from the Confederate capital *back* over the Potomac and capture Lee. Of all the strange communications that Lincoln received from military men during the war, this was the strangest. Not even McClellan had ever lost himself so completely to reality. Hooker's despatch arrived in Washington at a little after five in the afternoon on June 10. Lincoln answered it within the hour. He must have had a feeling of frustrated desperation as he wondered what he could say that would recall Hooker to his senses. In his reply, Lincoln again warned Hooker not to go south of the Rappahannock. If Hooker had Richmond invested at that moment, the President emphasized, he could not take it in twenty days, and in the meantime the Confederates would break his communications. Again he gave Hooker the best kind of strategic counsel: "I think Lee's army, and not Richmond, is your true objective point. If he comes toward the upper Potomac follow on his flank and on

[1] Lincoln to Hooker, June 5, 1863, *Works of Lincoln*, VIII, 291–292.

his inside track, shortening your lines while he lengthens his. Fight him, too, when opportunity offers. If he stays where he is, fret him and fret him." [2]

Two days after he wrote Hooker, Lincoln decided that he had better go to Hooker's headquarters and see the General. Ostensibly he wanted to witness a trial firing of some incendiary shells, but his undoubted purpose was to find out what was wrong with Fighting Joe. He left Washington by boat and got to Acquia, or part way there, when a telegram from Stanton induced him to turn back. Hooker had telegraphed that he was moving his headquarters so frequently that it would be hard for Lincoln to find him, and Stanton and Halleck thought that it was dangerous for the President to be traveling through an area that might at any moment become a fighting front. [3]

Hooker finally did what Lincoln wanted. He pulled back from the Rappahannock and moved northward on a line roughly parallel to Lee's line of march, following, as Lincoln had put it, on Lee's inside track. In the meantime, the advance units of the Confederate army were smashing through the Valley, threatening to gobble up Federal garrisons at Winchester and Martinsburg; other parts of Lee's army were still east of the mountains and moving toward the Valley. Lincoln thought that Hooker ought to save the garrisons by attacking some part of Lee's stretched out forces. On the evening of the fourteenth, Lincoln, looking very depressed, was at the War Department waiting for telegrams. He told Gideon Welles that his generals seemed to know little about

[2] Hooker to Lincoln, June 10, 1863, *Official Records,* XXVII, pt. 1, 34–35; Lincoln to Hooker, June 10, *Works of Lincoln,* VIII, 297.

[3] Lincoln to Hooker, June 12, 1863, *Official Records,* XXVII, pt. 1, 37; Hooker to Lincoln, June 12, *ibid.,* 37; General D. H. Rucker to Stanton, June 13, Stanton to Captain Ferguson, June 13, and Stanton to Lincoln, June 13, Lincoln MSS., vol. 113; Lincoln to Hooker, June 13, *C. C. W., Reports,* 1865, I, 259; MS. Journal of General M. C. Meigs, June 12, 13.

the situations in their fronts and that they rarely took advantage of enemy mistakes.[4]

That day Lincoln sent Hooker a telegram urging him to hit the Confederates at some point on their line of march. Again expressing his strategic thinking in salty, down to earth language, Lincoln wrote: "If the head of Lee's army is at Martinsburg and the tail of it on the plank road between Fredericksburg and Chancellorsville, the animal must be very slim somewhere. Could you not break him?" On the next day, Lincoln informed Hooker that the Confederates had captured Winchester and Martinsburg and were heading for the Potomac. Obviously laboring under great anxiety, Lincoln added: "I would like to hear from you." [5]

Hooker was laboring under great nervous strain himself. He was acting exactly as McClellan did in a crisis. Although he outnumbered the Confederates, he believed that he faced a superior enemy, and he called on the government to send him all available troops in the Washington area. He manifested McClellan's characteristic of trying to place the blame for his possible failure on the government. He told one officer that if he could not carry out his own plan others would have to give the orders for his movements; he would obey every order literally and let the responsibility rest on the authorities in Washington.[6] Like McClellan, he complained that he did not have the confidence of the government and was not being supported properly.

As he got closer to Washington in his northward movement, he fancied that Halleck was influencing Lincoln to withhold help from him. Finally he telegraphed Lincoln that he lacked Halleck's confidence and that the attitude of the general in chief would ruin any chance for victory in the op-

[4] Welles, *Diary*, I, 328.
[5] Lincoln to Hooker, June 14, 15, 1863, *Works of Lincoln*, VIII, 315, 317.
[6] Haupt, *Reminiscences*, 205–206.

erations ahead. He was asking indirectly for assurance from the President that Halleck would have no power to order his movements. Lincoln replied immediately and with a decision that Hooker had not expected. "To remove all misunderstanding," Lincoln telegraphed, "I now place you in the strict military relation to General Halleck of a commander of one of the armies to the general-in-chief of all the armies. I have not intended differently, but as it seems to be differently understood I shall direct him to give you orders, and you to obey them." [7]

With characteristic consideration, Lincoln wrote a letter to Hooker on the same day that he sent the telegram and despatched a special courier to the army to deliver the letter to Hooker. The President explained in the letter his reasons for making the order, and tried to reason Hooker out of his wild distrust of Halleck. Hooker did not lack Halleck's confidence in any degree to do him harm, said Lincoln. Halleck objected to Hooker reporting directly to the President but did not withhold support from Fighting Joe because of this practice. Lincoln thought that Halleck's criticism of Hooker's way of reporting was wrong. The arrangement would work all right, Lincoln asserted, if Halleck and Hooker were as frank to each other and to him as he was to them. Having reassured Hooker about the situation in his rear, Lincoln urged the General to look to the one in his front. He urged Hooker to strike a blow at the extended enemy army or its extended line of communications. He pointed out the obvious fact that Hooker was on the inside line of an arc from Virginia to Maryland, and Lee was on the outside. Hooker was closer to Richmond than Lee was and in an excellent position to attack the Confederate communications. In fact, said Lincoln, Hooker had the same opportunity that McClellan had had

[7] Hooker to Lincoln, June 16, 1863, *C. C. W., Reports*, 1865, I, 163; Lincoln to Hooker, June 16, *Works of Lincoln*, VIII, 323.

and lost after Antietam. Recalling that he had then urged McClellan to attack, Lincoln said: "Quite possibly I was wrong both then and now, but in the great responsibility resting upon me, I cannot be entirely silent. Now, all I ask is that you will be in such mood that we can get into our action the best cordial judgment of yourself and General Halleck, with my poor mite added, if indeed he and you shall think it entitled to any consideration at all." [8]

Lincoln's statement of the influence he intended to exert in the determination of strategic decisions was deceptively modest. He had not the slightest purpose of abandoning to Halleck the function of general in chief, which since second Manassas he—and not Halleck—had been exercising. Nor, as Lincoln knew, did Halleck desire to act as general in chief. In the present crisis, Lincoln was turning to Halleck more frequently than he did ordinarily for technical advice and information. In particular, he sent many orders to Hooker and other generals in the Virginia area through Halleck. He realized that Halleck could frame his thoughts in a form that the generals could understand, a result that did not always follow when he wrote the directives himself. Part of the humility in his letter to Hooker was real, part of it was assumed to calm the General's frenzied mind.

On June 23, Hooker was close enough to Washington to come into town for a flying visit. He conferred at the War Department with Lincoln, Stanton, and Halleck. The President looked sad and careworn at the meeting. How Hooker looked is not known. It was reported that he was drunk when he left the capital to return to the army and was drunk the next day. What happened at the conference is also unknown. One item that seems to have been discussed was whether or not an attempt should be made to hold Harper's Ferry at the

[8] Lincoln to Hooker, June 16, 1863, *Works of Lincoln*, VIII, 320–321.

northern end of the Valley. Halleck thought that it should be held, and Hooker, probably, that it should not. Lincoln agreed with Halleck. When Hooker got back to camp, he ordered a corps to move toward the Ferry.[9]

Shortly after Hooker departed, a rumor spread that he had sneaked back to Washington one night, probably for a drinking spree at his favorite haunts. Lincoln telegraphed him asking if the report was true. In a reply that was hardly respectful, Hooker denied it and asked if Lincoln had got the story from the newspapers. Calmly the President answered: "It did not come from the newspapers, nor did I believe it; but I wished to be entirely sure it was a falsehood." [1]

Three days after Hooker's visit, Lincoln was guardedly optimistic about the situation. He said to Gideon Welles: "We cannot help beating them, if we have the man. How much depends in military matters on one master mind! Hooker may commit the same fault as McClellan and lose his chance. We shall soon see, but it appears to me he can't help but win." [2] Hooker was not the man. Any resolution he had once possessed had disappeared. More and more, he was convinced that the Confederate army outnumbered him and that he could not fight it unless he got large reinforcements. He sent Butterfield, his chief of staff, to Washington to ask for all the disposable troops in the capital defences. Butterfield laid the request before Lincoln, who immediately sent for Halleck. The President said that he would be guided by Halleck's opinion. Halleck said that it was unsafe to detach any more men from Washington. Without a moment's hesitation, Lincoln stated that Halleck's decision was final.[3]

[9] Welles, *Diary,* I, 340; Heintzelman MS. Journal, June 25, 1863; Hebert, *Hooker,* 243.

[1] Hooker to Lincoln, June 26, 1863, and Lincoln to Hooker, June 27, *C. C. W., Reports,* 1865, I, 290–291.

[2] Welles, *Diary,* I, 344, June 26, 1863.

[3] *C. C. W., Reports,* 1865, I, 171.

If Hooker had deliberately wanted to provoke Lincoln, he could have chosen no more effective way than to ask for more troops and at the same time to refuse to attack until he received them. Hooker may not have been trying to anger Lincoln, but all the evidence indicates that he was looking for an excuse to get rid of his command. He was afraid to meet Lee. Hooker next asked Halleck for permission to abandon the defences of Harper's Ferry so that he could join the troops there to his army. When Halleck refused, Hooker asked to be relieved. In a petulant despatch to Halleck, he said that the government had charged him with too many missions: to cover Washington and Harper's Ferry and to encounter a superior enemy. Because he could not comply with all these conditions, he wanted to give up his post.[4] On Sunday, June 28, Lincoln told the Cabinet that Hooker had been relieved. The President said that for days Hooker had been acting like McClellan—refusing to execute orders and crying for reinforcements. Lincoln also announced that Meade had been appointed to command the army.[5]

The choice of Meade was made by Lincoln and Stanton. Halleck was not consulted. Apparently Lincoln and the Secretary decided upon Meade at a night conference at the War Department after Hooker's request to be relieved had arrived in Washington. Their selection was a logical one in the situation. They had to name a commander fast and one who was familiar with the army. Meade was one of the senior corps generals and had a solid reputation as a handler of troops. Many of the corps and division generals had recommended him to Lincoln for the command after Chancellorsville. His appointment would be well received by the army. Sometime

[4] Hooker to Halleck, June 26, 27 (two telegrams), 1863, *Official Records*, XXVII, pt. 1, 58, 60; Halleck to Hooker, June 27, two telegrams, *ibid.*, 59–60.
[5] Welles, *Diary*, I, 348.

during the conference, Stanton remarked that Meade was from Pennsylvania, where the crucial battle of the campaign would be fought. Lincoln is supposed to have said: "And will fight well on his own dunghill." [6]

Orders were prepared appointing Meade, and a special staff officer from the War Department went out to the army to deliver them to the new commander. The courier found Meade near Frederick, Maryland, half-dressed and asleep on a camp bed. With grim humor, he told Meade that he had bad news: that Meade was relieved from command of his corps. Meade said that he was not surprised, he had been expecting it. Then the officer informed him that he bore orders appointing him to command the army. Meade showed no elation. He said that he did not know the disposition of the army and that Reynolds would have made a better commander. But he agreed to accept the appointment. [7]

People were not dazzled or impressed by George Gordon Meade as they were by Burnside or Hooker. He lacked glamour. He was about six feet in height, gaunt, grizzled, and stern. On horseback, with a slouched hat pulled down almost to his large Roman nose, he reminded one observer of a grim helmeted knight. He was extremely nervous, probably dyspeptic, and given to frequent fits of temper in which he lashed out fiercely at all around him. His subordinates were his chief victims. One of his staff officers said that when Meade had something on his mind, he was like a firecracker, always going bang at somebody near him. He was known as "the old snapping turtle." [8] As a general, Meade was com-

[6] George C. Gorham, *Life and Public Services of Edwin M. Stanton,* II, 98–100; Heintzelman MS. Journal, June 28, 1862.

[7] Seward, *Reminiscences,* 238–241.

[8] Charles A. Page, *Letters of a War Correspondent,* 111; Dana, *Recollections,* 189–190; George R. Agassiz (ed.), *Meade's Headquarters, 1863–65; Letters of Colonel Theodore Lyman . . . ,* 73; Gordon, *War Diary,* 141.

petent in a routine sort of way. He handled troops well, he was above the average as a tactician, and he had a fair amount of courage in a crisis. He did not have enough boldness or originality to be a good strategist. His strategic plans showed no brilliance, not even much imagination.

Perhaps Meade was too gentle a person to be a successful general in a total war. Or perhaps his seeming gentleness was assumed to hide the fact that he lacked the hardness to wage hard modern war. He liked to think of war in the old way, as a conflict between men in uniform. Of economic warfare against enemy resources he had not the slightest appreciation and viewed it as brutality. Once, early in the war, he had been ordered to strip the farm of a man who was going to place his crops in the possession of the Confederates. He performed the mission, but he wrote to his wife: "It made me sad to do such injury, and I really was ashamed of our cause, which thus required war to be made on individuals." He thought that the government ought to conduct the war like an afflicted parent compelled, with a sad heart, to chastise an erring child.[9]

Meade received, along with the orders appointing him commander of the Army of the Potomac, written instructions on how to operate the army. Halleck drafted and signed the instructions, but they were Lincoln's strategic ideas put into military form by Halleck. They stated that Meade would not be hampered by minute instructions from Washington and would have wide freedom to move his army as he desired to meet changing situations. Lincoln realized that Meade's front was highly fluid. However, said Halleck, Meade always was to keep in mind that his army was the covering force for Washington as well as the striking force against the enemy. Therefore, he was to so maneuver and fight as to cover Wash-

[9] Meade to Mrs. Meade, December 5, 1861, February 23, 1862, Meade, *Life and Letters of Meade*, I, 234, 247.

ington and Baltimore. The instructions were agreeable to Meade. The Confederates were then in Pennsylvania. Meade told Halleck that he would move toward the Susquehanna River, keeping Washington covered, and give battle to the Confederates if they turned east.[1]

At the time Meade assumed command, the Confederate army was extended over a wide area in southern Pennsylvania. Lee, meeting no opposition, had sent his forces in separate columns against a number of key cities. Rightly Meade figured that if he concentrated his army some place west of the Susquehanna, Lee would have to concentrate also and risk battle. If Meade moved forward toward Lee's rear, the Confederates would have to pull back from Harrisburg and other places that they had occupied and prepare to meet the threat posed by a massed Union army. Meade reasoned also and again correctly that Lee would have to attack him. Lee was on the offensive in the country of the enemy. He could hardly retreat tamely to Virginia if confronted by a Federal army. He would have to fight, and if the Federals would not attack him, he would have to attack them. Meade decided to take a strong defensive position and receive Lee's attack. Tentatively he chose Pipe Creek in Maryland, just south of the Pennsylvania line, as the place where he would give battle.[2]

His analysis of what Lee would do proved accurate. Lee was surprised and disturbed when he learned that the Federal army was so close to him. Hurriedly he began to concentrate his army. He pulled his scattered forces back to Cashtown, from whence he could move east to make contact with the Federals. Some of his units went into Gettysburg, east of Cashtown. They reported that Gettysburg was the hub of a network of good roads, many of them leading toward the Po-

[1] Halleck to Meade, June 27, 1863, *Official Records*, XXVII, pt. 1, 61; Meade to Halleck, June 28, *ibid.*, 61–62.
[2] Meade to Halleck, July 1, 1863, *ibid.*, XXVII, pt. 1, 70–71.

tomac. Its strategic importance was great, and it was, therefore, important for Lee to occupy it. Lee had another reason
for wanting the town. His men found Federal soldiers there,
and for all Lee knew, Meade's whole army might be in the
vicinity. Lee put his army in motion toward Gettysburg. The
Federals that his troops had encountered were from Meade's
army. Although Meade had decided to fight at Pipe Creek, he
sent an advance force under Reynolds to Gettysburg to examine the terrain there. Reynolds reported that Gettysburg
was a stronger position than Pipe Creek and advised Meade
to make his battle at Gettysburg. Without hesitation, Meade
ordered his army forward. The two armies converged upon
Gettysburg at the same time. On July 1–3 they fought the
greatest battle ever waged in North America.

The fighting on the first day consisted largely of feeling out
operations by both sides. On the second Lee tried to break
the Union left and failed. On the third he attempted to crack
the center and failed. On July 4 there was no action. The
next day Lee pulled out of his line and started to withdraw
toward the Potomac. Gettysburg was a Union victory, but
Meade's conduct of the battle became the subject of bitter
controversy later. Butterfield, who continued to act as chief
of staff, charged that on the morning of July 2, before the
Confederates attacked, Meade directed him to prepare an
order for a retreat. Meade denied this, and the evidence
seems to support him. Apparently he told Butterfield to
gather information so that he could make a retreat order if
retreat became necessary.[3] On the night of July 2 Meade
called his officers into council. His enemies said that he asked
them whether the army should retreat and indicated that he
favored withdrawal. Meade denied this also, but here the evidence is not so clearly on his side. At some point in the proceedings a question arose as to the security of the army's

[3] *C. C. W., Reports,* 1865, I, 424–425, 436–439, 442–443, 466–468.

position. There was discussion about whether the position should be held as it was or minor adjustments made in it or given up altogether. Finally the generals voted by written ballot to hold it and fight. From the evidence, it is hard to say whether Meade proposed that the council consider abandoning the Gettysburg line or whether the question emerged naturally from the discussion. One general said that after the vote was taken, Meade said he disagreed with the decision. Meade and other officers replied that he had made no such remark, and Meade said he did not even think it.[4]

Part of the confusion concerning Meade's actions was due to the General's own uncertainty as to what he should do. Being unsure of his course, he gave different impressions of his purpose to different people. Some of his despatches to Washington must have caused Lincoln to wonder if Meade had a purpose. On the afternoon of July 2 he telegraphed Halleck that he was awaiting an attack by Lee. If he was not attacked, he said, and he could get information that he could attack with success he would do so. If he could not take the offensive or if the enemy passed to his rear, he would fall back to another position. That night, after the Confederates had assaulted and had been repulsed, he telegraphed that he would remain in his present position the next day but could not say until he knew more about the condition of his troops whether his operations would be defensive or offensive.[5]

Meade fought Gettysburg with great tactical skill. He placed his men well, and he used his reserves properly to bolster threatened places in his line. Nevertheless, he was content to fight a completely defensive battle. He showed no aggressive spirit. He launched no counterattacks after he re-

[4] *Ibid.*, 1865, I, 350–351; *Official Records*, XXVII, pt. 1, 13–14, 124–127, 139; Gibbon, *Personal Recollections*, 140–145; C. E. Slocum, *Life and Services of Major-General Henry Warner Slocum*, 135.

[5] Meade to Halleck, July 2, 1863, two despatches, *Official Records*, XXVII, pt. 1, 72.

pulsed the Confederate assaults. Like McClellan at Antietam, he was satisfied to see the enemy withdraw intact from his front. He felt that he had done something great by holding his ground and forcing Lee out of Pennsylvania. The day after the fighting stopped he issued an order to his troops in which he congratulated them for having "baffled" an enemy army of superior numbers. But our task is not yet accomplished, he said; we have to "drive from our soil every vestige of the presence of the invader." [6]

During the battle Lincoln was in the telegraph office of the War Department hour after hour day and night. When the news came that Lee's final attack had failed and that the Confederates were in retreat, Lincoln was jubilant. He reasoned correctly that Lee was withdrawing because he had been badly beaten and that Meade had victory in his grasp if he smashed after Lee. Then a copy of Meade's congratulatory order arrived in Washington. Lincoln snatched it eagerly. When he came to the sentence about driving the invader from "our" soil, his hands dropped to his knees and in an anguished tone he said: "Drive the invader from our soil! My God! Is that all?" [7]

[6] *Ibid.*, XXVII, pt. 3, 519.
[7] Bates, *Lincoln in the Telegraph Office*, 155–156; Rice, *Reminiscences of Lincoln*, 402.

Chapter 11

"Like a Duck Hit on the Head"

RIGHT after he read Meade's congratulatory order, Lincoln wrote a note to Halleck. He said that he did not like Meade's phrase about driving the invaders beyond the border. Now some other despatches from generals operating with Meade had come in. They all indicated a desire not to come to grips with Lee. Deeply disturbed, Lincoln wrote: "These things all appear to me to be connected with a purpose to cover Baltimore and Washington, and to get the enemy across the river again without a further collision, and they do not appear connected with a purpose to prevent his crossing and to destroy him. I do fear the former purpose is acted upon and the latter is rejected." If Halleck was satisfied that Meade was moving aggressively after the Confederates, Lincoln would be content. If Halleck was not, then Lincoln directed him to order Meade to move faster.[1]

Lincoln's analysis of Meade's purpose was completely correct. Meade was trying to get the Confederates over the Potomac without risking a battle. He did not say so in his communications to the government, and he probably did not admit even to himself that he was avoiding a showdown. But his fear of the result of a general engagement appeared in every despatch that he sent to the government. In one written

[1] Lincoln to Halleck, July 6, 1863, *Works of Lincoln*, IX, 18–19.

three days after Gettysburg, he told Halleck that he would
attack if he got an opportunity, trusting that if misfortune
overwhelmed him fragments of his army could reach Washington in time to help defend the city against the victorious
Confederates.[2] Such pessimistic talk was absurd. Meade was
thinking too much of what had happened to the attackers at
Gettysburg. He believed the same thing would happen to
him if he attacked. His defensive victory at Gettysburg ruined
him as an offensive general.

Lincoln sensed the absence of any aggressive purpose in
Meade's telegrams, and he feared that the General, unless
urged on from Washington, would let Lee escape. The President believed that if Meade could destroy the retreating
enemy the war would be ended. Halleck disagreed with Lincoln's opinion that Meade should seek a decisive battle. Un-
aggressive himself, Halleck thought that Meade was acting
properly in following Lee cautiously and using his army to
cover Washington. Nevertheless, he obeyed Lincoln's directions, and exhorted Meade to strike the Confederates before
they crossed the Potomac.[3] For a few days it seemed that
Meade would catch up to Lee and be able to attack him.
When the Confederates reached the river, high water prevented their crossing. Lincoln thought that now Meade
would surely close in for the final thrust. He was "anxious and
hopeful" for a victory, he told a friend.[4] But when Meade
still did not attack, Lincoln became downcast again. Waiting at the War Department for despatches from Meade, he
paced the floor nervously and said: "They will be ready

[2] Meade to Halleck, July 6, 1863, *Official Records*, XXVII, pt. 1,
80–81.

[3] Lincoln to Halleck, July 7, 1863, *Works of Lincoln*, IX, 22; Halleck
to Meade, July 8, *ibid.*, 22; Welles, *Diary*, I, 363–364; Halleck to Grant,
July 11, *Official Records*, XXIV, pt. 3, 498.

[4] Dennett, *Diary of Hay*, 66, July 11, 1863; Lincoln to J. K. Dubois,
July 11, *Official Records*, XXVII, pt. 3, 645.

to fight a magnificent battle when there is no enemy to fight." [5]

Again his analysis was correct. With the enemy trapped on the north side of the Potomac and fearful of being attacked, Meade called a council of his generals to discuss what he should do. He knew that he ought to attack, but always in his mind was the thought that if he did he would be defeated: the fruits of Gettysburg lost and the road to Washington open to the enemy. He seemed to be unable to comprehend that the Confederates had been badly beaten and were in no shape to resume the offensive.[6] The council voted not to attack until the strength of the Confederate position could be ascertained. Meade agreed with the decision. He began to probe cautiously the enemy line for a weak spot. While he was searching, the river fell, and Lee crossed to the Virginia side and safety.

Lincoln had been depressed by Meade's despatches describing the council. Then about noon on July 14 a telegram from Meade arrived announcing that Lee had escaped. Lincoln read it at the War Department. He was at once terribly angered and deeply saddened. To his secretary he said: "We had them within our grasp. We had only to stretch forth our hands & they were ours." [7] He left the Department to see Halleck. Gideon Welles walked across the White House lawn with him. In his diary, Welles recorded that he would never forget the President's voice and face as he talked about Meade's failure to destroy Lee. Lincoln said that he had expected and dreaded the awful news he had received: "And that, my God, is the last of this Army of the Potomac!" the President exclaimed. "There is bad faith somewhere. . . .

[5] Bates, *Lincoln in the Telegraph Office*, 157.

[6] *C. C. W., Reports*, 1865, I, 336; Gordon, *War Diary*, 142; Meade to Halleck, July 13, 1863, *Official Records*, XXVII, pt. 1, 91–92.

[7] Dennett, *Diary of Hay*, 66–67.

What does it mean, Mr. Welles? Great God! What does it mean?" Later in the day Lincoln got his feelings under control. Welles saw him again at the Department, lying on a sofa reading despatches and looking subdued but resolute.[8]

Right after Meade's despatch arrived, Halleck telegraphed Meade that Lincoln was greatly dissatisfied because Lee had escaped and that it would require an energetic pursuit of Lee to remove from the President's mind the impression that the pursuit so far had not been active enough. Taking Halleck's despatch as a censure, Meade asked to be relieved. Halleck replied that his telegram had not been intended to censure but only to stimulate Meade to action and that it was not sufficient cause for Meade to apply for relief.[9] Halleck showed Meade's request to Lincoln. The President immediately wrote a long letter to Meade. In many respects, it was the harshest letter to a general that he ever composed. He did not send it to Meade but retained it among his papers. Perhaps he felt that to rebuke Meade further would do no good and might do great harm. Most probably he wrote the document to release his own tortured feelings on paper.

Whatever the reasons, it was an excellent essay in military art; and it demonstrated that Lincoln appreciated a strategic principle that Meade and many generals seemed never to have heard of: that the destruction of the enemy armies was the primary objective of Union armies. Lincoln explained to Meade that he was sorry that anything he had said had pained the General but that he had been in such "deep distress" at the news of Lee's escape that he could not help expressing his disappointment. Ever since Gettysburg, said Lincoln, he had been oppressed by Meade's evident intention to herd the

[8] Welles, *Diary*, I, 370–371.
[9] Halleck to Meade, July 14, 1863, two telegrams, and Meade to Halleck, July 14, *Official Records*, XXVII, pt. 1, 92–94; Meade to Mrs. Meade, July 14, in Meade, *Life and Letters of Meade,* II, 134.

enemy over the river without fighting. Then when a flood detained Lee on the north bank, Meade "stood and let the flood run down, bridges be built, and the enemy move away at his leisure without attacking him." Meade did not seem to appreciate the magnitude of the misfortune involved in Lee's safe withdrawal, said the President: "He was within your easy grasp, and to have closed upon him would, in connection with our other late successes, have ended the war. As it is, the war will be prolonged indefinitely." If Meade could not attack Lee north of the Potomac, asked Lincoln, how could he with any chance of success, south of it? "Your golden opportunity is gone," Lincoln concluded, "and I am distressed immeasurably because of it." [1]

As distressed as he was about Meade, Lincoln at no time had any thought of removing him from command. He was grateful to Meade for having repelled the Confederate invasion, and he considered that the General had fought Gettysburg with tactical skill. Besides, if he got rid of Meade, who was there any better to put in his place? Speaking of Meade to Welles, Lincoln said: "He has made a great mistake, but we will try him farther." [2] To one of Meade's officers who had written to Lincoln defending his commander, the President replied with words that were a fair description of Meade: "General Meade has my confidence as a brave and skilful officer and a true man." [3] In time, Lincoln was even able to view Meade's actions after Gettysburg with grim humor. Many weeks later Meade came to Washington to confer with Lincoln and the Cabinet. During the discussions, there was naturally some talk of what had occurred at Gettysburg. Lincoln suddenly asked: "Do you know, general, what your at-

[1] Lincoln to Meade, July 14, 1863, *Works of Lincoln*, IX, 28–30.

[2] Welles, *Diary*, I, 374, July 17, 1863; Dennett, *Diary of Hay*, 69, July 19; McClure, *Lincoln and Men of War-Times*, 331–332.

[3] Lincoln to General O. O. Howard, July 21, 1863, *Works of Lincoln*, IX, 39.

titude towards Lee for a week after the battle reminded me of?" "No, Mr. President, what is it?" replied Meade. "I'll be hanged if I could think of anything else," said Lincoln, "than an old woman trying to shoo her geese across a creek."[4]

In the weeks right after Gettysburg, Lincoln gradually reconciled himself to the disappointing results of the battle. Meade, soothed and buttered up by Halleck, stopped talking about his being relieved. He complained, however, that he had an impression the government desired him to bring on a general engagement and that he was not ready for it, although he hoped to be able to advance at a later date. Hastily Lincoln informed Halleck that he did not think Meade should seek a decisive battle in Virginia, at least for the present. Making the same point that he had in the unsent letter to Meade, Lincoln said that if Meade had not been strong enough to attack north of the Potomac he certainly could not attack successfully south of it. The President obviously had no confidence that Meade could win a victory any place. He feared that the general who could not smash the enemy in his own country would be defeated if he fought a showdown battle in the enemy's country.[5]

In the letter to Meade that he did not send, Lincoln said that the destruction of Lee's army taken in connection with other recent Union victories, would have ended the war. He was referring to Grant's capture of Vicksburg on July 4. All during June Grant had maintained his bulldog grip on the great river fortress. His siege operations seemed slow to many critics in Congress and the press; some newspapers printed exaggerated stories of the deaths in his army from disease.

[4] W. A. Croffut, in *St. Paul and Minneapolis Pioneer Press*, December 7, 1884.

[5] Halleck to Meade, July 28, 1863, *Official Records*, XXVII, pt. 1, 104–105; Meade to Halleck, July 30, 31, *ibid.*, 106–107, 108–110; Lincoln to Halleck, July 29, *Works of Lincoln*, IX, 46–47.

Lincoln was beset by demands, including some from important Republicans, to remove Grant. The President refused to yield to the pressure. "I rather like the man," he was supposed to have said. "I think I'll try him a little longer." [6] On July 5, before the news of the fall of Vicksburg had arrived in Washington, Lincoln told one officer why he liked Grant: "He doesn't worry and bother me. He isn't shrieking for reinforcements all the time. He takes what troops we can safely give him . . . and does the best he can with what he has got. . . ." If Grant took Vicksburg, said Lincoln, "why Grant is my man and I am his the rest of the war." [7]

On July 7 Gideon Welles received a despatch from Admiral Porter announcing the capture of Vicksburg. Welles rushed to the White House to give Lincoln the news. The President was beside himself with joy. He said he would telegraph the wonderful information to Meade and Banks, the latter then besieging Port Hudson. "This will relieve Banks," exclaimed Lincoln. "It will inspire me." [8] He needed inspiration. He heard about Vicksburg when he was beginning to fear that Meade would let Lee get away. In those critical July days, he must have made many contrasts in his mind between the aggressive conduct of Grant and the halting action of Meade.

Definitely now he was Grant's man. He defended Grant against every criticism. To Burnside who complained that Grant had not returned some troops he had borrowed and had not said when he would, Lincoln replied: "General Grant is a copious worker and fighter, but a very meager writer or telegrapher." Undoubtedly Grant had meant to return the troops but had changed his purpose for some sufficient reason, said Lincoln, and had forgotten to tell Burn-

[6] William Conant Church, *Ulysses S. Grant . . .* , 180–181; Albert Deane Richardson, *A Personal History of Ulysses S. Grant*, 336–337.

[7] James F. Rusling, *Men and Things I Saw in Civil War Days*, 16–17.

[8] Welles, *Diary*, I, 364–365.

side.[9] Lincoln was obviously delighted to present this explanation of Grant's action. He had suffered so much from the literary profligacy of generals who accomplished nothing, who wrote well and fought badly, that he appreciated a spare man with the pen. Some people censured Grant for paroling the Vicksburg garrison instead of sending it and its commander, John C. Pemberton, north as prisoners of war. Grant's reason for concluding the parole arrangement with Pemberton was sound; he had wanted to induce a quicker capitulation and to avoid placing a sudden and large burden on the Federal prison system. One delegation of Grant critics appeared at the White House to protest the parole. They said that Pemberton's army would soon be in the field again. Lincoln told them the story of Sykes's dog, whom nobody liked. The boys who lived around Sykes fixed up a cartridge with a long fuse, put it in a piece of meat, which they dropped in front of Sykes's house, and whistled for the dog. He came out and swallowed the meat. The boys touched off the fuse, there was an explosion, and Sykes rushed from the house. He picked up a piece of dog and said mournfully: "Well I guess he'll never be much account again—as a dog." "And," Lincoln added, "I guess Pemberton's forces will never be much account again—as an army." [1]

A week after Vicksburg fell, Lincoln wrote Grant a gracious note of thanks. "I do not remember that you and I ever met personally," said Lincoln. "I write this now as a grateful acknowledgment for the almost inestimable service you have done the country." Lincoln then reviewed the Vicksburg campaign and his reaction to it. Revealing excellent strategic sense, he said that he had thought from the beginning that Grant should do what he finally did: go down the west

[9] Lincoln to Burnside, July 27, 1863, *Official Records*, XXIII, pt. 2, 561.
[1] Horace Porter, *Campaigning with Grant*, 27–28.

bank, cross, and operate below Vicksburg. However, continued Lincoln, he had also thought that when Grant got below the town he should have continued on, instead of turning north, and joined Banks at Port Hudson. Humbly and honestly, the President concluded: "I now wish to make the personal acknowledgment that you were right and I was wrong." [2]

Grant did not want to rest on his new laurels. He proposed a plan to take his army to Mobile and from it as a base to operate against the center of the Confederacy. Lincoln liked the idea and he appreciated Grant's desire to continue striking at the enemy's vitals, but he had to veto the plan. From his superior vantage point, he could see the whole picture of the war better than Grant. At the moment he was worried that France, which had seized the opportunity created by a divided America to seize Mexico, might move into Texas. To forestall the French, he wanted an expedition prepared to invade Texas and to occupy the line of the Rio Grande. He decided to send an army under Banks, who had captured Port Hudson, into Texas and to augment the size of Banks's force by adding to it units from Grant's army which had been sent to Grant from other departments. This would leave Grant's army so depleted that he could not undertake an operation of the magnitude of the one he had suggested against Mobile. Lincoln regretted having to keep Grant inactive, but he thought that Texas took precedence over Mobile. He wanted to tidy up affairs in the West before planning a move into the interior of the Confederacy. Grant, by capturing Vicksburg, had secured Union control of the whole Mississippi line and accomplished one of the great objectives of Lincoln's strategy. If Texas could now be made secure, the West would be in good shape. Mobile could wait. [3]

[2] Lincoln to Grant, July 13, 1863, *Works of Lincoln*, IX, 26.

[3] Lincoln to Stanton, and Lincoln to F. P. Blair, Sr., July 29 and 30,

In a considerate letter, Lincoln explained the purpose of his strategic planning to Grant. Mobile was a tempting prize, he said, but the Federal authority must be reestablished in Texas. Grant replied in a way that must have pleased Lincoln. The General said that he had inclined to a move against Mobile but that he could see the importance of a present move into Texas and that he indorsed it.[4] Lincoln probably did not know that while the Texas expedition was being planned Halleck and Stanton had considered a scheme to get Grant appointed commander of the Army of the Potomac. Grant heard about it, and asked Charles A. Dana to use his influence at the War Department to kill the proposal. Dana did, and Grant was profoundly grateful. He wrote Dana: "Whilst I would disobey no order I should beg very hard to be excused before accepting that command." [5]

While Grant was becoming the joy of Lincoln's heart because he fought hard and did not shriek for reinforcements, the commander of the other western army, Rosecrans, fought little and shrieked loudly. Rosecrans was developing into a first-rate epistolatory controversialist. He wrote angry letters to Washington at the slightest excuse and over the smallest details. He was increasingly convinced that the government was not supporting him properly and did not appreciate his achievements. After Lincoln had made him advance toward Chattanooga, when he had wanted to wait until Vicksburg's fate was settled before moving, Rosecrans moved forward and by skilful maneuvering forced the Confederates out of middle Tennessee and back to Chattanooga. His success came

1863, *Works of Lincoln,* IX, 47–49; Lincoln to Banks, August 5, *ibid.,* 56; Halleck to Banks, July 31, August 6, 10, *Official Records,* XXVI, pt. 1, 664, 672, 673; Banks to Halleck, August 15, *ibid.,* 682–683; Dennett, *Diary of Hay,* 77, August 9.

[4] Lincoln to Grant, August 9, 1863, *Works of Lincoln,* IX, 64–65; Grant to Lincoln, August 23, Lincoln MSS., vol. 121.

[5] Grant to Dana, August 5, 1863, Dana MSS.

when all interest was focused on Vicksburg and Gettysburg, and it was not noticed by the government as he thought it should be. Stanton wrote him that Meade had defeated Lee and Grant had taken Vicksburg and his noble army, if it would only advance, could end the war. Testily Rosecrans replied that Stanton did not seem to observe that the noble army had driven the enemy out of middle Tennessee. He said, probably taking a swipe at Grant, that he hoped the government would not overlook his victory because it was not written in letters of blood.[6]

During most of July, Rosecrans remained inactive. He was preparing for a final drive on Chattanooga, but he gave Washington no indication of when he would move. For all Lincoln knew, Rosecrans was stalled for the rest of the summer. Finally Halleck, at Lincoln's insistence, telegraphed Rosecrans that he must move. The patience of the authorities was exhausted, said Halleck, and the pressure for an invasion of East Tennessee was too strong for him or Rosecrans to resist. Rosecrans replied that he could not move beyond his means of supply and asked Halleck to tell Lincoln that he would advance eventually and with energy and prudence but that the two had to go together.[7] When by the first part of August he had not advanced a mile, Halleck ordered him to move forward immediately. Rosecrans asked if the order removed his discretion as to the time and manner of moving his troops. Halleck replied that the order was peremptory. Rosecrans then said that he was ready to move but if he had no discretion as to where he would cross the Tennessee River he wanted to be relieved. Justly irritated, Halleck told him to choose what routes of march he pleased but to get

[6] Stanton to Rosecrans, July 7, 1863, and Rosecrans to Stanton, July 7, *Official Records*, XXIII, pt. 2, 518.

[7] Halleck to Rosecrans, July 24, 25, 1863, *ibid.*, XXIII, pt. 2, 552, 554–555; Rosecrans to Halleck, July 25, two despatches, *ibid.*, 555–556.

ahead with his work and not to waste time quibbling over trivia.[8]

Rosecrans was not satisfied to bicker only with Halleck and Stanton. He took his troubles directly to Lincoln. He wrote the President that from Halleck's despatches he got the impression Lincoln was dissatisfied with his supposed inactivity. He explained why he had not moved faster: he had a long supply line to maintain and he lacked sufficient cavalry. Always one to go in detail into every issue past and present, Rosecrans then expounded on his failure to advance before Vicksburg fell. He repeated his curious reasoning that if he had gone forward then he would only have driven the Confederates in his front closer to Mississippi and made it easier for them to have attacked Grant. Lincoln replied in a long, carefully written letter. As he had done on previous occasions, he tried to calm the troubled mind of Rosecrans. He assured the General that he still had confidence in him and kindly feelings for him. Lincoln admitted that he had not liked Rosecrans's course during the siege of Vicksburg, that he had thought Rosecrans should aid Grant by taking the offensive. It had been by his direction, said Lincoln, that Halleck had ordered Rosecrans to move or to send part of his army to Grant. Lincoln recalled Rosecrans's despatch that the proper time for him to move was after Vicksburg fell, and said it had impressed him "very strangely." But all that was past, Lincoln continued. Vicksburg was in Federal possession, and the Confederates could reinforce their army facing Rosecrans from Mississippi. Therefore, Rosecrans's chance for a decisive stroke was lessened. Rosecrans could get into East Tennessee, Lincoln thought, but could he stay there? The President announced that he was leaving the decision as to what should

[8] Halleck to Rosecrans, August 4, 5, 7, 1863, *ibid.*, XXIII, pt. 2, 592, 597; Rosecrans to Halleck, August 4, 6, *ibid.*, 592, 594.

be done in Tennessee to Halleck and Rosecrans. Concluding with a touch of gentle ridicule, Lincoln begged Rosecrans to believe that he was not always watching him with an evil eye.[9]

Lincoln was telling Rosecrans to quit worrying and arguing and to fight. Rosecrans missed the point completely and ignored Lincoln's sage counsel. He sent the President another lengthy, quarrelsome communication, in which he insisted on raking the Vicksburg question over again. He disputed Lincoln's opinion that he should have kept the enemy in his front from reinforcing the enemy facing Grant. Why, he asked triumphantly, was it not equally correct that Grant should have prevented the Confederates in Mississippi from reinforcing their fellows in Tennessee?[1] Such pettifogging at a moment when action was needed must have nearly maddened the President.

In September Rosecrans finally moved forward. Again maneuvering his army with skill, he threatened the Confederate communications south of Chattanooga. The Confederate commander, Braxton Bragg, to escape being trapped in the city, evacuated it, and fell back to the south. Rosecrans was in possession of the prize which the Western army had long sought. At the same time, a small Union army under Burnside entered East Tennessee from the north. Most of the Union-sympathizing mountain area, which from the beginning of the war Lincoln had so desperately wanted to liberate, was now in Union hands. Rosecrans at this point misread the situation. Because Bragg was retreating, Rosecrans figured that the enemy was beaten and demoralized and that all he had to do to achieve a complete victory was to follow rapidly and force Bragg to battle. His proper course was to advance

[9] Rosecrans to Lincoln, August 1, 1863, Lincoln MSS., vol. 118; Lincoln to Rosecrans, August 10, *Works of Lincoln*, IX, 66–68.

[1] Rosecrans to Lincoln, August 22, 1863, *Official Records*, LI, pt. 1, 439.

but with caution. He should have remembered that he was pursuing an army that had not been defeated and that was intact as a fighting organization. Rosecrans forgot that he had not defeated Bragg on the field. Rashly he plunged southward. Bragg had retired only to find a favorable place to offer battle and to await reinforcements from Virginia. When he was ready to fight, he turned on Rosecrans, who was advancing in three separate columns. Suddenly Rosecrans realized the danger into which he was rushing. He hurriedly concentrated his army, just in time to receive Bragg's attack.

On September 19–20 Bragg hurled his troops at Rosecrans's lines in the battle of Chickamauga. On the first day Bragg won no success. On the second he made a complete breakthrough on the Union right. He made it because at a critical moment Rosecrans became excited and made a decision based on inaccurate information. It was reported to Rosecrans that one of his regiments in line was not properly supported. Without checking the report, which was not true, he ordered another regiment to move to the supposed weak spot. He either did not know the arrangement of his line or he forgot the location of his units. To obey the order, the second regiment had to pull out of line and march around and past still another regiment which was between it and the first one. This left a large gap in the Federal line through which the attacking Confederates poured. In a short time they swept the Union right from the field. Rosecrans and his two corps generals on the right tried vainly to stop the rout. Then, apparently affected by the panic of the troops, Rosecrans and the generals rode madly to Chattanooga. He was roundly criticized for leaving the field, but he could hardly have stayed when the battle on the right was lost. What was really bad was that while Rosecrans was fleeing to Chattanooga the Union left under George Thomas was fighting and holding its own. Rosecrans knew this, but he did not let it stay his bolt to safety. He should have ridden to his left and assumed command there. Instead he gave way to the frenzy of the moment and appeared as a general afraid to share the fate of his troops. That night, from Chattanooga, he ordered Thomas to retire to the city's fortifications.

At the end of the first day's fighting, Rosecrans informed the government that he had been attacked, had maintained his ground, and expected, with the blessing of Providence, to win on the morrow.[2] After the second day, he telegraphed Washington that he had met a serious disaster and was not sure that he could even hold Chattanooga.[3] His despatch announcing defeat arrived late at night on the twentieth. Early the next morning, Lincoln came into the bedroom of his secretary, John Hay, before Hay was up. The President sat on the bed and said that Rosecrans had been whipped and that he had expected the result. Lincoln had received a copy of Rosecrans's telegram at the Soldiers' Home outside the city where he had gone to spend the night. He had just gone to sleep when a courier arrived with the news. Immediately he had arisen and ridden into town, where he had spent most of the night at the War Department. All day Lincoln was in low spirits. He said to Gideon Welles that Bragg had been reinforced from Lee's army. Welles asked what Meade was doing with Lee weakened. Bitterly Lincoln replied: "It is the same old story of the Army of the Potomac. Imbecility, inefficiency—don't want to *do*—is defending the Capital." According to Welles, Lincoln then groaned: "Oh, it is terrible, terrible, this weakness, this indifference of our Potomac generals. . . ." Welles asked him why he did not remove Meade. Lincoln returned him the obvious answer: "What can I do

[2] Rosecrans to Halleck and to Lincoln, September 19, 1863, *ibid.*, XXX, pt. 1, 136.

[3] Rosecrans to Halleck, September 20, 1863, and to Lincoln, September 21, *ibid.*, XXX, pt. 1, 142–143, 149–150.

with such generals as we have? Who among them is any better than Meade?" [4]

Sometime during the day, probably late, Lincoln put on paper, in a letter to Halleck, his ideas about Rosecrans's situation. He said that it was extremely important to the Union cause that Rosecrans should hold Chattanooga because its possession kept the Confederates out of all Tennessee and broke their Western railroad connections. It was just as vital to the Confederates that they should secure Chattanooga, and they would, therefore, have to attack Rosecrans. The situation was really favorable to the Federals, Lincoln thought, because they could await the attack, strengthen their positions, and choose the place of battle. Rosecrans must be reinforced to the utmost of the government's ability, said Lincoln, because if the General could hold Chattanooga the rebellion would die—it could only "eke out a short and feeble existence, as an animal sometimes may with a thorn in its vitals." [5]

Lincoln took immediate steps to encourage and to strengthen Rosecrans. He telegraphed the General to be of good cheer and to hold his position. Like a good war director, he also asked Rosecrans to furnish the government with specific information about the location and condition of his troops. If he was going to help Rosecrans, Lincoln needed more detailed knowledge about Rosecrans's situation than the General's vague and frantic despatches had provided. At the same time, Lincoln directed Burnside to move to Chattanooga or some point in supporting distance of Rosecrans. [6]

Rosecrans's replies to the President's despatches did not furnish much additional information about his situation, and

[4] Dennett, *Diary of Hay*, 92; Welles, *Diary*, I, 438–440.

[5] Lincoln to Halleck, September 21, 1863, *Works of Lincoln*, IX, 131–132.

[6] Lincoln to Rosecrans, September 21, 22, 24, 1863, *ibid.*, IX, 132–133, 137.

his obvious confusion of mind must have alarmed Lincoln. On the twenty-second Rosecrans telegraphed that the fate of his army was in the hands of God, in whom he trusted, which was hardly reassuring to Lincoln; but the next day Rosecrans announced that he held Chattanooga and could be dislodged only by a very superior enemy army.[7] Lincoln was also puzzled, and angered, by what he considered the queer actions of Burnside. Even before Chickamauga, Burnside had been ordered to operate so as to be able to support Rosecrans. After the capture of Chattanooga, when Rosecrans had supposed Bragg was fleeing before him, one of Rosecrans's corps generals had informed Burnside that the Confederates were in full retreat. Burnside decided that Rosecrans had no need of him and started a move of his own toward Jonesboro, in a direction away from Chattanooga. Lincoln thought that Burnside was near Rosecrans and moving toward him. When he received a despatch from Burnside saying he was closing in on Jonesboro, Lincoln was horrified. "Damn Jonesboro," he said. It was the only time in the war that the workers in the military telegraph office heard him swear.[8] Orders were immediately sent to Burnside to go to Rosecrans. He promised to do so, and attempted to explain his side expedition to Lincoln. The President was in no mood to understand. He drafted a letter to Burnside in which he said that when he read the General's despatch he did not know whether he was awake or dreaming. After writing the letter, Lincoln decided not to send it. He probably thought it was too harsh and would wound Burnside without accomplishing any good purpose.[9] As it turned out, Burnside was unable to help Rose-

[7] Rosecrans to Lincoln, September 22, 23, 1863, *Official Records*, XXX, pt. 1, 161, 168.

[8] Burnside to Halleck, September 21, 1863, *ibid.*, XXX, pt. 3, 770; Bates, *Lincoln in the Telegraph Office*, 202.

[9] Burnside to Lincoln, September 23, 1863, *Official Records*, XXX,

crans. He had got himself so far away that he could not get to Rosecrans in a short time. Lincoln finally decided that it was best for Burnside to hold the territory he had occupied and to reinforce Rosecrans from some other source.[1]

On the night of the twenty-third, Lincoln again went to the Soldiers' Home. He felt confident that Rosecrans, at least for the time, could hold Chattanooga. John Hay went to the War Department to see if any important despatches had come in. He found a worried Stanton, who said that the news from Chattanooga was bad and that maybe Rosecrans could not maintain his position. Stanton asked Hay to find the President and bring him to the Department to attend a conference to discuss ways of relieving Rosecrans. Through a beautiful moonlight night, Hay rode out to the Home and aroused Lincoln from sleep. As Lincoln dressed, he remarked that the situation in Tennessee must be dangerous, because this was the first time Stanton had ever sent for him to come to the Department. Procuring a horse, Lincoln rode into town and went to the conference. Also present were Halleck, Seward, Chase, and several minor officials. By the time the President arrived, Rosecrans's despatch of the twenty-third announcing that he could hold Chattanooga had been received, and everybody felt easier. Nevertheless, it was determined to send reinforcements to Rosecrans and to get them from Meade, then doing nothing. The conferees decided to take about 20,000 troops from the Army of the Potomac, put them under Hooker's command, and transport them by rail to Tennessee. Railroad experts were called in to estimate how long it would take to move the reinforcements. Lincoln sat in on the planning of

pt. 3, 808–809; Lincoln to Burnside, September 25, *Works of Lincoln*, IX, 139–140.

[1] Burnside to Halleck, September 27, 1863, *Official Records*, XXX, pt. 3, 904–905; Stanton to Halleck, September 27, *ibid.*, 883; Lincoln to Burnside, September 27, two despatches, *Works of Lincoln*, IX, 141–142.

all the details, and did not leave the Department until day-break.[2]

Rosecrans's situation was perilous at Chattanooga and also in Washington. He was safe enough from attack by Bragg, but the Confederates were in position to sever his supply line along the Tennessee River. They could not drive him out of the city, but they might starve him out. In Washington, his reputation sank daily as more details were learned about Chickamauga and his behavior since the battle. Charles A. Dana was at Chattanooga sending almost daily and always devastating despatches about Rosecrans to Stanton. The Secretary was using all his influence to get Rosecrans removed and Thomas appointed to the command.[3] Lincoln himself had lost confidence in Rosecrans, and said so. As yet, he was not quite ready to remove the General because he was not sure whom to put in his place.[4] While he was deliberating on a successor, he continued to write encouraging despatches to Rosecrans, telling the General to hold Chattanooga at all cost and offering him bits of tactical advice, such as to "board at home," that is, draw supplies from the neighboring region, and prevent the Confederates from raiding his communications by quick, stabbing attacks in his front.[5]

By mid-October, Lincoln had decided what to do about Rosecrans. He did more than settle Rosecrans's fate. He made a complete and intelligent change in the command system in the West. All departments and armies in the West, including

[2] Dennett, *Diary of Hay*, 92–94; Bates, *Lincoln in the Telegraph Office*, 174–175.

[3] Dana to Stanton, September 27, 30, October 8, 12, 17, 1863, Dana MSS.; Stanton to Dana, September 30, Stanton MSS.

[4] Welles, *Diary*, I, 447, September 28, 1863.

[5] Lincoln to Rosecrans, October 4, 12, 1863, *Works of Lincoln*, IX, 154, 167.

Rosecrans's, were placed under the command of Grant. Grant was directed to go to Chattanooga and inspect the situation there. He had authority to retain Rosecrans in command or replace him with Thomas and to make any other change that he desired in the organization of the western forces.[6] Grant relieved Rosecrans by telegram before he got to Chattanooga and appointed Thomas to the command. Lincoln was pleased by Grant's decisive exercise of power and by the change in commanders. The President believed that Thomas was a good general and had acted like a hero at Chickamauga.[7] As for Rosecrans, Lincoln was glad to see him go. The President believed that Rosecrans had outlived his military usefulness. In one of his aptest similes, Lincoln said that since Chickamauga Rosecrans had lost his nerve and had acted "confused and stunned like a duck hit on the head." [8]

During the summer and early fall months when Lincoln had been largely occupied with Western problems, Meade had remained inactive in northern Virginia. After it became known that part of Lee's army had been sent to Bragg, Meade asked Halleck what the government thought he should do. He said that he was confident he could make Lee fall back but that his army was not large enough to follow Lee to Richmond and besiege the enemy capital. Halleck showed Meade's despatch to Lincoln and requested the President's views so that he could instruct Meade. Immediately Lincoln saw that Meade was thinking of Richmond as his primary objective and not Lee's army. Unhesitatingly Lincoln replied that Meade should advance on Lee "in manner of general

[6] Halleck to Grant, October 16, 1863, three despatches, and Halleck's orders of October 16, *Official Records*, XXX, pt. 4, 337, 404.

[7] Cleaves, *Rock of Chickamauga*, 180–183; Lincoln to R. A. Maxwell, September 23, 1863, Tracy, *Uncollected Letters of Lincoln*, 233–234.

[8] Dennett, *Diary of Hay*, 102, 106, 115.

attack" and if developments were favorable turn his movement into a real attack.[9] Halleck indorsed Lincoln's opinion,
and Meade said he would act on it. But after an initial advance, his customary timidity asserted itself. He informed
Halleck that he did not feel justified in going farther without
more positive authority from the government. Again he said
that if he attacked he would achieve nothing, even by a victory: Lee would fall back on Richmond and he could not follow him.[1] Meade refused to entertain the idea that he might
be able to attack and smash Lee; he could not conceive of
Lee's army as his objective.

Lincoln saw this despatch of Meade's also, and he wrote
Halleck a long letter about the course Meade ought to follow. It was one of his best strategic dissertations. He described
the situation in Virginia as he saw it: the two armies confronted each other across a river, each defending its own capital. Meade had about 90,000 men; Lee, 60,000. For battle,
Meade had three to Lee's two, but because it had been determined (by whom he did not say) that the side on the defensive had certain natural advantages the three could not
attack the two and were left standing on the defensive also.
If Lee's 60,000 could neutralize Meade's 90,000, Lincoln
wanted to know why 40,000 Federals could not neutralize
Lee and 50,000 of Meade's army be sent where they could be
of some use: "Having practically come to the mere defensive,
it seems to be no economy at all to employ twice as many men
for that object as are needed. . . ." With incisive sentences
that demonstrated he had come to full stature as a strategist,
Lincoln vetoed Meade's notion of following the Confederates
to Richmond:

[9] Meade to Halleck, September 14, 1863, *Official Records*, XXIX,
pt. 2, 179–180; Lincoln to Halleck, September 15, *Works of Lincoln*,
IX, 123–124.

[1] Meade to Halleck, September 18, 1863, *Official Records*, XXIX,
pt. 2, 201–202.

To avoid misunderstanding, let me say that to attempt to fight the enemy slowly back into his intrenchments at Richmond, and then to capture him, is an idea I have been trying to repudiate for quite a year.

My judgment is so clear against it that I would scarcely allow the attempt to be made if the general in command should desire to make it. My last attempt upon Richmond was to get McClellan, when he was nearer there than the enemy was, to run in ahead of him. Since then I have constantly desired the Army of the Potomac to make Lee's army and not Richmond, its objective point. If our army cannot fall upon the enemy and hurt him where he is, it is plain to me it can gain nothing by attempting to follow him over a succession of intrenched lines into a fortified city.[2]

Meade did not follow Lincoln's advice to make Lee's army his objective and to try to bring Lee to battle. He and Lee jockeyed for position in northern Virginia without once coming to actual contact. Once when he informed Halleck that he could not ascertain the enemy's position and strength, Old Brains urged him to act upon Napoleon's maxim: attack and he would find out. Haughtily Meade replied that if Halleck had orders to give he should issue them and cease inflicting his truisms on generals who had not asked for them. If his course was not approved, said Meade, he wanted to be relieved. Halleck humbly said that he had repeated truisms only to convey the wishes of the government and he regretted that they had displeased Meade.[3] Meade accepted Halleck's explanation, but he told his staff that he disliked the burden of command so much and his relations with Halleck were so unpleasant he wished the government would relieve him.[4]

Lincoln, in his eagerness to get Meade to fight, made a re-

[2] Lincoln to Halleck, September 19, 1863, *Works of Lincoln,* IX, 128–130.

[3] Halleck to Meade, October 10, 19, 1863, *Official Records,* XXIX, pt. 2, 228, 334; Meade to Halleck, October 18, *ibid.,* 346. See also Halleck to Meade, October 15, 18, *ibid.,* 328, 346.

[4] Agassiz, *Meade's Headquarters,* 36, 38–39.

markable proposition to Halleck. Pointing out that Lee had
been weakened more by the departure of some of his troops
to Bragg than Meade had by the departure of some of his to
Rosecrans, Lincoln said: "If General Meade can now attack
him on a field no worse than equal for us, and will do so with
all the skill and courage which he, his officers, and men possess, the honor will be his if he succeeds, and the blame may
be mine if he fails." Not even an offer by Lincoln to shoulder
the responsibility for failure could move Meade. He replied
with words whose equivalent Lincoln had heard many times
from many generals that he would attack provided he could
get the Confederates on an equal field and could ascertain
their exact position and was certain of his own communications.[5] A few days after penning this bellicose declaration,
Meade informed Halleck that the season for active campaigning was about over and that the army should be withdrawn
to near Washington. Halleck then asked Meade to come to
Washington to confer about future operations with Lincoln.
Meade saw the President on October 23. According to the
General, who left the only account of the meeting, Lincoln
was kind and considerate and found no fault, although he
was obviously disappointed that Meade had not got a battle
out of Lee. The President agreed that active operations for
the year might as well be ended.[6] He probably thought that
as Meade had not advanced in a period of good weather there
was no use wasting words to get him to go forward in bad
weather. It was undoubtedly on this occasion that Lincoln
told Meade that after Gettysburg the General had reminded
him of an old woman shooing geese across a creek. He did not

[5] Lincoln to Halleck, October 16, 1863, *Works of Lincoln,* IX, 171;
Halleck to Meade, October 16, and Meade to Halleck, October 16,
Official Records, XXIX, pt. 2, 332.

[6] Meade to Halleck, October 21, 1863, and Halleck to Meade, October 21, *Official Records,* XXIX, pt. 2, 361–363; Meade to Mrs. Meade,
October 23, in Meade, *Life and Letters of Meade,* II, 154.

tell Meade that, like Rosecrans, he was acting like a duck hit on the head, but he must have thought it. The President had about given up on Meade.

In November the weather continued unexpectedly good. Lincoln made another attempt to get Meade to fight, but Meade did not think the situation in his front was favorable enough for him to risk battle.[7] Instead he proposed that he be permitted to change his base of operations to Fredericksburg and to move from there against Richmond. He was still thinking in terms of the wrong objective and still trying to avoid going after the main one. Sharply and unhesitatingly, Lincoln disapproved of Meade's plan.[8] Late in the month Meade did attempt to attack Lee in rear, but when he found the Confederates in a strong position he called off his attack. He said that had he tried to storm Lee's lines he would have been defeated and would have sacrificed the lives of his men uselessly. He may have been right, but the idea of victory by attack never seemed to be in his mind. And like McClellan, he thought too much about casualties. His battle that did not come off was Meade's last move for the year. He went into winter quarters, bitterly convinced that the government would relieve him because he had not accomplished the impossible.[9]

From Meade and failure in the East, Lincoln turned expectantly to the West and Grant. Grant did not disappoint him. After relieving Rosecrans, Grant had come to Chattanooga to take direct charge of operations. He brought part of his army from Mississippi to join Thomas's force. Late in

[7] Lincoln to Halleck, October 24, 1863, *Works of Lincoln*, IX, 180; Halleck to Meade, October 24, and Meade to Halleck, October 24, *Official Records*, XXIX, pt. 2, 375–377.

[8] Meade to Halleck, November 2, 1863, and Halleck to Meade, November 2, *Official Records*, XXIX, pt. 2, 409–410.

[9] Meade to Lincoln, December 2, 1863, Lincoln MSS., vol. 133; C. C. W., *Reports*, 1865, I, 474–475; Agassiz, *Meade's Headquarters*, 60–61; Meade, *Life and Letters of Meade*, II, 160, 163–164.

November he hurled his combined armies at Bragg's lines
south of the city and broke them completely. Bragg, badly
beaten, had to retire into Georgia. Chattanooga, in Lincoln's
mind the bastion of all Tennessee, was secure. Grant did
more than smash the enemy grip on Chattanooga. Bragg had
sent a force under General James Longstreet northward to
attack Burnside in Knoxville. Grant, after he defeated Bragg,
despatched a force of his own under his trusted subordinate,
William T. Sherman, to deal with Longstreet. As Sherman
approached, Longstreet retired north toward the Virginia
border. Nearly all of East Tennessee was now unmistakably
in Union possession. The second of Lincoln's great strategic
objectives had been achieved and like the first—the opening
of the Mississippi—achieved by Grant.

Lincoln was delighted when he received the news of
Grant's success. He wired the General that he wanted to
tender him more than thanks, his "profoundest gratitude,"
for the victories which Grant's "skill, courage, and persever-
ance" had won.[1] Even in his great joy, Lincoln still was the
strategist. He wanted to complete Grant's work by running
down and destroying Longstreet, and he thought that the job
could be done if only he had good generals in the East. To
one of his secretaries he said: "Now, if this army of the Potomac was good for anything—if the officers had anything in
them—if the army had any legs, they could move thirty thousand men down to Lynchburg [in the Valley] and catch Longstreet. Can anybody doubt, if Grant were here in command
that he would catch him." Then Lincoln thought for a moment and added: "But I do not think it would do to bring
Grant away from the West."[2]

[1] Lincoln to Grant, December 8, 1863, *Works of Lincoln*, IX, 253–
254.

[2] Memorandum by John G. Nicolay, December 7, 1863, in Nicolay MSS.

Chapter 12

A Modern Command System

URING the winter months of 1863–64 the United States created a modern command system. Lincoln and Congress were its principal architects, but they merely put into institutional form the result of the nation's experience after three years of modern war. In a fundamental sense, the new arrangement represented the total military thought of the country. Congress authorized it, and Lincoln set it in operation. The central military figure in the system was Grant, and he was central by the united desires of Lincoln, Congress, and the people.

Grant, after the relief of Chattanooga, turned his mind for the first time to ideas of grand strategy. Heretofore he had thought only in terms of strategy for the particular area where his army operated. Now, either feeling a growing confidence in his military powers after his recent victories or wishing to demonstrate that he possessed the strategic ability to handle a larger command, Grant proffered advice to the government about the conduct of the war in other theaters. He revived his scheme to launch an offensive against Mobile. He proposed to hold the Tennessee line with a small force and to take his army down the Mississippi to New Orleans from where he would move to Mobile. Using Mobile as a base, he would invade and occupy key points in Alabama and Georgia, striking at the vital interior of what was left of the Confederacy.

[291]

Grant sent Charles A. Dana to Washington to lay the plan before Lincoln and to plead for its acceptance. Reasoning that his offensive would be more effective if at the same time the Army of the Potomac moved in Virginia, Grant also asked Dana to tell the President that the Eastern army ought to have a new commander, one who could coordinate its movements with the operations in the West. As a possible commander to replace Meade, Grant suggested one of his subordinate generals, William T. Sherman or William F. ("Baldy") Smith. Dana discussed Grant's proposals with Lincoln, Stanton, and Halleck. All three approved the Mobile move in principle, Dana reported to Grant, but they feared that if attempted at present it would lay East Tennessee, and possibly the whole state, open to enemy invasion. On the question of a new commander for the Potomac army, Lincoln and his advisers agreed that a change was desirable, and they inclined to Smith as the man for the job.[1]

Halleck explained officially to Grant Lincoln's reaction to the Mobile offensive. Before it could be undertaken, the President wanted the last remaining bands of Confederates in East Tennessee and other parts of the state chased out and the main enemy field army in north Georgia pushed back so far that it could never return to Tennessee. These conditions met, Lincoln would consent to a move on Mobile.[2] The President was taking no chances on the Confederates recovering Chattanooga and the region that he considered the bastion of the Union line in the West.

Halleck said nothing to Grant about the latter's recom-

[1] Dana, *Recollections*, 156–157; Wilson, *Under the Old Flag*, I, 315–317; Dana to Stanton, November 29, December 12, 1863, *Official Records*, XXXI, pt. 2, 72–73; Grant to Halleck, December 7, *ibid.*, pt. 3, 349–350; Dana to Grant, December 21, *ibid.*, pt. 3, 457–458.

[2] Halleck to Grant, December 21, 1863, *Official Records*, XXXI, pt. 3, 458.

mendation to replace Meade with a western general. The government, having indicated that it favored Smith, was probably waiting for Grant to say that he agreed with the choice of "Baldy." Grant said nothing, and Smith did not get the appointment. Later Smith charged that Lincoln had been ready to name him to the command but that Grant had persuaded the President to retain Meade. The evidence seems to support Smith. Apparently Grant suddenly changed his mind about Smith's capability for command. He discovered the trait in Smith's character that unfitted him to direct an army. Smith was a contentious controversialist who spent most of his time criticizing the plans of other generals, particularly those of his superiors. As Grant said later, the moment a superior differed with Smith he either had to yield completely to "Baldy" or abandon the idea of getting any further service out of him.[3] At the same time that he discarded Smith as a command possibility, Grant dropped the idea of securing the Eastern command for one of his officers. He probably decided that he could not spare Sherman, and he may have thought that it was unwise for him to push a Western general as leader of the Potomac army. Very possibly, he learned that he was about to be offered the position of general in chief, in which case he could dispose of the command situation in the East as he saw fit.

Early in January, Halleck informed Grant that most of the forces west of the Mississippi were to be placed under his command. Although Grant was being given increased authority, he was not to have a free hand in planning western operations. Lincoln was still determining the basic strategic pattern in the West. Carefully Halleck explained that the

---

[3] General W. F. Smith to General W. B. Franklin, April 28, 1864, Franklin MSS.; Wilson, *Rawlins*, 206–208; Grant to Halleck, February 20, 1865, *Official Records*, XLVIII, pt. 1, 917.

President thought it was necessary to break up the enemy
forces west of the river, especially those in Texas, before attempting any such move as the Mobile offensive. All operations in the West, said Halleck, were to be subordinated to
any movement Grant might choose to make from the Tennessee line, a plain hint that Lincoln thought Grant ought to
strike at the Confederate army in north Georgia. After brief-
ing Grant on the situation in the West, Halleck invited him
to present his views on the strategy that should be adopted in
all theaters of the war.[4] Halleck was seeking to draw out
Grant's strategic ideas for the benefit and guidance of the
President. At that time there was a great deal of talk in Congress and the press and among the general public about making Grant general in chief. Lincoln was perfectly willing to
appoint Grant to the office, because he thought Grant was by
far the best of the Union generals. But he naturally wanted to
know what strategy Grant, as general in chief, would employ
to subdue the Confederacy and particularly what movement
he would recommend for the important Eastern theater.

Grant realized by now that he would not be permitted to
undertake the Mobile offensive in the form that he had proposed it. In his reply to Halleck, he said that he thought the
most important line for him to secure was the one from
Chattanooga to Mobile and that he could secure it by moving both from Mobile and from his present position in Tennessee. Grant was still trying to get Lincoln's approval for
the Mobile plan by dangling before the President the bait
of a simultaneous movement from Chattanooga against the
Confederate army in Georgia, an operation which he knew
Lincoln favored. As to his views on over-all strategy, Grant
said that he had heretofore abstained from suggesting what
should be done in other theaters "or even to think much

4 Halleck to Grant, January 8, 1864, *Official Records*, XXXII, pt. 2,
40–42.

about the matter," but that he would give his ideas to Halleck in another letter.[5]

Grant's plan for a dual movement from Chattanooga into Georgia and from New Orleans to Mobile and from there into the interior of Alabama was not too sound. The government did not have enough troops in the West to constitute two major striking forces. Furthermore, if the army at Chattanooga was weakened to build up the force destined for Mobile, there was always the possibility that the Confederates might be able to recover East Tennessee. Grant's scheme violated the strategic principle of doing one big thing at a time. Lincoln saw the weakness in the plan and vetoed it. Halleck informed Grant that no operation would be permitted that endangered East Tennessee. Expressing Lincoln's thoughts, Halleck pointed out that Chattanooga was a central position for the armies of both sides. If the Confederates held it, they could menace Tennessee and Kentucky. If the Federals held it, they could protect the two states and operate from it on central, interior lines against the long Confederate defence periphery.[6]

A few days after he submitted his ideas about Western strategy to the government, Grant sent Halleck a plan for proposed operations in the East. He recommended giving up the attempt to capture Richmond by moving against it in Virginia. Instead, he suggested that a force of 60,000 be thrown by the Navy onto the North Carolina coast, from whence it could advance into the interior of the state and threaten the railroad lines connecting Richmond with the deep South. The Confederates would then have to abandon the capital in order to protect their communications. No place in his letter to Halleck did Grant say that the force in North Carolina or the Army of the Potomac in Virginia

[5] Grant to Halleck, January 15, 1864, *ibid.*, XXXII, pt. 2, 99–101.
[6] Halleck to Grant, January 18, 1864, *ibid.*, XXXII, pt. 2, 126–127.

would seek a showdown battle with the enemy. His plan was merely one to seize Richmond.

Lincoln must have been disappointed when he saw Grant's communication. The General's scheme was faulty in several vital respects. The force of 60,000 could not be raised without taking troops from the Army of the Potomac, which would have weakened that army to the point where Lee could have delivered a stroke at Washington. The force operating in North Carolina would have been in a position of great potential danger, because the Confederates could have rapidly concentrated troops from Georgia and Virginia to attack it. The worst feature of Grant's plan was that it was aimed at a false object. Like Meade, Grant was thinking of Richmond and not Lee's army as the primary objective. The conclusion is plain that Halleck's request for his views caught Grant unprepared. He had done some thinking about over-all strategy, but little of a systematic nature. Asked to suggest a plan for the Eastern theater, he presented a hastily-prepared and not a very good one.[7] Later he would willingly discard it—after he talked to Lincoln, the civilian strategist who never forgot that the destruction of enemy armies was the proper objective.

When Halleck read Grant's plan, he knew Lincoln would not like it. Halleck was so familiar with Lincoln's strategic ideas that he could tell how the President would react to almost any proposal. He informed Grant that he would lay the scheme before Lincoln but that the President would disapprove it. Using almost the same words that Lincoln had employed in several letters to Meade, Halleck emphasized that Lee's army, not Richmond, should be the objective of the Potomac army. He pointed out to Grant that the force for North Carolina could not be enlisted without taking 30,000 men from Meade's army and that when Lee learned

[7] Grant to Halleck, January 19, 1864, *ibid.,* XXXIII, 394–395.

that the army facing him had been depleted he would move on Washington, forcing the government to recall the whole Carolina expedition for the defence of the capital. The easiest way to defeat Lee, said Halleck, again expressing a Lincoln idea, was to fight him near Washington. At the end of his letter to Grant, Halleck said that the final decision as to operations in the Eastern theater would probably depend, under Lincoln, upon Grant.[8] Halleck meant that Grant would soon be called to Washington to become general in chief and would then have the opportunity to learn firsthand Lincoln's strategic concepts.

Late in February, Congress passed a bill reviving the rank of lieutenant general and empowering the President to appoint to it one officer from among the present major generals in the regular army. The new rank was the highest one in the army and had previously been held by only two men, by George Washington on a permanent basis and by Scott as a brevet or nominal rank. The law stated that the lieutenant general might be authorized, under the direction of the President and during his pleasure, to command the armies of the United States.[9] Congress, of course, had no power to say what officer Lincoln was to appoint as lieutenant general, but everybody knew it was to be Grant. His friends had introduced and pushed the bill, and during the discussions of it numerous members had said that the measure was intended to make Grant general in chief. There is no clear evidence to show that Lincoln had suggested that the bill be introduced, but he may well have done so. Certainly he approved of the act and was eager to ratify Congress's choice, and the nation's, of Grant as director of the armies.

Apparently Lincoln felt doubtful of Grant in only one respect: he thought that maybe the General had presidential

---

[8] Halleck to Grant, February 17, 1864, *ibid.*, XXXII, pt. 2, 411–413.

[9] *Congressional Globe*, 38 Cong., 1 Sess., pt. 1, 586–594.

ambitions and would let his political aspirations affect his generalship. In the early months of 1864, both Republicans and Democrats were casting covetous eyes at Grant as a White House possibility and trying to commit him as a member of their organizations. A Grant boom was in the making. Grant, however, had assured two of Lincoln's friends in January that he had no desire to be a candidate for anything and that as a soldier he thought he had no right to utter political views.[1] Presumably the friends relayed this information to Lincoln, who had it when the lieutenant general bill was passed. But the President was not quite satisfied; he feared that perhaps Grant's head was being turned by the adulation he was receiving. According to one story, he called in a close friend of Grant's and asked him if the General wanted to be president. The man said Grant did not, and showed Lincoln a letter from Grant disclaiming any political designs. Lincoln said he was glad to hear it, because when the presidential grub got to gnawing at a man nobody could say when it would stop.[2]

On March 4, Grant wrote W. T. Sherman that he had received orders to go to Washington to receive his commission. He said that he would accept no appointment that required him to make the capital his headquarters.[3] He reached Washington at five in the afternoon of the eighth. Nobody was at the railroad station to meet him. With two members of his staff, he made his way to Willard's Hotel. That night there was a reception at the White House, to which Grant was invited. He arrived at about nine-thirty. A great buzz of conversation arose from the crowd when he entered, and from the noise and Grant's appearance Lincoln guessed who it was. He came up and said: "This is General Grant, is it?" Grant

[1] Grant to I. N. Morris, January 20, 1864, Grant MSS.; General John Palmer to Lyman Trumbull, January 24, Trumbull MSS.

[2] Richardson, *Grant*, 384–385.

[3] Grant to Sherman, March 4, 1864, *Official Records*, XXXII, pt. 3, 18.

replied: "Yes." The two exchanged a few words, and then Lincoln turned the General over to the eager guests. Grant was embarrassed by the attention he received. Later in the evening, Lincoln drew Grant into the Blue Room for a conference with himself and Stanton. The President told Grant that tomorrow he would formally present him with his commission. Lincoln said he would make a short speech which he would read from a manuscript and thoughtfully suggested that as Grant was not accustomed to public speaking he could write out his speech of acceptance and read it. Lincoln asked Grant to make two points in his reply: to say something that would obviate other generals being jealous of him and to include something that would please the Army of the Potomac.[4]

The next day at one p.m. in the room where the Cabinet met, Lincoln gave Grant the commission. As he handed the official document to the General, Lincoln said: "With this high honor devolves upon you also a corresponding responsibility. As the country herein trusts you, so, under God, it will sustain you. I scarcely need add, that with what I here speak for the nation goes my own hearty personal concurrence." Grant had written his remarks of acceptance on a half-sheet of notepaper. He read his speech poorly. He did not incorporate in it Lincoln's recommended points of the night before. Lincoln's secretary thought that perhaps Grant thought it was wise to begin his career as general in chief by disregarding any suggestions from Lincoln. More probably, Grant did not know how to express gracefully the sentiments proposed by the President.[5] On the following day, the War Department issued orders announcing that Halleck, at his own request,

[4] MS. memorandum, March 8, 1864, by John G. Nicolay, in Nicolay MSS.; Welles, *Diary*, I, 538–539.

[5] *Works of Lincoln*, X, 33–34; MS. memorandum, March 9, 1864, by J. G. Nicolay, in Nicolay MSS.; Nicolay and Hay, *Lincoln*, VIII, 340–342.

had been relieved as general in chief and that Grant
was assigned to the command of the armies of the United
States.[6]

The new general in chief was now formally installed in
office, but important details of the new command system remained to be worked out. At first Grant had thought he
would make his headquarters in the West, but after coming
to Washington he changed his mind and decided to remain
in the East. His reasons, as given after the war, were that all
the important political pressures centered in Washington and
that he was the only person who could withstand their influence on military operations. Any subordinate that he appointed to the Eastern command would have to yield, at least
partially, to the politicians and hence would be unable to
carry out Grant's plans. As additional reasons, Grant stated
that the best and most dangerous of the enemy armies was in
the Eastern theater and that it was here the Union most
needed a decisive victory.[7]

Grant said nothing in his writings after the war about Lincoln's wishes as to the location of supreme headquarters. Although the factors he listed as deciding him to stay in the
East were valid ones and present in his mind in 1864, it is
obvious that Lincoln had some influence upon Grant's decision. Certainly the location of headquarters was a matter
Grant would have discussed with Lincoln. And certainly the
President would have said that he wanted Grant in the East,
which was the logical place for him to be—at or near Washington, the nerve-center of the war, and close to the person of
the commander in chief. Indeed, if Grant had not voluntarily

[6] Orders of March 10, 1864, *Official Records*, XXXIII, 663; Halleck
to Stanton, March 9, Lincoln MSS., vol. 147.

[7] Ulysses S. Grant, *Personal Memoirs of Ulysses S. Grant*, II, 116–
118; Adam Badeau, *Military History of Ulysses S. Grant . . .* , II,
11–14.

decided to establish headquarters in the East, Lincoln undoubtedly would have ordered him to do so.

Although Grant realized headquarters would have to be in
the East, he was determined that he would not stay in the political atmosphere of Washington. The only other place in
the Eastern theater where he could go and be at an important
center of military communications was to the Army of the
Potomac. So Grant set up headquarters with that army in the
field and traveled with it wherever it went. Meade continued
as commander of the army, but Grant became its directing
strategic head. Grant's presence with the Army of the Potomac removed him from Washington and from daily personal contact with Lincoln. He was, however, usually so close
to the capital that he could easily go to it to see Lincoln, or
the President could journey to Grant's field quarters. Furthermore, Grant was always in telegraphic communication
with the President. To facilitate the exchange of intelligence
between Lincoln and Grant, a new command office, the chief
of staff, was created. It is not known who suggested the office.
Lincoln may have proposed it; but if he did not, he at least
knew who should be chief of staff and appointed Halleck.
From his years of experience with Old Brains, Lincoln appreciated that Halleck was the ideal officer for the post.

Halleck was not completely a chief of staff in the modern
sense. Primarily he was a channel of communication between
Lincoln and Grant and between Grant and the departmental
commanders. Halleck had the happy faculty of being able to
communicate civilian ideas to a soldier and military ideas to
a civilian and make both of them understand what he was
talking about. He could interpret Lincoln's strategic concepts to Grant and Grant's military language to the President.
Because of Halleck, Lincoln and Grant never misunderstood
each other, as Lincoln and McClellan had. Grant rarely

wrote to Lincoln. He sent most of his despatches to Halleck, who turned them over to Lincoln with, when necessary, an analysis or explanation. Halleck also served as a liaison between Grant and the generals commanding departments. Under Grant there were seventeen different commands and 533,-000 men. It was an immense job in itself for Grant to formulate general strategic directions for the departments. If he had had to read all the reports from the subordinate commanders and frame and write minute instructions for them, Grant could not have devoted any attention to strategic planning. At his request, the despatches of departmental generals were sent to Halleck, who either transmitted them to Grant or summarized their contents for the general in chief. Grant sent most of his orders to subordinates through Halleck. Often Grant would tell Halleck in general terms what he wanted done and direct the chief of staff to put his purpose in detailed, written instructions to the subordinate concerned, or he would delegate complete authority to Halleck to handle a situation of a routine nature.

Halleck thought of himself as a coordinator of information who had no responsibility except in matters of advice and administration. Hooker sneered that Halleck's position was like that of a man who married with the understanding he would not sleep with his wife.[8] In some respects, Halleck's job was as unrewarding and unpleasant as Hooker thought, but for the most he performed it well. Part of the credit for the smooth working of the new command system belonged to him. And the system did work. The arrangement of commander in chief, general in chief, and chief of staff gave the United States a modern system of command for a modern war.

[8] Grant to Halleck, April 26, 1864, Grant MSS.; Halleck to Grant, May 2, *Official Records*, XXXVI, pt. 2, 328–329; Halleck to W. T. Sherman, July 16, *ibid.*, XXXVIII, pt. 5, 150; Joseph Hooker to Zachariah Chandler, May 3, Chandler MSS.

It was superior to anything achieved in Europe until von Moltke forged the Prussian staff machine of 1866 and 1870.[9]

The presence of Grant with the Army of the Potomac created an unusual command relationship between Grant and Meade. When McClellan had taken the field in 1862, Lincoln had relieved him as general in chief on the correct grounds that one man could not direct the operations of many armies and lead one in battle. Grant's position, however, was different from McClellan's. Technically, Grant did not command the Army of the Potomac. Actually, he commanded it in a partial sense. He traveled with it and issued strategic and sometimes tactical orders to Meade. Some of his orders to Meade were verbal, given as they sat before the campfire at night or on the battle line; others were written. On rare occasions, Grant gave orders to Meade's subordinates without going through Meade. It might be said that Grant was the strategic commander of the Potomac army; Meade its tactical commander.

The arrangement freed Grant from the heavy burden of administering the Eastern army and from the labor of checking on tactical details of its operations. It left him time to think about grand strategy and plan operations for other theaters. Without such an arrangement, as Grant said several times, he could not have exercised the functions of general in chief. When Grant assumed the chief command, Meade had offered to give up his command, so that Grant could appoint a man of his own. Grant asked Meade to stay on, having decided that it would lower the morale of the Eastern army if a Western general were named to lead it. After working with Meade a short time, Grant came to have a high opinion of him. He said that of all the officers he knew Meade and Sher-

⁹ Maurice, *Statesmen and Soldiers of the Civil War*, 96–98; Badeau, *Grant*, II, 32, 81.

man were the most capable of commanding large armies. The relationship between Grant and Meade could have been awkward and inefficient. Because of Grant's liking for Meade and his tact in handling the touchy general, it worked with a fair degree of efficiency.[1]

When Grant wrote his memoirs after the war, he gave the impression that Lincoln let him run the war absolutely as he pleased. In Grant's picture, Lincoln was a military innocent who did not understand what Grant was doing and did not want to understand. At his first interview with the President, related Grant, Lincoln said that he was not a military man, did not want to interfere in military affairs, and did not want to know Grant's plans. All he wanted was a general in chief who would take responsibility and call on him for any needed help. Then, Grant continued, Lincoln brought out a map of Virginia on which he had marked every position of the contending armies and said he wanted to submit a plan of his own. He pointed to two streams emptying into the Potomac and proposed that an army should be landed between them and operate on one of them as a line of communications. Grant said that he listened respectfully and did not suggest that the streams would protect Lee's flanks and shut the Federal army up in a potential trap. He did not then or later, said Grant, tell Lincoln what his plans were.[2]

Grant wrote under the influence of the postwar Grant and Lincoln myths. Grant had become the Great General, Lincoln the Great Emancipator. There was nothing in the Lincoln legend to recall that he had been a great war leader because he was also Lincoln the Great Strategist. Grant had forgotten much in the years after the war, and his account was

[1] Grant, *Memoirs*, II, 116–118; Badeau, *Grant*, II, 186–192; Porter, *Campaigning with Grant*, 114–115; Grant to Stanton, May 13, 1864, *Official Records*, XXXVI, pt. 2, 695; Grant to W. T. Sherman, April 26, 1864, Grant MSS.

[2] Grant, *Memoirs*, II, 122–123.

wide of the truth. It is improbable that Lincoln proposed the plan described by Grant, which involved a movement of the Army of the Potomac from the Rappahannock-Rapidan line to the Potomac. For months Lincoln had urged Meade to attack Lee on the Rappahannock line and had disapproved a plan by Meade to shift operations farther east to Fredericksburg. He would hardly have suggested a scheme involving such a retrograde movement as one to the Potomac. But even if Lincoln had put forward the plan ascribed to him by Grant, it was not as bad an idea as Grant pretended. There was little possibility that the Army of the Potomac, superior in size to the enemy army and with water communications at its back, could have been trapped by Lee anywhere near the Potomac.

Grant's vision of himself conducting the war with a free hand has been generally accepted by historians. It is true that Lincoln permitted Grant more latitude in determining strategy than he had given McClellan or Halleck. To a friend, who asked if Grant did not have too much power, Lincoln replied: "Do you hire a man to do your work and then do it yourself?" [3] One reason why Lincoln let Grant have great strategic authority was that he believed the General was a great soldier. A biographer of Grant's quoted the President, undoubtedly in exaggerated terms, as saying: "Grant is the first General I have had. You know how it has been with all the rest. . . . They all wanted me to be the General. . . . I am glad to find a man that can go ahead without me." Lincoln meant that Grant took the resources the government could give him and tried to accomplish his assigned mission with what he had, instead of, like other generals, picking out something he lacked and claiming he could not win until he got it.[4] But Lincoln did not mean, as many writers have in-

[3] Gilmore, *Personal Recollections*, 228.
[4] Church, *Grant*, 231–232, 248–249.

ferred from such remarks and as Grant claimed in his memoirs, that he did not want to know what Grant's plans were or that he yielded to Grant the function of strategic planning. What Lincoln really said to Grant in their various interviews was that he did not want to know the details of Grant's plans. He knew what Grant's basic strategic ideas were, because Grant told him, and he was satisfied to know the general pattern. He approved of Grant's strategy and let the General execute it because Grant conformed his plans to Lincoln's own strategic ideas. Fundamentally, Grant's strategy was Lincolnian.

Lincoln's influence upon Grant's thinking was clearly evident in Grant's plan for operations in the Eastern theater. After he talked to Lincoln in Washington, Grant dropped completely his scheme to send an army into North Carolina. His new plan was to make Lee's army the objective and to go after it in Virginia and destroy it. In words that Lincoln might have written, Grant instructed Meade: "Wherever Lee goes, there you will go also." [5] The movement against Lee was part of a grand strategic design that could be described in modern terms as Operation Crusher. While the Army of the Potomac followed Lee to the death in northern Virginia, a smaller force under General Butler was to move from Fortress Monroe up the James River toward Richmond and menace and if possible capture the capital. Butler was also to destroy the railroads south of Richmond which supplied Lee's army. If Butler could seize Richmond, Lee could not hope to escape Grant by falling back into the city's entrenchments to stand a siege; if, on the other hand, Butler did not secure Richmond and Lee eluded Grant and reached the town the Confederates would find their communications to the deep South destroyed and would have to fight the

[5] Grant to Meade, April 29, 1864, *Official Records*, XXXIII, 827–829.

combined forces of Grant and Butler outside the fortifications.[6]

In the Western theater, Grant planned two large offensives. The army near Chattanooga, now commanded by Sherman, was to move into northern Georgia, charged with the objective of destroying the opposing enemy army and damaging the economic resources of the region around Atlanta. At the same time, an army under Banks was to move from New Orleans to Mobile. Grant hoped eventually to unite the forces of Sherman and Banks and thus fulfill his ambition to secure the Chattanooga-Mobile line.[7] In his instructions to Meade and Sherman, Grant explained that his strategic purpose was to work all the armies toward a common center. He meant that he was going to pulverize the Confederacy with blows from all directions. In his final report, he analyzed his plan in more detail. Before 1864, he said, the Eastern and Western armies had acted like balky teams, no two ever pulling together, which enabled the Confederates to shift troops advantageously on interior lines from one theater to another. He decided to employ the greatest possible number of troops and to hammer continuously at the armies and resources of the enemy at every possible point until by attrition if nothing else the Union won.[8] This was the simple and effective strategy that Lincoln had urged upon Buell and Halleck as early as 1861.

It is impossible to say what proportion of the strategy of Operation Crusher originated with Grant and what with Lincoln. The basic idea was undoubtedly Grant's. And yet Lincoln had some influence on the working out of the plan. From March 26–May 4, Grant was in the field with the Army

[6] Grant to B. F. Butler, April 2, 18, 1864, *ibid.*, XXXIII, 794–795, 804–805; Grant's report, *ibid.*, XXXIV, pt. 1, 13–14.

[7] Grant to Sherman, April 4, 1864, *ibid.*, XXXII, pt. 3, 245–246; Grant to N. P. Banks, April 17, *ibid.*, XXXIV, pt. 3, 190–192.

[8] *Ibid.*, XXXIV, pt. 1, 8–9.

of the Potomac, getting it ready for the spring campaign. Once a week he came to Washington and conferred with Lincoln. In these meetings, the two went over the general features of Grant's plans. Lincoln told John Hay that Grant's strategy reminded him of suggestions he had often made to Halleck, Buell, and other generals to move all Federal forces against the enemy line at the same time so as to bring into action the Federal advantage of superior numbers and prevent the Confederates from shifting troops from one point to another. Lincoln said he had recognized Grant's application of this idea of his when Grant told him that he intended to make the whole Federal line useful: that those troops not fighting could help the fighting by advancing. Grasping the point immediately, Lincoln had said to Grant: "Those not skinning can hold a leg." [9]

In his memoirs, Grant gave a characteristic misleading account of the interview at which Lincoln made this remark. The General said Lincoln uttered it at their last meeting before Grant took the field, which would have been around the last of April or first of May. According to Grant, Lincoln had learned from somebody else that a movement all along the line was intended and seemed to think it was something new in war. Grant had to explain the matter to him, whereupon the astonished President made his skinning statement.[1] Hay recorded his conversation with Lincoln in his war diary; Grant wrote his version years after the war. Even without Hay's contemporary evidence, Grant's story can be disproved. The General liked Lincoln's figure of speech so much that he appropriated it as his own and repeated it at a much earlier date than the time he claimed to have heard it from Lincoln. In a letter to Sherman on April 4 in which he instructed Sherman what to do in Georgia and explained the other strategic

[9] Dennett, *Diary of Hay*, 178–179, April 30, 1864.
[1] Grant, *Memoirs*, II, 141–143.

moves he was planning, Grant said that he was sending a small force under General Franz Sigel on a raid into western Virginia. Sigel might not accomplish much, Grant said, but at least the enemy would have to detach troops against him. If Sigel could not skin, added Grant with obvious relish, he could hold a leg.[2]

One of Grant's projected offensives, the attack on Mobile, did not come off. Banks had started an offensive of his own up Red River in Louisiana in April, and by exercising his talents for mismanagement to the utmost had got himself so badly defeated that he was unable to engage in the Mobile movement. Angered and disgusted by the news of Banks's failure, Grant telegraphed Halleck that Banks ought to be removed. Halleck showed Grant's despatch to Lincoln. In an election year, the President, who was the leader of the political party committed to prosecuting the war to victory as well as commander in chief, could not and would not hastily relieve a general who was so important a political figure as Banks. Halleck told Grant that Lincoln wanted to wait for further information on the Red River reverse before taking any action. Grant then suggested that Banks be left in command in Louisiana but that his troops be placed under the field direction of another general. Lincoln saw that Grant wanted to get rid of Banks but that he was dodging the responsibility of asking specifically for his removal. Rightly thinking that Grant ought to shoulder the responsibility, Lincoln asked Halleck to tell Grant that Banks would be removed if Grant insisted on it as a military necessity or that Banks would be shelved at New Orleans if Grant would name an officer to take command of his troops. Unless Grant would do one of these things, Halleck explained, Lincoln would not risk alienating Banks's friends. Forced to act up to the obligation

[2] Grant to Sherman, April 4, 1864, *Official Records*, XXXII, pt. 3, 245–246.

of his position, Grant recommended that General E. R. S. Canby be given the command of the army in Louisiana, and Lincoln appointed him.[3]

Lincoln was glad that he had managed to ease Banks out of field service without ousting him from his departmental command. Banks could do no harm in New Orleans, and he was still tied politically to the administration. Lincoln confessed to Gideon Welles that he had erred in thinking at one time that Banks was a capable general. He had "cousined" up to Banks, said Lincoln, but Banks had failed him. With mock sadness, Lincoln quoted Thomas Moore's verse beginning:

> *Oh, ever thus from childhood's hour,*
> *I've seen my fondest hopes decay.*[4]

Grant was forty-two years old in 1864. He was five feet eight in height and weighed about one hundred thirty-five pounds. His eyes were dark gray, his hair and short full beard were chestnut brown. His left eye was a little lower than the other, and he had a wart on his right cheek. His frame was slightly stooped. There was little magnetism in his appearance and personality. He never inspired troops to frenzies of applause or affection, as did McClellan and Burnside. At first sight, most people were not impressed by him; many found him a comic figure.[5] A sensitive observer who first saw Grant soon after he came to Washington said the General was an extraordinary person but did not look it. Young Charles Francis Adams, Jr., of a family not given to uttering praise lightly, wrote his father in London that Grant

[3] Grant to Halleck, April 22, 29, 30, 1864, *ibid.*, XXXIV, pt. 3, 252–253, 331, 357; Halleck to Grant, April 22, 29, 30, May 3, *ibid.*, 293, 331–332, 357, 409; order appointing Canby, May 7, *ibid.*, 491.

[4] Welles, *Diary*, II, 26.

[5] Church, *Grant*, 219–220; Porter, *Campaigning with Grant*, 14–16; Rusling, *Men and Things*, 135–136.

could pass for a dumpy, slouchy little subaltern who was fond of smoking. But he knew how to manage men quietly, Adams added, and he possessed exquisite judgment. In a penetrating evaluation, Adams said that in a crisis all would instinctively lean on Grant.[6] Another keen student of human nature, Colonel Theodore Lyman of Meade's staff, saw immediately past Grant's exterior to the real man. He noted that Grant's face had three expressions: deep thought, extreme determination, and great simplicity and calmness. Summing Grant up, Lyman said that the General looked as if he had determined to butt his head through a brick wall and was about to do it.[7]

Grant's war service before 1864 had been an ideal training experience for the job of general in chief. He was a better war director because he had come up the hard and long way. He had started as a small unit commander and then had gone on to bigger commands as he had proved on the field that he could handle larger responsibilities. He learned self-confidence from his successes and patience and determination from his failures. His experience with small commands was fortunate for Grant. It taught him the importance of looking after such things as ammunition supplies and means of transportation—the prosaic vital things that can make or break an army. Most valuable of all, he first encountered the problems of army administration on a small scale and mastered one set before he met another and more complex one. He learned administration from the regimental level up, which was a better way than if he had suddenly been placed in charge of a huge army as McClellan had been.

At the beginning of the war, Grant knew as much about the theory and history of war as the average West Point graduate and regular army officer, which was not very much. He

[6] C. F. Adams, Jr., to C. F. Adams, Sr., May 29, 1864, W. C. Ford (ed.), *A Cycle of Adams Letters*, II, 133–134.

[7] Agassiz, *Meade's Headquarters*, 80–81.

did not, after the conflict started, study the higher art of war from books, but he studied it closely from the events he witnessed and experienced. At Henry and Donelson, he saw the moral value of being on the offensive, and he learned at Shiloh the danger of neglecting the principle of precaution. In nearly all of his early operations, he demonstrated that he understood one of the most important of all strategic principles, that of making the destruction of the enemy army his primary objective. Grant absorbed some of his knowledge of war from other officers, and on many occasions used the brains of others, which is what a great general should do. As Sherman well expressed it, Grant possessed "in an eminent degree that peculiar and high attribute of using various men to produce a common result. . . ." [8] His brilliant victories at Vicksburg and Chattanooga were partly the result of his own developing strategic powers and partly of his ability to use the powers of his subordinates to accomplish his purpose. When he became general in chief, Grant was about as perfectly trained and formed for the post as any general could be.

Grant was, judged by modern standards, the greatest general of the Civil War. He was head and shoulders above any general on either side as an over-all strategist, as a master of what in later wars would be called global strategy. His Operation Crusher plan, the product of a mind which had received little formal instruction in the higher art of war, would have done credit to the most finished student of a series of modern staff and command schools. He was a brilliant theater strategist, as evidenced by the Vicksburg campaign, which was a classic field and siege operation. He was a better than average tactician, although like even the best generals of both sides he did not appreciate the destruction that the increasing firepower of modern armies could visit on troops advancing across open spaces.

[8] Wallace, *An Autobiography*, 662–664.

Lee is usually ranked as the greatest Civil War general, but this evaluation has been made without placing Lee and Grant in the perspective of military developments since the war. Lee was interested hardly at all in "global" strategy, and what few suggestions he did make to his government about operations in other theaters than his own indicate that he had little aptitude for grand planning. As a theater strategist, Lee often demonstrated more brilliance and apparent originality than Grant, but his most audacious plans were as much the product of the Confederacy's inferior military position as his own fine mind. In war, the weaker side has to improvise brilliantly. It must strike quickly, daringly, and include a dangerous element of risk in its plans. Had Lee been a Northern general with Northern resources behind him, he would have improvised less and seemed less bold. Had Grant been a Southern general, he would have fought as Lee did.

Fundamentally Grant was superior to Lee because in a modern total war he had a modern mind, and Lee did not. Lee looked to the past in war as the Confederacy did in spirit. The staffs of the two men illustrate their outlook. It would not be accurate to say that Lee's general staff were glorified clerks, but the statement would not be too wide of the mark. Certainly his staff was not, in the modern sense, a planning staff, which was why Lee was often a tired general. He performed labors that no general can do in a big modern army —work that should have fallen to his staff, but that Lee did because it was traditional for the commanding general to do it in older armies. Most of Lee's staff officers were lieutenant colonels. Some of the men on Grant's general staff, as well as the staffs of other Northern generals, were major and brigadier generals, officers who were capable of leading corps. Grant's staff was an organization of experts in the various phases of strategic planning. The modernity of Grant's mind was most apparent in his grasp of the concept that war was becoming total and that the destruction of the enemy's economic resources was as effective and legitimate a form of warfare as the destruction of his armies. What was realism to Grant was barbarism to Lee. Lee thought of war in the old way as a conflict between armies and refused to view it for what it had become—a struggle between societies. To him, economic war was needless cruelty to civilians. Lee was the last of the great old-fashioned generals, Grant the first of the great moderns.

Chapter 13

"I Begin to See It"

By the first of May, Grant was ready to send the Army of the Potomac smashing over the Rapidan at Lee. As the General was about to take the field, Lincoln wrote him a friendly note of appreciation and encouragement. The President's letter was a perfect statement of the command relationship he expected to exist between him and Grant. It also proves that Lincoln knew the general features of Grant's strategy and had learned them from Grant and that he was content to leave the execution of the details to the General:

Not expecting to see you again before the spring campaign opens, I wish to express to you in this way my entire satisfaction with what you have done, so far as I understand it. The particulars of your plans I neither know nor seek to know. You are vigilant and self-reliant, and pleased with this, I wish not to obtrude any constraints or restraints upon you. While I am very anxious that any great disaster or capture of our men in great numbers shall be avoided, I know these points are less likely to escape your attention than they would be mine. If there is anything wanting which is within my power to give, do not fail to let me know it. And now, with a brave army and a just cause, may God sustain you.

Grant replied from the field, expressing profuse thanks for the support he had received from Lincoln and ending his letter by saying: "Should my success be less than I desire, and expect, the least I can say is, the fault is not with you." [1] Grant was not going to throw off the responsibility for failure on Lincoln.

Grant struck the Confederate army almost immediately after he crossed the Rapidan. For several days he sent no reports to Washington. Lincoln knew that Grant was fighting, but his only information of Grant's progress came from newspaper despatches of reporters with the army.[2] People who saw the President at this time recalled later his calm confidence of victory and his faith in Grant. He was supposed to have told a Congressman who asked how Grant was coming that the General had crawled into the Wilderness, as the region right south of the Rapidan was called, drawn up the ladder and pulled the hole in after him and that everybody would have to wait until he came out. To another person, he spoke admiringly of Grant's coolness and persistency in a crisis and said that once Grant got his teeth into anything nothing could shake him off.[3]

The recollections of his friends were accurate. As was usual with him when an important operation was starting, Lincoln tried to find out everything that he could about what was happening. He drifted from office to office talking to people about Grant and asking them if they had heard any rumors. One night he was so busy gathering news that he went without sleep.[4] One of his secretaries aptly summarized Lincoln's attitude by saying that he watched every report of the campaign with "quiet, unswerving interest." [5] By the end of the

[1] Lincoln to Grant, April 30, 1864, *Works of Lincoln,* X, 90–91; Grant to Lincoln, May 1, Lincoln MSS., vol. 153.

[2] Stanton to B. F. Butler, May 6, 8, 1864, Marshall, *Correspondence of Butler,* IV, 168, 175.

[3] Porter, *Campaigning with Grant,* 98; Francis B. Carpenter, *The Inner Life of Abraham Lincoln: Six Months at the White House,* 283.

[4] Welles, *Diary,* II, 25, May 7, 1864.

[5] J. G. Nicolay to Therena Bates, May 15, 1864, Nicolay MSS.

first week of the fighting in the Wilderness, despatches of a more definite nature began to arrive in Washington. Lincoln learned that Grant had hit Lee in one hard, slugging battle after another and, despite heavy losses, had inched forward. More confident than ever of victory, Lincoln said to John Hay: "How near we have been to this thing before and failed. I believe if any other general had been at the head of that army it would have been now on this side of the Rapidan. It is the dogged pertinacity of Grant that wins." [6]

Grant was not as close to victory as Lincoln thought. The General had planned to bring Lee to decisive battle someplace between the Rapidan-Rappahannock line and Richmond. While the Army of the Potomac ran down Lee, Butler was to advance up the south side of the James destroying Lee's railroad communications with the lower South and possibly capturing Richmond. Grant had always figured that he might have to move the Potomac army to south of the James: if he could not force Lee to battle or if Lee, with his army crippled but intact, retreated to Richmond. In the latter case, Grant would follow him and unite with Butler for the kill. Grant tried to destroy Lee in northern Virginia by attacking him in front and at the same time enveloping the Confederate right with a flanking movement. Every one of Grant's attempts failed. Lee, showing great defensive skill and aided by the rugged terrain of the Wilderness, held off the Union frontal assaults and shifted forces to his right to foil the enveloping movements. Grant bent Lee's right back in each battle, but he never got around it and he never broke the Confederate line in front. In a month of bloody fighting, the two armies moved across northern Virginia in a general line running from north to southeast. Although Grant was getting nearer to Richmond all the time, he was not achieving his objective of making Lee fight a showdown battle. The

[6] Dennett, *Diary of Hay*, 180, May 9, 1864.

Union casualties were tremendous: over 50,000 men killed and wounded. Lee's losses were smaller in number but probably a larger proportion of his total. Had Grant been willing to continue this kind of fighting indefinitely, he might have eventually killed the greater part of the Confederate army and a large part of his own. Grant, however, did not want to bleed his way to victory. He was willing to incur heavy losses if they were necessary to victory, but he would not take them merely to inflict corresponding losses on the enemy or if he could win by fighting in some other way. He did not believe in butchery as a principle of war.

As he fought his way through the Wilderness and across northern Virginia, Grant began to doubt that his plan would succeed. He told the government that he would take no backward step and that he could whip Lee if Lee would fight. The trouble was that Lee would not fight the kind of battle Grant wanted him to—a decisive battle that would settle the issue of the campaign at once. The Confederate commander refused to risk his army in open battle. Always Lee fought from behind field entrenchments, and it was obvious to Grant that he would not come out from them and probably could not be forced out. Early in the campaign, Grant considered that if he could not bring Lee to battle north of Richmond he would have to shift operations to south of the James.[7]

By the first week in June, Grant stood about nine miles northeast of Richmond. He was at the end of the line he had said he would fight it out on if it took all summer. His plan had failed. Instead of destroying Lee at a distance from Richmond, he had only driven the Confederates closer to their capital. If he continued his movement to envelop Lee's right, the Confederate army would retire into the ring of fortifications around Richmond and stand a siege. Grant was willing

[7] Grant to Halleck, May 8, 10, 11, 26, 1864, *Official Records*, XXXVI, pt. 1, 2–3, 4, 8–9.

to destroy Lee's army by the slow method of siegecraft if that was the only way he could do it, but he preferred the quicker decision of battle. He decided to make one more attempt to force battle on Lee. He telegraphed Halleck that without greater sacrifice of life than he was willing to sustain he could not accomplish his strategic objective by operating outside of Richmond. Therefore, he was going to leave the Richmond area, march straight south through the Peninsula, and come out south of the James. From there, he would move to seize Petersburg, which was the hub of all the railroads connecting Richmond with the eastern Confederacy. Butler was supposed to have cut these roads at the beginning of the campaign, but had been defeated and driven back into a pocket between the James and Appomattox rivers.

Holding the railroads, Grant would be in position to cut off Lee's supplies from the deep South. Lee would have to fight for his communications; he would have to leave the safety of Richmond and fight the decisive engagement that Grant wanted.[8] Lincoln approved of Grant's change in plan. Although the President had said nothing to Grant about the casualties of the campaign, he must have agonized over them, and he certainly knew the depressing effect they had on popular morale. Grant's new scheme promised lighter losses and quicker results. When Grant informed the government that he had started to cross the James, Lincoln telegraphed him: "I begin to see it; you will succeed. God bless you all." [9]

Again Grant failed to force Lee to battle. He succeeded in masking his withdrawal from Lee's front and crossing the James before the Confederate commander realized what was happening. Then Grant drove at Petersburg and its railroads, which were guarded by only a small enemy force. He did not

[8] Grant to Halleck, June 5, 1864, *ibid.*, XXXVI, pt. 1, 11–12.
[9] Grant to Halleck, June 14, 1864, *ibid.*, XL, pt. 2, 18–19; Lincoln to Grant, June 15, *Works of Lincoln*, X, 126.

capture the town because the defenders put up a stubborn fight and his generals in charge of the attack, not fully apprised by Grant that he wanted them to go into Petersburg, conducted the assault feebly. The Confederates halted Grant long enough to give Lee time to move down from Richmond. He arrived just as the thin defence lines were about to buckle.

With the main Confederate army on the scene, Grant had no chance to take Petersburg by assault. Lee's troops dug themselves into entrenchments for miles above and below Petersburg. The situation was the same as in the Wilderness or in the fighting north of Richmond: Lee was behind field fortifications and would not risk a battle. All that Grant could do now was to try to secure possession of the Petersburg railroads by engaging in a modified siege operation. He put his own army into entrenchments from which with constant probing attacks he could feel and threaten Lee's line in front. While keeping Lee occupied at all points, he aimed to swing his left around the Confederate right until he could get it on the railroads in rear of Petersburg. Then at last he could make Lee fight. Although Grant was disappointed by the result of his campaign, he was as confident as ever of ultimate victory. In a letter to a friend, he pointed out that Lee's army and the Confederate army facing Sherman were so weak that they could not fight outside of fortifications and that the great losses of Confederate manpower could not be replaced. If the Northern people, said Grant, would only continue to support the war success was certain.[1]

Lincoln was deeply disappointed that the campaign to destroy the Confederate army in Virginia had ended in a siege. Feeling perhaps some doubts of Grant's generalship and wanting to see for himself what had happened, the President decided to pay Grant a visit in camp. He left Washington by

[1] Grant to J. R. Jones, July 5, 1864, MS. in Chicago Historical Society.

boat on June 20 and returned on the twenty-third.[2] At Grant's headquarters at City Point, he reviewed troops, and in the evening sat with Grant and the staff before the General's tent, telling some of his favorite stories. Grant assured Lincoln that his failure to defeat Lee in battle was but a temporary setback and that from his present position he would eventually bring Lee to bay. Impressed by Grant's confidence, Lincoln said to a staff officer: "When Grant once gets possession of a place, he holds on to it as if he had inherited it." [3] When Lincoln got back to Washington, his associates noted that he was in better spirits than when he had departed and that he had as much faith as ever in Grant.[4]

Soon after the siege started, Grant had to deal with a serious problem of military administration in which Lincoln was directly involved. When Grant moved to Petersburg, he absorbed Butler's forces into his command. Before, Butler had been a departmental commander and the head of the Army of the James, with a large measure of freedom of action. While technically continuing to be the commander of his army, he now became, in effect, a corps commander under Grant. The difficulty was that Butler was not competent to direct a corps in battle. He could administer one excellently, but he could not fight it. In addition, Butler's commission was junior only to Grant's. If at any time Grant had to leave Petersburg to go to Washington, Butler would become commander of the Armies of the Potomac and the James, a prospect which made many officers shudder. Grant considered Butler's presence undesirable and dangerous and suggested to Halleck that Butler ought to be shifted to some command where he could do no harm. He would not formally recom-

[2] Lincoln to Mrs. Lincoln, June 24, 1864, *Works of Lincoln*, X, 134; Welles, *Diary*, II, 55.

[3] Porter, *Campaigning with Grant*, 216–224.

[4] Welles, *Diary*, II, 58; Pease and Randall, *Diary of Browning*, 673; Beale, *Diary of Bates*, 378.

mend that Butler be relieved, said Grant, because he had no specific complaint to make against him—but could not Halleck find a way to get rid of him? Halleck detested Butler and was eager to oblige Grant. But he told Grant that he had heard any attempt to dispose of Butler would have to be a matter of "consultation," which meant that Lincoln would enter the picture. Cunningly Halleck advised that Butler could be shelved by leaving him in command of his former department with headquarters at Fortress Monroe and putting his troops under the field command of an officer like "Baldy" Smith.[5]

Grant grasped at Halleck's suggestion. He asked Old Brains to obtain an order from Lincoln assigning Butler's troops to Smith. Halleck then drafted an order stating that by the direction of the President Butler's army was to be organized into a corps under Smith's command and that Butler was to retire to Fortress Monroe to act emptily as departmental commander.[6] Lincoln at first approved the order and then withdrew his indorsement. Apparently he consented to its issuance without fully understanding its significance. Halleck may have told him verbally only the general nature of the document. Whatever the facts of the case, the President suddenly realized that an order relieving an important political general was about to go out in his name. He moved quickly to put the responsibility for shelving Butler where it belonged. Before Halleck could send the order to Grant, he received a note from Stanton asking him to bring it and Grant's letter requesting the new command arrangement to Lincoln. After Halleck talked to Lincoln, he changed the language of the order. In the revised version, the one that went to Grant, the phrase "by

[5] Grant to Halleck, July 1, 1864, and Halleck to Grant, July 3, *Official Records*, XL, pt. 2, 558–559, 598.

[6] Grant to Halleck, July 6, 1864, *ibid.*, XL, pt. 3, 31; Halleck's order of July 7, *ibid.*, 59.

order of the President" was deleted. If Butler was to be ousted, it would have to be by the authority of the general in chief.[7]

Butler heard about the order from his friends in Washington. Immediately he rushed to City Point to confront Grant. Grant said the order was a mistake, and promised to write to Halleck, and did, asking that it be suppressed. Jubilantly Butler informed his friends and his wife that he was stronger than ever and would have a more important command.[8] The unfortunate Smith, once more done out of a command, charged that Grant backed down before Butler because Butler threatened to expose that Grant had been drunk in Butler's presence. Smith also said that Butler told Grant he could prevent the Republican convention from nominating Lincoln and could control the Democratic convention. Fearful of subjecting Lincoln to the political vengeance of Butler, Grant suspended the order.[9]

Smith's statements were based largely on his own angry suspicions and were far from the truth. Undoubtedly Butler did talk strongly to Grant, but it is improbable that he uttered the threats described by Smith. He could not have said anything about Lincoln's nomination, because the Republican convention had already met, in June, and named Lincoln as the party candidate. What Butler probably did say to Grant, and it was all he had to say, was to point out that the order did not bear Lincoln's name and that Grant would have to take the responsibility for issuing it. Grant knew how important the support of Butler, a prominent Democrat, was

[7] Stanton to Halleck, July 7, 1864, *ibid.,* XL, pt. 3, 59; revised order of July 7, *ibid.,* 69.

[8] Grant to Halleck, July 10, 1864, *ibid.,* XL, pt. 3, 122–123; Butler to J. W. Shaffer, July 9, *ibid.,* 114; Butler to Mrs. Butler, July 10, Marshall, *Correspondence of Butler,* IV, 481–482.

[9] William Farrar Smith, *From Chattanooga to Petersburg . . . ,* 32–59, 174–178.

to the administration in an election year, and he realized that if Lincoln had withheld his name from the order the President did not want Butler sloughed off, at least at the moment. By dispensing with the order, Grant demonstrated that he appreciated the vital relationship in a democracy between war and politics.

Lee made an early attempt to weaken Grant's hold on Petersburg by increasing the Confederate forces in the Valley and directing them to move northward and threaten Washington. The Confederate commander hoped that the pressure on Washington would cause the Union government to detach troops from Grant for the defence of the city. As leader of the Valley force, Lee appointed Jubal A. Early. When Early began his movement, there were few Federal troops in the Valley or around Washington. The army that should have been in the Valley to meet Early's threat was in West Virginia. As a part of his Virginia plan of operations, Grant had sent a force under David Hunter to the Valley to destroy supplies which might go to Lee's army. When the Confederates had concentrated against Hunter, he had retreated westward over the mountains into West Virginia instead of falling back down the Valley. Washington was more weakly defended when Early struck than in 1862 when Jackson began his movement. Early met no opposition as he advanced, and by the first week in July he had started to cross the Potomac.

Grant was informed of the progress of Early's movement by his own intelligence service and from Washington. He reasoned that Lincoln would be sensitive about the safety of the capital and might want the general in chief to come and direct its defence. Grant was so far away from the area of Early's operation that he was not in a good position to make quick decisions about what measures should be taken to defeat Early. Even Grant's information about the Union forces in the Valley was not accurate. He did not understand that

Hunter had got himself so far removed from the Valley that he could take no part in its defence. Grant telegraphed Halleck that the forces in the Valley should be able to get in Early's rear and trap him. He saw no danger to Washington, said Grant, but if Lincoln thought it advisable he would come with reinforcements to the capital, leaving operations at Petersburg to stand on the defensive.[1]

Grant's telegram arrived in Washington at five minutes after one on the afternoon of July 10. Lincoln answered it one hour later. Writing with the enemy north of the Potomac and approaching the capital, the President was calm in spirit. He informed Grant that the government had no force fit or large enough to take the field against Early. Washington could probably be held against an attack, Lincoln said, but Baltimore could not. Lincoln then told Grant what he thought the General should do: "Now, what I think is, that you should provide to retain your hold where you are, certainly, and bring the rest with you personally, and make a vigorous effort to destroy the enemy's forces in this vicinity. I think there is a fair chance to do this, if the movement is prompt. This is what I think upon your suggestion, and is not an order."[2] Again, as in 1862, Lincoln was thinking in offensive terms about the Confederate force in the Valley. He was not worried as much about the safety of Washington as he was about the possibility of running down the invaders and removing finally the enemy menace in the Valley area.

Grant, after some reflection and a conference with his chief of staff, decided to send two corps to Washington but not to go himself. He thought, and so telegraphed Halleck, that if he left Petersburg his action would be interpreted by the Northern people and the enemy as a sign of weakness in the

[1] Grant to Halleck, July 9, 1864, *Official Records*, XXXVII, pt. 2, 134.

[2] Lincoln to Grant, July 10, 1864, *Works of Lincoln*, X, 155–156.

Union cause. The reinforcements he was despatching, he said, ought to be well able to cope with Early. His telegram came in to Washington early in the morning on July 11. That day Early was approaching the defences of the city; in the afternoon he would feel out their strength. Lincoln replied to Grant at eight o'clock. Without hesitation and with complete confidence in his general in chief, Lincoln accepted Grant's decision and approved of Grant's arrangements. He only feared that the Confederates would get over the Potomac before the Federal forces could converge on them. The next day the commander in chief was actually under enemy fire. Early probed at the capital fortifications with strong reconnaissances. Lincoln went out to Fort Stevens to see the fighting and stood on the parapet while bullets whizzed around him and a soldier was killed at his side.[3]

Lincoln's foreboding that Early would escape proved correct. Finding the defences too strong to assault and fearful of being trapped by the superior Federal forces gathering around him, Early recrossed the Potomac and retired up the Valley. Lincoln spoke harshly of the timid pursuit conducted by General H. G. Wright of Grant's Sixth Corps, who was in charge of the troops following Early, saying that Wright acted as though he were afraid he might catch the Confederates.[4] Wright, however, was not at fault. Early got away because the tangled command system in the Washington military area did not make anybody responsible for catching him. As Charles A. Dana pointed out to Grant, there was really no commander or central authority to direct operations against Early. Hunter, the former commander of the Valley forces, was working his way back from West Virginia; one general

[3] Grant to Halleck, July 10, 1864, *Official Records*, XXXVII, pt. 2, 155; Lincoln to Grant, July 11, *ibid.*, 191; Wilson, *Rawlins*, 243–244; Dennett, *Diary of Hay*, 209, July 11; John H. Cramer, *Lincoln Under Enemy Fire*.

[4] Dennett, *Diary of Hay*, 210, July 14, 1864.

commanded the defences of Washington and another those of Baltimore; Wright commanded the Sixth Corps; Halleck refused to give any orders to any of these officers unless told to do so by superior authority; and Lincoln was issuing no orders to Halleck. If Grant did not direct positively and explicitly what should be done, said Dana, everything would be at loose ends.[5]

Halleck was in an ugly mood, probably brought on by the recent appearance of the enemy near Washington and the realization that he, who once had been general in chief, was powerless to order anybody to do anything. In his bitterness, Halleck openly criticized Grant. Grant sent a staff officer to Washington after Early retired to bring back to Petersburg the two corps he had sent to the capital. Halleck refused to order the corps returned without written instructions from Grant. Sneeringly he asked the staff officer when Grant was going to accomplish something at Petersburg and denounced Grant for going south of the James and for stripping Washington of troops.[6]

Grant now realized that he would have to unify the command system in the Washington area by putting the troops in the capital and the adjacent departments under the control of one general. Early was still in the Valley and was sure to strike again. Only a central command of all the forces around the city could prevent a recurrence of the confusion prevailing in the recent raid. If Early could make periodic sweeps at Washington and escape each time because of the divisions in the Federal command system, Grant would always have to be detaching troops from Petersburg to chase after the Confederates. He would never be able to corner Lee.

[5] C. A. Dana to Grant, July 12, 1864, *Official Records*, XXXVII, pt. 2, 223.

[6] Grant to Halleck, July 14, 16, 1864, *ibid.*, XXXVII, pt. 2, 300–301, 350; MS. Diary of General Cyrus B. Comstock, July 15. See also Halleck to W. T. Sherman, July 16, *Official Records*, XXXVIII, pt. 3, 150–151.

Furthermore, Grant knew that if Early got close to Washington again Lincoln would become dissatisfied with the defence setup for the capital. The President had voiced no criticisms of Grant's arrangements to check Early and had accepted without argument Grant's decision to stay at Petersburg. But another time around Lincoln might not be so patient. He might demand that Grant come to Washington to direct operations against the enemy or take part of Grant's army away from Petersburg for service in the Valley.

Grant had just received a despatch from Lincoln that showed how closely the commander in chief followed the course of operations and how quickly he would question a move that he thought was faulty. At the War Department, Lincoln had seen a telegram from Grant to Sherman in which Grant said he was about to make a "desperate effort" at Petersburg to secure a position he could hold with a relatively small number of troops. Lincoln sent Grant a telegram cautioning the General not to attack in such a way as to incur heavy casualties: "Pressed as we are by lapse of time I am glad to hear you say this; and yet I do hope you may find a way that the effort shall not be desperate in the sense of great loss of life." [7]

Grant wrote to Halleck proposing that Washington and the three departments around it be merged together under the command of General William B. Franklin, who had not had an important post since he had been a corps commander under McClellan and Burnside. Halleck replied that Franklin would not be satisfactory to Lincoln because the President believed that Franklin had disobeyed Burnside's orders at Fredericksburg.[8] Grant then wrote directly to Lincoln, ex-

[7] Grant to W. T. Sherman, July 16, 1864, *Official Records,* XXXVIII, pt. 5, 149; Lincoln to Grant, July 17, *Works of Lincoln,* X, 160.

[8] Grant to Halleck, July 18, 1864, and Halleck to Grant, July 21, *Official Records,* XXXVII, pt. 2, 374, 408.

plaining how he planned to change the Washington command system and why he had suggested Franklin as commander. Franklin happened to be available, said Grant, but he did not insist on Franklin's appointment. Any general in whom he and Lincoln had confidence would do, Grant continued, and Meade might be a good man for the job. If Meade was chosen, Grant recommended that General W. S. Hancock, a corps commander in the Army of the Potomac, be named to command that army. Grant said that he would not like to put on paper his reasons for proposing a new commander for the Potomac army but that General John A. Rawlins of his staff was bearing his letter to Washington and could tell Lincoln what the reasons were.[9] They were not as sinister as Grant made them sound, but they were serious. Meade's vicious temper was threatening to destroy his usefulness as a general. He abused and insulted corps generals to their faces at headquarters and made most of them his bitter enemies. They retaliated by criticizing his generalship. The situation was so tense and so dangerous to command harmony that Grant feared he would have to relieve Meade.[1] But he wanted to ease Meade out graciously, because he liked the Old Snapping Turtle and had confidence in him. Putting Meade in command of the Washington area would solve two problems: it would remove him from the Army of the Potomac without demoting him to a minor assignment and it would place an experienced officer in charge of the capital defences.

Rawlins arrived in Washington on the morning of July 26 and delivered Grant's letter to the President. After reading it, Lincoln asked Stanton to telegraph Grant asking when the General could meet Lincoln at Fortress Monroe for a confer-

[9] Grant to Lincoln, July 25, 1864, *ibid.*, XXXVII, pt. 2, 433–434.

[1] C. A. Dana to Stanton, July 7, 1864, *ibid.*, XL, pt. 1, 35–36; MS. Diary of C. B. Comstock, July 7.

ence. An exchange of telegrams between City Point and
Washington resulted in fixing the meeting for the morning
of the thirty-first.[2] Before Lincoln left Washington, news
from the Valley indicated that Early was about to strike again.
To meet the new crisis, the President directed that Halleck
be placed temporarily in command of Washington and the
surrounding departments. Lincoln's order stated that because
of the difficulties and delays in communication between City
Point and Washington orders for the operations against Early
would have to be issued directly from the capital and Halleck would have full authority to take any measures necessary
for the defence of the entire Washington military area.[3] What
Lincoln and Grant discussed at their conference is not disclosed by any records. Indeed, it is possible that they did not
meet at all but that Lincoln called off his trip as Early again
approached the Potomac.

If they did get together at Fortress Monroe, they assuredly
discussed the Washington command problem. And yet on
August 1, the day after the meeting was to have taken place,
Grant wrote to Halleck suggesting a new command arrangement for Washington and the Valley, which he would hardly
have done if he and Lincoln had discussed the subject on the
previous day and reached an agreement. The tone of Grant's
letter suggests that he had been thinking about the Washington question since he had recommended Meade as the capital
commander and that suddenly, without ever seeing Lincoln,
he had hit upon a new plan which he immediately communi-
cated to the government. Grant now proposed that General

[2] Stanton to Grant, July 26, 1864, Lincoln to Grant, July 28, Grant
to Lincoln, July 28, in *Works of Lincoln*, X, 174, 177–178; Grant to
Stanton, July 26 and Stanton to Grant, July 27, *Official Records*,
XXXVII, pt. 2, 444, 463; Grant to B. F. Butler, July 30, *ibid.*, XL,
pt. 3, 676.

[3] Grant to Halleck, July 26, 1864, *Official Records*, XXXVII, pt. 2,
445; Stanton to Halleck, July 27, *Works of Lincoln*, X, 175–176.

Philip H. Sheridan, his cavalry leader, go to Washington and take temporary command of the forces in the departments making up the Washington military area: the Departments of Washington, the Susquehanna, West Virginia, and the Middle Department. The four departments were to be merged into one division. Hunter, the commander of the West Virginia Department and the senior general in the area, was to be administrative head of the division, but Sheridan would take active command of the troops in the field. Grant's instructions to Sheridan were that he was to go where Early went and follow the Confederates to the death.[4]

Grant's despatch arrived in Washington late at night on the first. Lincoln probably saw it the next day. That night the President slept on Grant's communication, and on the third he sent Grant a telegram which was as important and as wise a document as any he wrote to any general in the war. He approved of Grant's purpose to move Sheridan relentlessly after Early, he said. "This I think, is exactly right as to how our forces should move, but please look over the despatches you may have received from here, ever since you made that order, and discover, if you can, that there is any idea in the head of any one here of 'putting our army south of the enemy,' or of following him to the 'death' in any direction. I repeat to you, it will neither be done nor attempted, unless you watch it every day and hour, and force it." [5]

Lincoln's telegram reveals his masterly ability as a director of war. Grant had the mistaken notion that from Petersburg he could estimate from the reports of others a military situation at Washington and direct movements in the Valley by the relatively slow means of the military telegraph. Grant was too far away to judge the situation around Washington or to

[4] Grant to Halleck, August 1, 1864, *Official Records*, XXXVII, pt. 2, 558.
[5] Lincoln to Grant, August 3, 1864, *Works of Lincoln*, X, 180.

control movements in that area. Lincoln was right in saying that Grant first ought to come to Washington, examine the situation firsthand, and directly issue the orders to get his movement started. For some reason, probably because he feared being held at the capital, Grant did not want to go to Washington. But in avoiding Washington, he was dodging his responsibility as general in chief. Lincoln's telegram sharply recalled Grant to the obligations of his office. Lincoln here "interfered" in military affairs because the head of the army was not performing his proper military function, and the result of Lincoln's interference, the ultimate smashing of Confederate power in the Valley, was another demonstration that Lincoln was a better strategist than any of the generals. And the episode was another refutation of the myth that Lincoln kept his hands entirely off the military machine and let Grant run it as he pleased.

When Grant received Lincoln's despatch, he realized he would have to bow to the President's will. He telegraphed Lincoln that he would leave for Washington in two hours and would spend several days with the forces being gathered for operations against Early at Monocacy Junction (near the capital) under Hunter's command. But he went with great reluctance.[6] Grant reached Monocacy on the fifth and conferred with Hunter, who said Halleck did not seem to have confidence in him and asked to be relieved. Grant gratefully agreed to the request, because it would enable him to put Sheridan in complete command of the new division.[7] In the meantime, Sheridan, following instructions from Grant, had reported in Washington and was instructed there to go to Monocacy. Before he left, he talked to Lincoln. In his memoirs, Sheridan gave a misleading account of the events lead-

[6] MS. Diary of C. B. Comstock, August 4, 1864; Grant to Lincoln, August 4, *Official Records*, XLII, pt. 2, 38.

[7] Grant, *Memoirs*, II, 317–321; MS. Diary of C. B. Comstock, August 5, 6, 1864.

ing up to his appointment. He said that Lincoln opposed merging the departments around Washington into one command, which was not true. Closer to the truth was his statement that Lincoln said Stanton thought Sheridan was too young to command an important department.[8] Sheridan was thirty-three years old and looked younger because he was five feet five in height and weighed only one hundred and fifteen pounds. In a story which ungraciously decreased Sheridan's stature an inch, Lincoln was supposed to have said to the General later in the war: "General Sheridan, when this peculiar war began I thought a cavalryman should be at least six feet four high; but I have changed my mind—five feet four will do in a pinch."[9]

At Monocacy, Grant gave Sheridan instructions for the campaign against Early and then left for Washington. He went to the War Department to see Stanton. The Secretary sent a note to Lincoln saying Grant was with him and asking if the General should come to the White House or would Lincoln come to the Department. Back came Stanton's note with a characteristic Lincolnian indorsement saying the President would call at the Department in a few minutes.[1] Lincoln and Grant doubtless discussed the appointment of Sheridan and Grant's plan to destroy the enemy forces in the Valley. Grant left for City Point on August 7, and on that day an order was issued combining the four departments in the Washington area into the Middle Division under the temporary command of Sheridan.[2] An aftermath of Grant's visit to Washington was that he became convinced Halleck was his enemy and would not cooperate with his plans. He tried to get rid of Halleck by proposing to Stanton that Old

[8] P. H. Sheridan, *Personal Memoirs of P. H. Sheridan*, I, 461–466.

[9] *Ibid.*, I, 346–347; Bates, *Lincoln in the Telegraph Office*, 67.

[1] Stanton to Lincoln, August 5, 1864, Stanton MSS.

[2] *Official Records*, XLIII, pt. 1, 719; MS. Diary of C. B. Comstock, August 7, 1864.

Brains be sent to replace McDowell in the exile command of the Pacific coast. Trying to mask his purpose, he said that McDowell was inefficient and Halleck would be a good man for the post. When Stanton, probably seeing through the subterfuge, replied that there were no complaints of McDowell and that Halleck could not be spared from Washington, Grant backed down.[3]

Although Lincoln had felt it necessary to call Grant to account in the Sheridan affair, he had lost none of his faith in the General or in Grant's plan to hammer at Petersburg until Lee was forced to battle. In mid-August, the President demonstrated strikingly that in a crisis he would support Grant to the hilt. He stood by Grant on a military issue that was related to the general political situation and at a moment when he could have found good political reasons for not sustaining the General. Northern morale was low in the summer. Victory over the Confederacy seemed more remote than ever, and the popular will to continue the war was weakening. There was much talk about a negotiated peace, and Lincoln himself thought that the depressed mood of the people might result in his defeat in the coming presidential election.

In August the government had announced that a new and heavy draft of troops would be made. Threats of forcible opposition to any more conscription were heard in the Eastern cities. Halleck was excitedly convinced that there would be widespread resistance to the draft, and he proposed that a substantial part of Grant's army be withdrawn to put down the riots he expected to occur. When Grant heard what Halleck was advising, he protested to Washington that for military reasons he could not afford to lose any troops, that if he weakened his army he risked losing his hold on Petersburg. His telegram reached Washington at seven in the morning on

[3] Grant to Stanton, August 15, 20, 1864, *Official Records*, L, pt. 2, 945, 951; Stanton to Grant, August 18, *ibid.*, 949; Wilson, *Rawlins*, 257.

August 17. Lincoln must have seen it soon after it was received in Halleck's office, for he answered it at ten. Although Lincoln also feared there would be opposition to the draft and although he could have taken the stand that it was a military necessity to replenish the armies, the President immediately agreed with Grant. In a telegram of steel, he said to Grant: "I have seen your despatch expressing your unwillingness to break your hold where you are. Neither am I willing. Hold on with a bulldog grip, and chew and choke as much as possible." [4] When Grant read the telegram, he laughed delightedly and said: "The President has more nerve than any of his advisers." [5]

[4] Grant to Halleck, August 15, 1864, *Official Records*, XLII, pt. 2, 193–194; Lincoln to Grant, August 17, *Works of Lincoln*, X, 193.

[5] Porter, *Campaigning with Grant*, 279.

Chapter 14

Lincoln and the Hour of Victory

IN the remaining months of 1864, Lincoln watched intently and sometimes anxiously over the conduct of the vast Union war effort, but he intervened in the management of it only at rare intervals because in general he was satisfied with Grant's direction. He felt that victory was certain if the people would continue to support the war. September was a month of triumph for the Union cause. Sheridan, after weeks of indecisive maneuvering, caught Early at Winchester and drubbed him soundly. The Confederates retreated southward, and the enemy menace in the Valley was at least temporarily removed. The delighted President, who could have well claimed much of the credit for Sheridan's success, gave all the honor to Sheridan. He telegraphed the General: "Have just heard of your great victory. God bless you all, officers and men. Strongly inclined to come up and see you." [1] The despatch epitomized Lincoln's humility of spirit. A communication that he addressed to Grant a few days later epitomized the close but restrained supervision he maintained over operations in all theaters. Lincoln feared, and his apprehension was a prudent and proper one for a director of war to have, that Lee might reinforce Early for a destructive attack on Sheridan, then halfway up the Valley and in an exposed position if assaulted by a superior enemy. Lincoln tele-

[1] Lincoln to Sheridan, September 20, 1864, *Works of Lincoln*, X, 227.

graphed Grant: "I hope it will have no constraint on you, nor do harm any way, for me to say I am a little afraid lest Lee send reinforcements to Early, and thus enable him to turn upon Sheridan." Grant reassured Lincoln by saying he was taking steps to prevent Lee from helping Early by attacking Lee. Grant himself was not scoring any spectacular triumphs, but he was steadily pushing his siege lines around Petersburg always closer to the vital railroads whose loss would force Lee out to battle.[2]

The most important victory of September was the capture of Atlanta by the army under the command of Sherman. Sherman had started his movement into Georgia at the same time that Grant had crossed the Rapidan. His mission was to defeat and if possible destroy the Confederate army opposing him and to destroy the economic resources of north Georgia. In the first phase of his operation, Sherman advanced rapidly, partly because Joseph Johnston, the Confederate commander, did not fight him as hard as Lee fought Grant. Lincoln was pleased with the vigor of Sherman's moves and expressed to Sherman, through Stanton, his admiration of the General.[3] In the summer months Sherman's advance slowed down a little, but he kept going forward. On September 2, he occupied Atlanta.

His success came at a time when the government desperately needed a victory. Northern morale was breaking because the conquest of the Confederacy seemed hopeless, although in a purely military sense the destruction of the Confederacy was then as certain as anything can be in war. But hardly ever is war purely military, especially in a democracy where it is dependent on the resolution of the people to

[2] Lincoln to Grant, September 29, 1864, *ibid.,* X, 236; Grant to Lincoln, September 29, *Official Records,* XLII, pt. 2, 1090–1091; Grant to J. R. Jones, October 4, 1864, MS. in Chicago Historical Society.

[3] Stanton to Sherman, May 20, 1864, *Official Records,* XXXVIII, pt. 4, 260–261.

support and fight it. In the summer and fall of 1864, the North had only to keep battering at the weakened walls of what was left of the Confederacy until they collapsed. At a moment when victory was more sure than at any previous time in the war the Northern will to fight was at its lowest point. With Grant stalled at Petersburg and Sherman apparently stopped before Atlanta, the war seemed to be approaching an intolerable stalemate. Then came the news of Sherman's capture of Atlanta to thrill and rejuvenate the war spirit of the Northern masses. Sherman's success guaranteed that the war would be continued and Lincoln reelected in November. The President, who realized better than anybody the significance of Atlanta, issued a proclamation tendering the nation's thanks to Sherman and his army.[4]

Sherman had Atlanta but he had not accomplished his primary objective of destroying the Confederate army, which moved to a position west of the city. Curiously enough, the defeated Confederates now had the initiative over Sherman. They struck at his communications extending back to Tennessee and retired to safety when he tried to catch them. Their obvious purpose was to annoy and harass Sherman without risking their forces in a decisive battle. Sherman knew that if he attempted to run them down they would lead him away on a wild-goose chase to Alabama. As long as he stayed in Atlanta, Sherman was restricted to a barren defensive strategy. To recover the initiative, Sherman proposed a bold plan to Grant. He would send General George Thomas with about 30,000 troops back to Tennessee with instructions to take command in the state and gather enough forces to hold the Tennessee line against enemy attack. With the main part of the army, Sherman would march across Georgia, de-

[4] "Order of Thanks and Rejoicing," September 3, 1864, *Works of Lincoln*, X, 213.

stroying economic resources as he went, and come out at Savannah or Charleston on the coast, where the Navy could open up a base for him.[5] Grant submitted Sherman's scheme to the government without directly giving it his approval. He said that originally it had been intended for Sherman to connect with a Union army moving up from Mobile, thus securing a line from Chattanooga to the Gulf. This move had been called off because the Union army in Louisiana had never been able to get to Mobile. Grant thought it would be advantageous to operate on a line from Atlanta to Savannah provided the Navy could establish a coastal base for Sherman.[6]

Actually Grant did not like Sherman's plan as much as he indicated to the government. The general in chief feared that if Sherman set out for the coast the Confederate field army in Georgia would invade Tennessee, and he well knew how Lincoln would react to a movement that might weaken the defences of the bastion of the West. Grant wanted Sherman to defeat the Confederate army before he left Atlanta. Sherman, however, insisted that he could never destroy the enemy from Atlanta but if he smashed across Georgia the Confederates would have to follow him or attack Thomas in Tennessee. Whichever course the Confederates took, Sherman was sure they would be defeated. Grant finally approved Sherman's plan on condition that Sherman could guarantee the safety of the Tennessee line.[7] Lincoln, of course, saw the exchange of telegrams between Grant and Sherman. He instructed Stanton to tell Grant that he felt much solicitude about Sherman's proposed movement and was impressed with

[5] Sherman to Grant, October 1, 1864, *Official Records*, XXXIX, pt. 3, 3.

[6] Grant to Halleck, October 4, 1864, *ibid.*, XXXIX, pt. 3, 63–64.

[7] Grant to Sherman, October 11, 1864, two despatches, *ibid.*, XXXIX, pt. 3, 202; Sherman to Grant, October 11, *ibid.*, 202.

Grant's objections to it. Obviously the President feared Sherman's plan would open Tennessee to invasion.[8] Just as obviously he was willing to trust Grant's judgment as to what should be done. If Grant said Sherman could go ahead, Lincoln would agree. When Grant said that Sherman's plan was the best that could be devised for the West and told Sherman to start his movement, Lincoln, with some misgivings, accepted the decision.[9] By mid-November, Sherman, who more than any Civil War general grasped the concept of total war, was ready to flame across Georgia, bringing the destructiveness of modern war to the heart of the Confederacy and demonstrating to the Southern people that the Union possessed a power which could not be resisted. What he was going to do might not be war, Sherman explained to Grant, but it was certainly statesmanship.[1]

While Grant and Sherman were maturing their plans, the presidential campaign was roaring to a close. Among the charges thrown at Lincoln by the Democrats was that he had interfered improperly in military matters. A Congressman who was close personally to both Lincoln and Grant asked Grant for permission to use a letter by the General denying the accusation. Grant replied that anything he had ever written the President could be used by Lincoln in any way. In one of his rare expressions of humor, the General added: "I think, however, for him to attempt to answer all the charges the opposition will bring against him will be like setting a maiden to work to prove her chastity." [2]

The election in November was a resounding triumph for Lincoln. Writing to congratulate Lincoln on his reelection,

[8] Stanton to Grant, October 12, 1864, *ibid.*, XXXIX, pt. 3, 222.

[9] Grant to Stanton, October 13, 1864, and to Sherman, November 1, 2, *ibid.*, XXXIX, pt. 3, 239, 576, 594.

[1] Sherman to Grant, November 6, 1864, *ibid.*, XXXIX, pt. 3, 660.

[2] E. B. Washburne to Grant, September 20, 1864, and Grant to Washburne, September 21, *ibid.*, XLII, pt. 2, 934, 935.

Grant accurately observed that the quiet order prevailing in the election was a demonstration of Union strength and of more value to the Union cause than a won battle. In a letter to a friend, Grant said that the result of the election and the tightening effect of the blockade had doomed the Confederacy. Its government, he noted, was now "collecting old men and little boys" for the armies: "It is better that it should be so. When the job is done then it will be well done." [3]

Before Sherman set out for Savannah, the commander of the Confederate army in Georgia, General John B. Hood, decided to invade Tennessee. Hood's purpose was to draw Sherman back after him and defeat the Federals in the mountains. Sherman, however, refused to be drawn; he trusted Thomas to deal with Hood. As Hood marched into Tennessee, Sherman marched across Georgia. Hood's one chance of victory was to get into Tennessee and smash the small army there before Thomas could concentrate enough men to hold the state. But instead of moving rapidly, Hood moved slowly, and on his way to Thomas's base at Nashville he suffered a bad defeat at Franklin. After Franklin, Hood had no chance to win, and he should have retired to Georgia. Like a doomed figure in a tragedy, he chose to go on to Nashville and defeat. With his little army, he took position on the hills south of the city and waited—for what he could not have given a rational answer.

In Nashville, "Old Pap" Thomas was gathering an army that would eventually number almost 70,000. Thomas was a good general, a hard-hitting attacker, but he always took a long time to get ready to attack. He moved like a sledgehammer when he moved, but he never advanced until his army was prepared down to the last knapsack. All during December Thomas stayed in his works at Nashville. He was ready-

[3] Grant to Stanton, November 10, 1864, *ibid.*, XLII, pt. 3, 581; Grant to J. R. Jones, November 13, MS. in Chicago Historical Society.

ing a paralyzing blow at Hood, but he did not fully inform the government what he was planning. To Lincoln it seemed that Thomas was avoiding battle with the Confederates. The President did not know that the battered Confederate army was incapable of offensive action; he feared that while Thomas dallied at Nashville Hood would strike for Kentucky. Finally, Lincoln directed Stanton to take up Thomas's inaction with Grant. The Secretary telegraphed Grant that Lincoln was worried by Thomas's disposition to lay in his fortifications indefinitely, which looked to the President like the old McClellan-Rosecrans strategy. Grant, who knew how slow Thomas was, immediately sent several sharp despatches to Thomas urging him to attack at once. Thomas replied that he wanted to build up his cavalry before attacking and that he would launch an offensive as soon as possible.[4] Not impressed by Thomas's pledge of early action and completely misjudging Thomas's generalship, Grant informed the government that Thomas was excellent on defence but did not know how to fight offensively and would probably never attack Hood. Grant advised that Thomas be relieved and the command of his army be given to John M. Schofield, one of his corps generals.[5]

Lincoln was astonished at Grant's recommendation to remove Thomas. When he had asked Grant to spur Thomas to action, he had never dreamed that the general in chief would go to the length of ousting Thomas from command. Although the President was disturbed by Thomas's slowness, he saw no reason to relieve him. He greatly admired Thomas and had ever since Chickamauga. Nevertheless, he did not want to oppose Grant on the issue of Thomas. The general

---

[4] Stanton to Grant, December 2, 1864, *Official Records*, XLV, pt. 2, 15–16; Grant to Thomas, December 2, 6, 8, *ibid.*, 17, 70, 97; Thomas to Grant, December 2, 6, *ibid.*, 17–18, 70.

[5] Grant to Stanton, December 7, 1864, *ibid.*, XLV, pt. 2, 84, 96.

in chief, Lincoln believed, ought to have the right to choose his field commanders. Halleck transmitted to Grant Lincoln's reactions to the proposed removal. If Grant wished Thomas relieved, he was to issue an order to that effect, and nobody in the government would oppose the order. But, added Halleck, the responsibility for relieving Thomas would have to be Grant's, because nobody in the government wanted Thomas removed. Undeterred by Lincoln's obvious disapproval of what he was asking, Grant then prepared an order relieving Thomas and appointing Schofield to the command.[6]

Grant telegraphed the order to Halleck with instructions to send it to Thomas. Before it went over the wires, two despatches from Thomas arrived in Washington stating that as he was moving out to attack Hood a sleet storm had set in to halt all operations. Halleck, showing a good sense of responsibility, informed Grant of the import of Thomas's communications and asked Grant if he still wanted to transmit the removal order. Grant agreed to suspend the order until the weather cleared and Thomas had a chance to prove he meant to fight.[7] Several days passed before Thomas could move, and Grant became impatient again. He started for Washington to see Lincoln. From the capital, he intended to go to Nashville and personally relieve Thomas. He reached Washington on December 15 and went into conference at the War Department with Lincoln, Stanton, and Halleck. The President tried to talk Grant out of removing Thomas and, voicing good army doctrine, said that Thomas on the ground was better able to judge his situation than was Grant five hundred

[6] Halleck to Grant, December 9, 1864, *ibid.*, XLV, pt. 2, 96; Grant's order of December 9, *ibid.*, 114.

[7] Thomas to Halleck, December 9, 1864, and to Grant, December 9, *ibid.*, XLV, pt. 2, 114; Grant to Halleck, December 9, *ibid.*, 115–116; Halleck to Grant, December 9, *ibid.*, 116; Grant to Halleck, December 9, *ibid.*, 116; Grant to Thomas, December 9, 11, *ibid.*, 115, 143.

miles away in Washington. But Grant, unreasonably angry at Thomas, insisted on relieving him. With great reluctance, Lincoln let Grant have his way. As the general in chief was about to start, a telegram arrived at the War Department from a military telegraph official with Thomas's army announcing that on the fifteenth Thomas had attacked Hood, smashed the enemy line, and would complete his work the next day with a great victory. The telegram was received at eleven o'clock, and Stanton immediately drove to the White House to tell Lincoln the good news. The President had retired, but Stanton had him called. Lincoln appeared at the head of the second story landing in his nightshirt and holding a candle to hear the tidings. His face broke into a glad smile.[8]

Nobody recorded how Grant felt when he heard of Thomas's victory. He called off his trip to Nashville and congratulated Thomas in a not quite gracious message. Lincoln also telegraphed congratulations to Thomas. The President sent his despatch on the sixteenth without knowing the full results of Thomas's battle. Always the complete strategist, he exhorted Thomas not to be satisfied with a partial victory: "You made a magnificent beginning; a grand consummation is within your easy reach. Do not let it slip." [9] Thomas did not let it slip much. On the sixteenth he broke Hood's line completely, and the Confederate army started a long retreat back to Mississippi. As it withdrew, Thomas hit it repeatedly with the most devastating cavalry pursuit of the war. Only remnants of Hood's army escaped, and it was never an army again. The victory at Nashville was the only one in the war so complete that the defeated army practically lost its existence. It was also a complete vindication of Lincoln's faith in

[8] Lucius E. Chittenden, *Recollections of President Lincoln and His Administration*, 363; Bates, *Lincoln in the Telegraph Office*, 315–317; *Official Records*, XLV, pt. 2, 196.

[9] Grant to Thomas, December 15, 1864, *Official Records*, XLV, pt. 2, 195; Lincoln to Thomas, December 16, *Works of Lincoln*, X, 315–316.

Thomas. Again the President had been more right than Grant.

While Hood was marching to destruction in Tennessee, Sherman was moving across Georgia in the fabled march to the sea. He aimed to emerge at some point on the coast like Savannah or Port Royal where the Navy could pick him up and carry him to Virginia to join Grant in a final crushing movement against Lee.[1] At first, Sherman himself was not sure which coastal port he would go to, and until he decided Lincoln and Grant knew only the general objective of his movement. Discussing Sherman with the General's brother, a United States Senator, Lincoln said: "I know what hole he went in at, but I can't tell what hole he will come out of." [2] Although Sherman was virtually unopposed and untroubled by supply difficulties because he lived off the country, Lincoln feared for his safety. The President worried that the Confederates would concentrate enough forces to trap Sherman in the interior of Georgia. Grant assured Lincoln that Sherman had a large enough army to protect himself against any attack and, as Grant expressed it, strike bottom on salt water.[3]

By December 10, Sherman was in front of Savannah and laid the city under siege and certain capture. The Confederates evacuated it on the twenty-first, and Sherman had his base on the ocean. In a dramatic telegram to the government, he presented Savannah to the nation as a Christmas present. Lincoln was delighted with Sherman's success and his despatch. He wrote the General a letter of appreciation which was, at the same time, an admirable analysis of the effect of Sherman's movement on Southern morale:

[1] Grant to Sherman, December 6, 1864, *Official Records,* XLIV, 636–637.

[2] McClure, *Lincoln and Men of War-Times,* 219–220, footnote.

[3] Grant to Sherman, December 18, 1864, W. T. Sherman MSS., Acq. Box 4.

Many, many thanks for your Christmas gift, the capture of Savannah.

When you were about leaving Atlanta for the Atlantic coast, I was anxious, if not fearful; but feeling that you were the better judge, and remembering that "nothing risked, nothing gained," I did not interfere. Now, the undertaking being a success, the honor is all yours; for I believe none of us went further than to acquiesce.

And taking the work of General Thomas into the count . . . , it is indeed a great success. Not only does it afford the obvious and immediate military advantages; but in showing the world that your army could be divided, putting the stronger part to an important service, and yet leaving enough [Thomas] to vanquish the old opposing force of the whole,—Hood's army—it brings those who sat in darkness to see a great light. But what next?

I suppose it will be safe to leave General Grant and yourself to decide.[4]

Sherman and Grant were already planning the "next." They decided that instead of having Sherman go to Grant by sea he would go by land, marching up through the Carolinas and wrecking more of the Confederacy's dwindling economic resources. By taking the land route to Virginia, Sherman could get to Grant faster than by sea, and he could aid Grant before he reached him by destroying the Carolina railroads that supplied Lee's army.[5] The Grant-Sherman plan was a masterly strategic concept. Executing a gigantic rightwheel, Sherman would move to Lee's rear and accomplish important secondary objectives as he went. If Sherman's destruction of Lee's communications did not force Lee to come out and

[4] Lincoln to Sherman, December 26, 1864, *Works of Lincoln*, X, 325–326. For Sherman's pleased reaction to Lincoln's letter, see Sherman to Lincoln, January 6, 1865, *Official Records*, XLVII, pt. 2, 19.

[5] Grant to Sherman, December 6, 18, 27, 1864, *Official Records*, XLIV, 636–637, 740–741, 820–821; Sherman to Grant, December 16, 24, *ibid.*, 726–728, 797–798; Sherman to Halleck, December 24, *ibid.*, 798–800.

fight, the Confederate army in Petersburg would perish for want of supplies or be trapped helplessly when Sherman and Grant joined.[6] Lincoln spoke accurately when he said it would be safe to leave the next decision to his two best generals.

December, the month of victories, saw the last two of Lincoln's political generals, Banks and Butler, leave the military scene. Since 1863, Lincoln had refused to keep political generals in field commands when they showed they were incapable. He had readily agreed, even in an election year, to Grant's suggestion that Banks be shelved in Louisiana. In the Butler case in the summer of 1864, he had been willing to let Butler be removed from field command if Grant took the responsibility for the act. His reluctance to relieve Butler on his own authority was largely due to political sensitivity, although he may well have thought that Grant had presented no actual evidence of Butler's incompetency.

In the winter of 1864–65, Banks came to Washington and tried to get his former command restored. Lincoln said that it could not be done, that he liked Banks personally but there was no place for him in the field. When Banks still pressed for an active assignment the President said bluntly that he did not wish to be argued with anymore.[7] Butler was relieved of command because in December he gave such a demonstration of his unfitness for field service that Lincoln felt it was imperative to get rid of him. Grant planned, with the cooperation of the Navy, a combined land and naval attack on Fort Fisher, which guarded Wilmington, North Carolina, the last important port open in the Confederacy. Wilmington was in Butler's department, and the General announced that he was going to accompany the expedition, as he had a right to, although Grant did not want him to go. Grant

[6] Sherman to Stanton, March 12, 1865, *ibid.*, XLVII, pt. 2, 793–794.
[7] Harrington, *Banks*, 163–164.

had designated another officer to lead the land forces, but Butler, the superior ranking officer, now took over the command. The attack on Fort Fisher failed, and largely because Butler botched the operation. Lincoln immediately asked Grant to explain the cause of the defeat. The General replied that the attack had been "a gross and culpable failure" and the person to blame would soon be known.[8] Unofficially from Halleck and Grant and others, Lincoln learned Butler was the person. Grant now felt strong enough to ask again that Butler be relieved. In his letter of request, he did not mention Fort Fisher but stressed Butler's general incompetence, of which Fort Fisher was the unnamed proof. This time Grant got what he wanted. Back shot an order from Washington relieving Butler, and the document bore the authority: "by direction of the President."[9]

Even before Butler was removed, Grant started to prepare another expedition against Fort Fisher. Lincoln took a direct hand in planning the second operation. Mindful that Grant had said the Navy had not cooperated too efficiently with Butler, Lincoln instructed Secretary Welles to see that interservice coordination was better in the next attack.[1] The second expedition succeeded, and one reason why it did was that the land and water services worked together.

As the spring of 1865 opened, Lincoln was serenely confident of victory near at hand. He knew that Virginia would be the key theater when warmer weather brought more active operations. If Grant could defeat Lee, the few remaining centers of Confederate resistance would collapse. The President continued to watch Grant's actions approvingly but al-

[8] Lincoln to Grant, December 28, 1864, and Grant to Lincoln, December 28, *Official Records*, XLII, pt. 3, 1087.

[9] Grant to Stanton, January 4, 1865, and Halleck to Grant, January 7, *ibid.*, XLVI, pt. 2, 29, 60.

[1] Gideon Welles to Grant, December 29, 1864, *ibid.*, XLII, pt. 3, 1091.

ways closely. When Lincoln did not like or understand something Grant was doing, he promptly called the General to account. As the spring operations were getting under way, Grant experienced twice the vigilant control Lincoln was likely to exercise over the military machine. By late February, Sheridan had cleared the Valley of Confederates. Grant directed Sheridan to bring most of his cavalry to Petersburg for the final move against Lee. In an answering despatch, Sheridan told Grant that he was on his way and was leaving 2,000 cavalrymen in the Valley as a scouting force for the infantry there. Lincoln saw Sheridan's telegram at the War Department but apparently he saw only part of it or a garbled version of the whole, because he understood from it that only 2,000 troops of all arms were being left behind. He thought that Sheridan was carting off the whole Valley army to Petersburg. Deeply disturbed, Lincoln telegraphed Grant asking him to explain why the Valley line was being exposed to possible invasion. Grant replied that Sheridan's 2,000 figure referred to cavalry only and that adequate defensive forces were present in the Valley. The General's despatch crossed one from Lincoln in which the President said he had found out the true facts of the case and apologized to Grant for troubling him.[2]

Grant's second encounter with Lincolnian authority was of the General's own asking. During a conference between some Union and Confederate officers to arrange an exchange of prisoners, General Longstreet, a friend of Grant's before the war, remarked that Lee would like to meet Grant to conclude a military convention to end hostilities. Longstreet's message was conveyed to Grant, who asked Stanton for instructions.[3] Grant's action was perfectly proper, and Lincoln

[2] Lincoln to Grant, February 25, 27, 1865, *Works of Lincoln*, XI, 40–41; Grant to Lincoln, February 26, *Official Records*, XLVI, pt. 2, 704.

[3] Grant to Stanton, March 3, 1865, *Official Records*, XLVI, pt. 2, 801–802.

understood that the General was not seeking to exceed his authority by becoming a peace negotiator. Nevertheless, the President thought Grant ought to be instructed explicitly that he was to confine his activities to fighting. Lincoln himself composed the directive Grant had asked for, although Stanton's name was signed to it: "The President directs me to say that he wishes you to have no conference with General Lee unless it be for capitulation of General Lee's army, or on some minor or purely military matter. He instructs me to say that you are not to decide, discuss, or confer upon any political questions. Such questions the President holds in his own hands, and will submit them to no military conferences or conventions. Meanwhile you are to press to the utmost your military advantages." [4]

Late in March, as Grant was about to start his final turning movement around the Confederate right, he invited Lincoln to come down to City Point for a visit. Lincoln eagerly accepted, and with a party of officials and friends and Mrs. Lincoln left Washington on the twenty-third. Traveling in the steamer *River Queen*, Lincoln reached City Point late the next day. [5] The President stayed with Grant's army for thirteen days and enjoyed nearly every minute of it. His motives for making the trip to Virginia were partly to have a sort of vacation (observers noted how deadly worn he looked); partly to see his son Robert, who was on Grant's staff; and mainly military. He wanted to see Grant defeat Lee and end the war. He wanted to witness victory. As he confessed to Stanton after being a few days at City Point, he knew he

---

[4] Stanton to Grant, March 3, 1865, *Works of Lincoln*, XI, 43; Stanton to Grant, March 3, 5, *Official Records*, XLVI, pt. 2, 802, 841; Grant to Stanton, March 4, *ibid.*, 823–824.

[5] Grant to Lincoln, March 20, 1865, *Official Records*, XLVI, pt. 3, 50; Lincoln to Grant, March 20, 23, *Works of Lincoln*, XI, 59–61; Lincoln to Stanton, March 25, two despatches, *ibid.*, 61–62.

ought to be at home but he had to see "nearer to the end" of Grant's movement.[6]

The President slept on the *River Queen* and spent his evenings on ship, but during the day he was all over camp, walking among the soldiers, and visiting the wounded in the hospitals. On one of his strolls, he saw some men cutting timber to build a cabin and picked up an ax and swung it on a log while the soldiers cheered. He liked to sit in the adjutant general's hut and read the despatches that came in from the front announcing the progress of the fighting. When not examining telegrams he would lean back in his chair with his legs twisted comfortably and talk for hours with the junior officers.[7]

Every day Lincoln received reports from Grant, Meade, and other generals as to how the move around Lee's right was going. He relayed the substance of the reports to Stanton, who in turn informed the President what was happening in other theaters.[8] On March 25, Lincoln saw an actual battle from close range. Lee decided to try to break the Union lines in front of Petersburg by hurling an attack on the key Union position of Fort Stedman. The attack failed, and the commander in chief watched it thrown back from where he stood on a ridge safely in the rear. He said the spectacle was more satisfactory than would be a review he was to witness later.[9] Several officers who saw Lincoln at City Point recalled later that he was nervous and sad, kept asking when the army would move, and seemed to think that Grant would not be able to turn Lee out of Petersburg. According to Sheridan,

[6] Lincoln to Stanton, March 30, 1865, *ibid.*, XI, 63–64.

[7] Richardson, *Grant*, 461; Badeau, *Grant*, III, 137–139.

[8] Lincoln to Stanton, March 31, April 1, 2, 1865, *Works of Lincoln*, XI, 64–70; Stanton to Lincoln, March 31, *Official Records*, XLVI, pt. 3, 332.

[9] Richardson, *Grant*, 463.

Lincoln expressed a fear that as Grant moved his left around Petersburg, Lee would come down and capture City Point.[1] Lincoln probably was nervous, not because he feared failure but because he sensed the approach of victory and was impatient for the final result. His alleged remark to Sheridan did not mean that he thought Lee would seize City Point or that Grant had neglected to provide for the defence of the place. Rather, it was the statement of a careful war director who was wondering if every contingency had been provided for. Two days after Fort Stedman, General Sherman came up to City Point from North Carolina to confer with Grant and Lincoln. The President discussed reconstruction problems with Sherman, which showed how close Lincoln thought the war was to being over. In his memoirs, Sherman wrote that Lincoln was worried that some setback to Sherman's army might occur during the General's absence and that he anxiously urged Sherman to return to North Carolina. Sherman interpreted this to mean a certain doubt of victory in Lincoln's mind, but he too was misreading the President.[2] Lincoln was really saying to the generals: let's get on the job and get this thing over.

On April 1 Grant crashed around Lee's right and stood astride the last railroad artery connecting Richmond and the lower South. Lee could no longer stay in Petersburg, and on the second he evacuated the town, retreating to the West; Richmond was also evacuated. Union forces occupied both cities on the third. On the previous day Grant, without definitely indicating that he was about to capture Petersburg, had invited Lincoln to join him at the front. Early on the morning of the third he notified Lincoln that he was in

---

[1] Porter, *Incidents and Anecdotes*, 281–282; Sheridan, *Memoirs*, II, 130–131.

[2] William T. Sherman, *Memoirs of General William T. Sherman By Himself*, II, 324–331.

Petersburg. The President, not too much surprised by the news, started for Petersburg immediately. When he met Grant, Lincoln said: "Do you know, general, that I have had a sort of a sneaking idea for some days that you intended to do something like this." [3] Lincoln spent an hour and a half with Grant and then returned to City Point. On the fourth, he went into Richmond, almost unattended and unguarded, and stayed the night. When Stanton reproached him for exposing himself by accompanying a pursuing army, Lincoln promised: "I will take care of myself." [4]

He was sure now that in a few days the war in Virginia would be over. He could go back to Washington. Lee's army was fleeing westward with Grant hard on its tired heels and certain to envelop it before it could reach safety. In fact, with Sherman pushing up from North Carolina, there was no place of safety anywhere for Lee. Grant assured the President that Lee would have to surrender by April 11 at the latest. On the night of the sixth, Lincoln explained the situation to a group of guests on the *River Queen*. Getting out his maps, the President pointed out the route of Lee's march, the position of each pursuing Union corps, and the probable place where the Confederates would have to yield.[5]

The seventh was Lincoln's last complete day at City Point. Sheridan, smashing victoriously at the Confederates, telegraphed Grant: "If the thing be pressed I think Lee will surrender." Grant sent Sheridan's despatch to Lincoln. The

[3] Grant to Colonel T. S. Bowers, April 2, 1865, and Lincoln to Grant, April 2, *Official Records*, XLVI, pt. 3, 449; Lincoln to Stanton, April 3, two despatches, *Works of Lincoln*, XI, 70; Grant, *Memoirs*, II, 458–459.

[4] Stanton to Lincoln, April 3, 1865, and Lincoln to Stanton, April 3, *Official Records*, XLVI, pt. 3, 509.

[5] Marquis de Chambrun, "Personal Recollections of Mr. Lincoln," *Scribner's Magazine*, XIII, 1893, 27.

President telegraphed Grant: "Let the *thing* be pressed." [6] It was his last important order and like most of his orders a good one.

On April 8, a Saturday, Lincoln boarded the *River Queen* and started home. As the ship swung out from the pier, Lincoln stood a long time looking back at the land.[7] He may have been thinking of the weary years of defeat—of McClellan, Burnside, Hooker—or of the hour of victory and Grant and Sherman. That day John Wilkes Booth registered at the National Hotel in Washington.

[6] Lincoln to Grant, April 7, 1865, *Works of Lincoln*, XI, 77; Sheridan, *Memoirs*, II, 187.

[7] Chambrun, "Recollections of Mr. Lincoln," 34.

Bibliography

AGASSIZ, GEORGE R. (ed.): *Meade's Headquarters, 1863–65: Letters of Colonel Theodore Lyman* (Boston, 1922).

ANGLE, PAUL M. (ed.): *New Letters and Papers of Lincoln* (Boston, 1930).

ARNOLD, ISAAC N.: *The Life of Abraham Lincoln* (Chicago, 1885).

ATKINSON, C. F.: *Grant's Campaigns of 1864 and 1865* (London, 1905).

BACHE, RICHARD MEADE: *Life of General George Gordon Meade* . . . (Philadelphia, 1897).

BADEAU, ADAM: *Military History of Ulysses S. Grant, from April, 1861 to April, 1865* (3 vols., New York, 1868–1881).

BALLARD, COLIN R.: *The Military Genius of Abraham Lincoln: An Essay* (London, 1926).

BARNARD, JOHN G.: *The Peninsula Campaign and Antecedents* . . . (New York, 1864).

BATES, DAVID H.: *Lincoln in the Telegraph Office* . . . (New York, 1907).

BATES, SAMUEL P.: *The Battle of Chancellorsville* (Meadsville, Pennsylvania, 1882).

BEALE, HOWARD (ed.): *Diary of Edward Bates, 1859–1866 (Annual Report of American Historical Association, 1930, IV,* Washington, 1933).

BENNETT, JAMES GORDON: Manuscripts (Library of Congress).

B[ICKHAM], W[ILLIAM] D.: *Rosecrans' Campaign with the Fourteenth Army Corps* (Cincinnati, 1863).

BIGELOW, JOHN, JR.: *The Campaign of Chancellorsville* (New Haven, 1910).

BROOKS, NOAH: *Washington in Lincoln's Time* (New York, 1895).

[355]

BUEL, CLARENCE C. and JOHNSON, ROBERT U. (eds.): *Battles and Leaders of the Civil War* (4 vols., New York, 1887–1888).

BUTLER, BENJAMIN F.: *Autobiography and Personal Reminiscences of Major-General Benjamin F. Butler: Butler's Book* (Boston, 1892).

BUTTERFIELD, JULIA A. (ed.): *A Biographical Memorial of General Daniel Butterfield* (New York, 1903).

CAMERON, SIMON: Manuscripts (Library of Congress).

CARPENTER, FRANCIS B.: *The Inner Life of Abraham Lincoln: Six Months at the White House* (New York, 1867).

CHAMBRUN, MARQUIS DE: "Personal Recollections of Mr. Lincoln," *Scribner's Magazine*, XIII, 26–38 (January, 1893).

CHANDLER, ZACHARIAH: Manuscripts (Library of Congress).

CHASE, SALMON P.: Manuscripts (Library of Congress).

——: *Diary and Correspondence of Salmon P. Chase* (*Annual Report of American Historical Association*, 1902, II, Washington, 1903).

CHITTENDEN, LUCIUS E.: *Recollections of President Lincoln and His Administration* (New York, 1891).

CHURCH, WILLIAM CONANT: *Ulysses S. Grant . . .* (New York, 1897).

CLEAVES, FREEMAN: *Rock of Chickamauga: The Life of General George H. Thomas* (Norman, 1948).

Committee on the Conduct of the War: Reports (8 vols., Washington, 1863–1866).

COMSTOCK, CYRUS B.: Manuscript Diary (Library of Congress).

CONGER, ARTHUR L.: "President Lincoln as War Statesman," *Wisconsin Historical Publications, Proceedings*, 1916, 106–140 (Madison, 1917).

——: *The Rise of U. S. Grant* (New York, 1931).

COPPEE, HENRY: *Grant and His Campaigns* (New York, 1866).

COX, JACOB DOLSON: *Military Reminiscences of the Civil War* (2 vols., New York, 1900).

CRAMER, JESSE GRANT (ed.): *Letters of Ulysses S. Grant to his Father and his Youngest Sister, 1857–78* (New York, 1912).

CRAMER, JOHN H.: *Lincoln under Enemy Fire* (Baton Rouge, 1948).

CROFFUT, WILLIAM A.: Manuscripts (includes manuscripts of General Ethan Allen Hitchcock), (Library of Congress).

—— (ed.) : *Fifty Years in Camp and Field: the Diary of Major-General Ethan Allen Hitchcock* (New York, 1909) .

DAHLGREN, JOHN A.: Manuscripts (includes Journal of Captain Ulric Dahlgren) , (Library of Congress) .

DANA, CHARLES A.: Manuscripts (Library of Congress) .

——: *Recollections of the Civil War . . .* (New York, 1902) .

DENNETT, TYLER (ed.) : *Lincoln and the Civil War in the Diaries and Letters of John Hay* (New York, 1939) .

DODGE, GRENVILLE M.: *Personal Recollections of President Abraham Lincoln, General Ulysses S. Grant and General William T. Sherman* (Council Bluffs, 1914) .

DOSTER, WILLIAM E.: *Lincoln and Episodes of the Civil War* (New York, 1915) .

DOUBLEDAY, ABNER: *Chancellorsville and Gettysburg* (New York, 1882) .

ECKENRODE, H. J. and CONRAD, BRYAN: *George B. McClellan: The Man Who Saved the Union* (Chapel Hill, 1941) .

ELLIOTT, CHARLES W.: *Winfield Scott: The Soldier and the Man* (New York, 1937) .

"Federal Generals and a Good Press," *American Historical Review*, XXXIX, 284–297 (January, 1934) .

FLOWER, FRANK A.: *Edwin McMasters Stanton . . .* (New York, 1905) .

FORD, HARVEY S. (ed.) : *Memoirs of a Volunteer, 1861–1863* (New York, 1946) .

FORD, WORTHINGTON C. (ed.) : *A Cycle of Adams Letters* (2 vols., Boston, 1920) .

FRANKLIN, WILLIAM B.: Manuscripts (Library of Congress) .

FRY, JAMES B.: *Operations of the Army under Buell* (New York, 1884) .

FULLER, J. F. C.: *The Generalship of Ulysses S. Grant* (London, 1929) .

GIBBON, JOHN: *Personal Recollections of the Civil War* (New York, 1928) .

GILMORE, JAMES R.: *Personal Recollections of Abraham Lincoln and the Civil War* (Boston, 1898) .

GORDON, GEORGE H.: *A War Diary of Events in the War of the Great Rebellion, 1863–1865* (Boston, 1882).

GORHAM, GEORGE C.: *Life and Public Service of Edwin M. Stanton* (2 vols., Boston, 1899).

GRANT, ULYSSES S.: *Personal Memoirs of Ulysses S. Grant* (2 vols., New York, 1885–1886).

——: Manuscripts (Illinois State Historical Library).

GREENE, FRANCIS V.: "Lincoln as Commander-in-Chief," *Scribner's Magazine*, XLVI, 104–115 (July, 1909).

HALLECK, HENRY W.: *Elements of Military Art and Science . . .* (New York, 1861).

HARRINGTON, FRED HARVEY: *Fighting Politician, Major General N. P. Banks* (Philadelphia, 1948).

HAUPT, HERMAN: *Reminiscences of General Herman Haupt* (Milwaukee, 1901).

HAY, THOMAS ROBSON: "President Lincoln and the Army of the Potomac," *Georgia Historical Quarterly*, X, 277–301 (December, 1926).

HEBERT, WALTER H.: *Fighting Joe Hooker* (Indianapolis, 1944).

HEINTZELMAN, SAMUEL P.: Manuscript Journal (Library of Congress).

HILLIARD, GEORGE S.: *Life and Campaigns of George B. McClellan* (Philadelphia, 1865).

HOWARD, OLIVER OTIS: *Autobiography of Oliver Otis Howard* (2 vols., New York, 1908).

HOWE, M. A. DE WOLFE (ed.): *Home Letters of General Sherman* (New York, 1909).

HUMPHREYS, ANDREW A.: *The Virginia Campaign of '64 and '65* (New York, 1883).

HURLBERT, WILLIAM H.: *General McClellan and the Conduct of the War* (New York, 1864).

JOHNSON, ANDREW: Manuscripts (Library of Congress).

JOHNSON, R. W.: *A Soldier's Reminiscences in Peace and War* (Philadelphia, 1886).

JOHNSTON, R. M.: *Bull Run: Its Strategy and Tactics* (Boston, 1913).

JULIAN, GEORGE W.: *Political Recollections, 1840–1872* (Chicago, 1884).

KELLEY, WILLIAM D.: *Lincoln and Stanton* (New York, 1885).

KETCHUM, HIRAM: *General McClellan's Peninsula Campaign* (New York, 1864).

LAMON, WARD HILL: *Recollections of Abraham Lincoln, 1847–1865* (Washington, 1911).

LANDER, FREDERICK W.: Manuscripts (Library of Congress).

LARNED, DANIEL REED: Manuscripts (Library of Congress).

LEWIS, LLOYD: *Sherman: Fighting Prophet* (New York, 1932).

LIDDELL HART, B. H.: *Sherman: Soldier, Realist* (New York, 1930).

LINCOLN, ROBERT TODD: Manuscripts (Library of Congress).

LIVERMORE, MARY A.: *My Story of the War . . .* (Hartford, 1889).

LIVERMORE, THOMAS L.: *Numbers and Losses in the Civil War in America, 1861–65* (Boston, 1901).

LIVERMORE, WILLIAM ROSCOE: *The Story of the Civil War* (2 vols., New York, 1913).

MCCLELLAN, GEORGE B.: Manuscripts (Library of Congress).

——: *McClellan's Own Story* (New York, 1887).

MCCLURE, ALEXANDER K.: *Abraham Lincoln and Men of War-Times* (Philadelphia, 1892).

MCCORMACK, THOMAS J. (ed.): *Memoirs of Gustave Koerner, 1809–1896* (2 vols., Cedar Rapids, 1909).

MARBLE, MANTON: Manuscripts (Library of Congress).

MARSHALL, JESSIE A. (ed.): *Private and Official Correspondence of Benjamin F. Butler During the Period of the Civil War* (5 vols., Norwood, Massachusetts, 1917).

MAURICE, SIR FREDERICK: "Lincoln as a Strategist," *Forum,* LXXV, 161–169 (February, 1926).

——: *Statesmen and Soldiers of the Civil War: A Study of the Conduct of War* (Boston, 1926).

MEADE, GEORGE: *Life and Letters of George Gordon Meade* (2 vols., New York, 1913).

MEIGS, MONTGOMERY: Manuscripts (Library of Congress).

——: "General M. C. Meigs on the Conduct of the War," *American Historical Review,* XXVI, 285–303 (January, 1921).

MENEELY, ALEXANDER HOWARD: *The War Department, 1861* (New York, 1928).

MICHIE, PETER S.: *General McClellan* (New York, 1901).

Military Historical Society of Massachusetts: *Papers of,* I, *The Peninsula Campaign of General McClellan in 1862* (Boston, 1881).

——: *Papers of,* II, *The Virginia Campaign of General Pope in 1862* (Boston, 1886).

——: *Papers of,* IV, *The Wilderness Campaign, May–June 1864* (Boston, 1905).

——: *Papers of,* X, *Critical Sketches of Some of the Federal and Confederate Commanders* (Boston, 1895).

MORSE, JOHN T. (ed.): *Diary of Gideon Welles* (3 vols., Boston, 1911).

MYERS, WILLIAM STARR: *A Study in Personality: General George Brinton McClellan* (New York, 1934).

NEVINS, ALLEN: *Frémont, Pathmarker of the West* (New York, 1939).

NICOLAY, JOHN G.: Manuscripts (Library of Congress).

NICOLAY, JOHN G. and JOHN HAY: *Abraham Lincoln: A History* (10 vols., New York, 1904).

—— (eds.): *Complete Works of Abraham Lincoln* (12 vols., New York, 1905).

O'CONNOR, RICHARD: *Thomas: Rock of Chickamauga* (New York, 1948).

PAGE, CHARLES A.: *Letters of a War Correspondent* (Boston, 1899).

PALFREY, FRANCIS WINTHROP: *The Antietam and Fredericksburg* (New York, 1882).

PEARSON, HENRY GREENLEAF: *James S. Wadsworth of Geneseo* (New York, 1913).

PEASE, THEODORE C. and RANDALL, JAMES G. (eds.): *Diary of Orville Hickman Browning,* I (Springfield, 1927).

PIATT, DONN: *Memories of the Men Who Saved the Union* (New York, 1887).

POORE, BEN: PERLEY: *The Life and Public Services of Ambrose E. Burnside* (Providence, 1882).

PORTER, DAVID D.: *Incidents and Anecdotes of the Civil War* (New York, 1885).

PORTER, HORACE: *Campaigning with Grant* (New York, 1897).

RAYMOND, HENRY J.: *The Life and Public Services of Abraham Lincoln* . . . (New York, 1865).

RAYMOND, HENRY W. (ed.): "Excerpts from the Journal of Henry J. Raymond," *Scribner's Monthly*, XIX, 57–61 (November, 1879), 419–424 (January, 1880), 703–710 (March, 1880).

RICE, ALLEN THORNDIKE (ed.): *Reminiscences of Abraham Lincoln by Distinguished Men of His Time* (New York, 1888).

RICHARDSON, ALBERT DEANE: *The Secret Service, The Field* . . . (Hartford, 1865).

——: *A Personal History of Ulysses S. Grant* (Hartford, 1885).

ROPES, JOHN CODMAN: *The Army Under Pope* (New York, 1881).

——: *The Story of the Civil War* (2 vols., New York, 1933).

RUSLING, JAMES F.: *Men and Things I Saw in Civil War Days* (New York, 1899).

RUSSELL, WILLIAM H.: *My Diary, North and South* (Boston, 1863).

SANDBURG, CARL: *Abraham Lincoln: The War Years* (4 vols., New York, 1945).

SCHOFIELD, JOHN M.: *Forty-Six Years in the Army* (New York, 1897).

——: Manuscripts (Library of Congress).

SCHUCKERS, JACOB W.: *Life and Public Services of Salmon Portland Chase* (New York, 1874).

SCHURZ, CARL: Manuscripts (Library of Congress).

——: *Reminiscences of Carl Schurz* (3 vols., New York, 1907–1908).

SEWARD, FREDERICK W.: *Reminiscences of a War-Time Statesman and Diplomat, 1830–1915* (New York, 1916).

SHANKS, WILLIAM F. G.: *Personal Recollections of Distinguished Generals* (New York, 1866).

SHERIDAN, P. H.: Manuscripts (Library of Congress).

——: *Personal Memoirs of P. H. Sheridan* (2 vols., New York, 1888).

SHERMAN, WILLIAM T.: Manuscripts (Library of Congress).

——: *Memoirs of William T. Sherman By Himself* (2 vols., New York, 1891).

SLOCUM, C. E.: *The Life and Services of Major-General Henry Warner Slocum* (Toledo, 1913).

SMITH, THEODORE C.: *Life and Letters of James A. Garfield* (2 vols., New Haven, 1925).

SMITH, WILLIAM E.: *The Francis Preston Blair Family in Politics* (2 vols., New York, 1933).

SMITH, WILLIAM FARRAR: *From Chattanooga to Petersburg Under Generals Grant and Butler* (Boston, 1893).

STANTON, EDWIN M.: Manuscripts (Library of Congress).

STINE, J. H.: *History of the Army of the Potomac* (Philadelphia, 1893).

SWINTON, WILLIAM: *Campaigns of the Army of the Potomac* (New York, 1866).

TAYLOR, EMERSON GIFFORD: *Gouverneur Kemble Warren . . .* (Boston, 1932).

THORNDIKE, RACHEL (ed.): *The Sherman Letters . . .* (New York, 1894).

TOWNSEND, E. D.: *Anecdotes of the Civil War in the United States* (New York, 1884).

TRACY, GILBERT A. (ed.): *Uncollected Letters of Abraham Lincoln* (Boston, 1911).

TRUMBULL, LYMAN: Manuscripts (Library of Congress).

VILLARD, HENRY: *Memoirs of Henry Villard, Journalist and Financier* (2 vols., Boston, 1904).

WADE, BENJAMIN F.: Manuscripts (Library of Congress).

WALKER, FRANCIS A.: *History of the Second Army Corps in the Army of the Potomac* (New York, 1886).

WALLACE, LEW: *Lew Wallace, An Autobiography* (2 vols., New York, 1906).

WALTERS, JOHN BENNETT: "General William T. Sherman and Total War," *Journal of Southern History,* XIV, 447–480 (November, 1948).

War of the Rebellion: A Compilation of the Official Records of the Union and Confederate Armies (128 vols., Washington, 1880–1901).

WASHBURNE, ELIHU B.: Manuscripts (Library of Congress).

WEBB, ALEXANDER: *The Peninsula* (New York, 1881).

WILLIAMS, KENNETH P.: *Lincoln Finds a General* (2 vols., New York, 1949).

WILLIAMS, T. HARRY: *Lincoln and the Radicals* (Madison, 1941).

WILSON, JAMES HARRISON: *The Life of Charles A. Dana* (New York, 1907).

——: *Under the Old Flag* (2 vols., New York, 1912).

——: *The Life of John A. Rawlins* (New York, 1916).

Index